The RACELESS.

T0228664

"*The Raceless Antiracist* is a scholarly yet down-to-earth deep dive into the most vexing issue of our time. It is universally acknowledged that color-coded human races are an illusion and that racism is a highly destructive problem. Yet race is used universally all day, every day. The illusion of race is almost always used in strategies to resolve the difficulties racism creates. *The Raceless Antiracist* shows the way out of the maze. I am tempted to call it a masterwork. However, it seems that Dr. Mason's masterwork is ever in process and developing on a practical, empirical, and interpersonal level. The book should be required reading for all educators, activists, politicians, and anyone interested in justice and global harmony."

—Arnett Duncan, EdD, Executive Director, Kweli Educational Enterprises, Inc.

"One of the most important books of the twenty-first century. A challenge to racists and antiracists, the colorblind and color-conscious, 'woke' and 'anti-woke' alike, *The Raceless Antiracist* is the solution to social division we've been waiting for. Dr. Sheena Michele Mason expertly guides us toward finally shedding the pernicious fiction of race, recognizing our common humanity, and realizing our true potential—together."

—Angel Eduardo, Senior Writer, Foundation for Individual Rights and Expression, and Board Chair, Foundation Against Intolerance & Racism

"The concept of race is itself a tool of oppression, and celebrating it, however well-intentioned, is promoting the white supremacist project. *The Raceless Antiracist* is a wonderfully clear and accessible guide and call to arms, explaining why it is that if we want to get rid of racism, we've got to get rid of race, and charting the way forward to a truly post-racist world."

—David Livingstone Smith, author of *Making Monsters: The Uncanny Power of Dehumanization*

"Sheena Michele Mason is a timely and refreshing voice in the antiracist soundscape. *The Raceless Antiracist*, at once descriptive and didactic, educates and even invites its readers to a more nuanced, honest look at the inner workings of what we'd otherwise call 'race.' The sooner the togetherness wayfinder makes its way into graduate seminars, journal articles, academic books, popular press, and public discourse . . . the better!"

—Russell Galloway, Graduate Teaching Assistant, PhD Student, University of Alabama

"Dr. Sheena Michele Mason has penned a moving and courageous elegy to an age-worn belief and custom—the noxious notion and practice of race as a scientific reality. Mason argues that if we are ever to progress as a species, we must rid ourselves of the hidebound notion of race and its concomitant pseudoscientific methodologies that consign all to a more limited humanity. Mason ushers in shimmering new possibilities of collaboration, communion, and collective care."

—Hoda Mahmoudi, Research Professor and Chair, The Bahá'í Chair for World Peace, University of Maryland, College Park

"*The Raceless Antiracist* is a vital and timely intervention in a world suffering from a crisis of equitable solutions to the extreme challenges we face. Sheena Michele Mason's togetherness wayfinder charts a path toward addressing the inequities and damages of racism while simultaneously emphasizing the positive power of our collective humanity to come together for our future and future generations. Pursuing and committing to the sincere social justice the wayfinder can facilitate is about actually sustaining the conditions for our survival and the survival of all biological life on the earth."

—Virginia Kennedy, Adjunct Lecturer, SUNY Oneonta

The
RACELESS
Antiracist

Why Ending *Race* Is the Future of Antiracism

SHEENA MICHELE MASON

Foreword by Starlette Thomas

Pitchstone Publishing
Durham, North Carolina

Pitchstone Publishing
Durham, North Carolina
www.pitchstonebooks.com

Library of Congress Cataloging-in-Publication Data

Names: Mason, Sheena Michele, author. | Thomas, Starlette, writer of foreword
Title: The raceless antiracist : why ending race is the future of
   antiracism / Sheena Michele Mason ; foreword by Starlette Thomas.
Other titles: Why ending race is the future of antiracism
Description: Durham, North Carolina : Pitchstone Publishing, [2024] |
   Includes bibliographical references and index. | Summary: "Within the
   dusty catalog of long-discarded theories about the universe and
   humankind's place in it, one idea continues to permeate the popular
   imagination as much today as it did at its ignominious invention: the
   idea of "race." As a society, we treat the "racial" categories that were
   invented centuries ago as if they are, in truth, inescapable and
   permanent aspects of reality. We organize, divide, and judge people
   based on our belief in "race"-and we often define ourselves and our
   relationships with others based on this same belief. Many scholars and
   activists argue that this type of racialization is necessary because
   even if "race" is not real, racism is. While such an approach might help
   lessen some effects of racism, it inevitably strengthens the very
   foundation of racism. As Sheena Michele Mason argues in The Raceless
   Antiracist, fighting racism by reifying the idea of "race" and operating
   within the practice of racialization is like trying to stop a flood by
   dousing it with water. To end racism, we must end the very idea of
   "race" itself, our practice of racialization, and the attending power
   imbalances that are part and parcel of race/ism"— Provided by publisher.
Identifiers: LCCN 2023041228 | ISBN 9781634312523 (paperback) | ISBN
   9781634312530 (ebook)
Subjects: LCSH: United States—Race relations. | Racism—United States. |
   Anti-racism—United States. | Race—Philosophy. | Race
   relations—Philosophy. | BISAC: SOCIAL SCIENCE / Race & Ethnic Relations
   | SOCIAL SCIENCE / Ethnic Studies / American / African American & Black
   Studies
Classification: LCC E184.A1 M31354 2024 | DDC 305.800973—dc23/eng/20231004
LC record available at https://lccn.loc.gov/2023041228

To Kisha, Tati, Sky Bear, Jojo, and the rest of my village.
To the future, the past, and today.

Contents

Acknowledgments

Abolition, the world-making of fugitive hope, occurs
in the mundane places of our subjectivity,
or the minutiae of our living.

—Marquis Bey, *Black Trans Feminism*, 2022

Thank you to Lakisha, my wife. Kisha, you make the best parts of life even better and the most challenging parts of life at least tolerable. In many ways, this book would not have come into fruition without your unshakeable love and support. You help me remember that my ideas are worth sharing. I dedicate this book to you and our children—to us. I dedicate this book to all of us.

Thank you to the Graduate School faculty of the English and Philosophy Departments at Howard University for nurturing my mind and spirit. A special thanks to Dr. Jacoby Adeshei Carter. Your consistent encouragement and support have helped to nurture my intellectual, emotional, and spiritual growth. May you mentor countless more students who will thrive under your tutelage. And may more of those students find themselves eliminativists (i.e., abolitionists).

Thank you to all of the people I cite throughout this book and countless others. I did not arrive on this journey in a vacuum. I am forever indebted to the authors, artists, and activists that continue to inspire me.

Thank you to the Mercatus Center at George Mason University for the Pluralism and Civil Exchange Grants and for my time as a visiting fellow in the Program on Pluralism and Civil Exchange. Your support helped bring this book and other educational tools into fruition.

Thanks to my colleagues and students at SUNY Oneonta for encouraging me and engaging with my ideas. A special thanks to my former students Tenisha Terry-Moultrie, Aine McCarthy, Hazharat Haruna, Delielah Tinsley, Shane Moran, and Brook Mucurio for providing enlightening feedback over the last couple of years.

And to Rev. Dr. Starlette Thomas, aka the Raceless Gospel, and Dr. Tade Souiaiaia, may your lights shine even brighter.

Foreword

You've opened this book and entered a new world. Progress will be made as you thumb each page door. Turn each slowly as there is a new creation behind them. You'll need to keep up because there are more words behind them. Words that fall in line behind them. This is a movement. Hurry up and get in line then.

No mere pencil pushing here. These well-researched words are ones you can count on and stack up against the color-coded caste system that is "race." Each page is a countdown to when we begin again. A whole new cosmos is starting now and in 10 . . . 9 . . . 8 . . .

There are more words where these came from that will make you question where "race" came from. No talk of the birds and the bees. "Race" is an unnatural union for which you'll find no biological support. Not tucked under skin but smuggled in through colors that hide behind them the true motivations of colonialism, colonization, capitalism, patriarchy, and more. There are always more and more parts to this machinery, this technology that legitimates violence while covering up its function.

"Race" is a source of our social dysfunction and in your hands, you hold a treatise, comprehensive instructions for our social healing and deliverance. Here are words that help us to find out who we really are to ourselves and each other—apart from racialization and "race/ism." In turn, we'll put "race" behind us and enter a new way of being and belonging—not rooted in skin-deep relations or calls for flesh fights where we root for our side of the false binary of "black" and "white." The togetherness wayfinder, a word combination that unlocks the future we need though sight unseen—the end of "race" and, thus, racism.

Aided and abetted by religious institutions, media, and government, it can be difficult to believe. But just keep reading and counting with me . . . 7 . . . 6 . . . 5. "Race" is but a four-letter word that has gotten in front of and ahead of us for hundreds of years. But Dr. Sheena Michele Mason courageously puts it in its place from the theory of racelessness to a practical apparatus that supports a future imagination and reality without "race/ism" and its attendant "racial/st" ideology. So, let's practice, because it won't be as easy or appear in 3 . . . 2 . . . 1. Keep reading and keep your eyes open as "race" is stripped of its authority and slowly but surely undone.

Starting at the tip of your tongue, read this book aloud and it will work its way down until you can move about freely, reclaim your body, and join us in creating a future without race/ism. Because we don't need more of "race" or, in turn, its progeny. Instead, we need less of this topical treatment of human being and belonging, rooted in the pseudoscience of European "Enlightenment" thinking. We need to "race" less and self-liberate from these competing identities. This can come only when we reconcile ourselves to the reality that "race" will not save us.

"Race," in the United States, supports a hierarchy of being that was created in enthusiastic support of "white" supremacy—the system of belief that people deemed "white" constitute a superior "race" that should dominate society to the detriment of other people who get assigned "nonwhite" identities. It wasn't made to reconcile us but to ensure that we live in comparison—side by side but never together. Instead, it is the invented problem to keep us going back and forth, back and forth, less aware of where our efforts should be focused: the centers of power that profit from our predetermined thoughts and ways of resistance. Us versus them, race's dehumanization knows no ends. It has no boundaries.

Consequently, we need words that hem it in, that get in front of and behind it, that are not just antiracism or antiracist but antirace.

We need words that don't maintain "race" or rearrange it but remove it from time and space. *The Raceless Antiracist: Why Ending Race Is the Future of Antiracism* offers that language and removes the linguistic barrier that impedes freeing speech. This is our time to take our bodies back, reclaiming these fleshy places from "racial/st" language that "eraces" us. We can finally see ourselves as we are and have always been, which is not to be confused with a colorblind lens. Yet, we must admit that we are not physically colored beige, that is, mixed-race, black, brown, red, yellow, or white. Because we don't come from colors but countries, right?

Race/ism has wronged us for so long. There is much work to do to ensure that we get this right. Thus, we need tools and a framework that does more than tinker with institutions, industries, and our inherited hatreds. Dr. Mason provides this while doubling as instructor and mechanic, popping the hood of American society and having a look under while shining a light using statistics, personal narratives, and a searing philosophical and literary lens. She empowers the reader with the needed language, a new tongue, and the tools that enable us to believe that we can do this work and bear witness. The togetherness wayfinder can deliver us from the body of this social death. Can I get a witness?

Perhaps that was a bit premature. But I am confident of this: "race" cannot be repurposed or rehabilitated for relationships with self and neighbor. No, we will have to rid ourselves of it, step back and away from it. Race/ism must be reexamined, and Dr. Mason is called to do this, to reorient us to life after race/ism. She can and does walk us through this page after page.

Dr. Mason has created an opportunity for us to think again, to be reeducated and to reconsider how we relate to ourselves, our neighbors, and the world at large when it comes to "race." She names and makes plain the work: we cannot effectively stop the causes of race/ism while maintaining the belief in human "races" and practice of racialization.

While some would argue that there is no future without "race," "race" abolitionists from all walks of life are saying and proving that there is. Again, I say, *there is a future without race/ism.* Repeat after me and join the chorus with Dr. Mason as director. This is not a rehearsal.

Lifting words that raise our view, she is taking us higher, to the true version of ourselves located far, far away from racialization and all the tricks of its trade. No longer bound by what theologian Brian Bantum calls a "tragic incarnation," we cannot even consider the thought of it. Race/ism has literally captured our imaginations. Yet, the togetherness wayfinder requires just that, listening to the sound of freedom up above our heads. It is the sound of a new humanity. May you have ears to hear it and eyes to see it.

With our North Star in view, we are being directed away from this contrived reality of unjust power imbalances. Dr. Mason works "as if walls did not exist," to employ the words of philosopher Howard Thurman. Magically, she binds this vision to the pages of this book, compresses liberation into letters and holds it steady with punctuation marks. Can you feel it moving?

You must have turned the page quickly. Because this book is going somewhere. The future of antiracism, a future without race/ism: next page.

Reverend Dr. Starlette Thomas
Director of the Raceless Gospel Initiative

The pursuit of liberation from "race" is an especially urgent matter for those people who, like modern blacks in the period after transatlantic slavery, were assigned an inferior position in the enduring hierarchies that raciology creates. However, this opportunity is not theirs alone. There are very good reasons why it should be enthusiastically embraced by others whose antipathy to race-thinking can be defined, not so much by the way it has subordinated them, but because in endowing them with the alchemical magic of racial mastery, it has distorted and delimited their experiences and consciousness in other ways. They may not have been animalized, reified, or exterminated, but they too have suffered something by being deprived of their individuality, their humanity, and thus alienated from species life. Black and white are bonded together by the mechanisms of "race" that estrange them from each other and amputate their common humanity.

—Paul Gilroy, *Against Race*, 2000

Preface

You write in order to change the world, knowing perfectly well that you probably can't, but also knowing that literature is indispensable to the world. . . . The world changes according to the way people see it, and if you alter, even but a millimeter the way people look at reality, then you can change it.

—James Baldwin

In this book, I present pathways toward a future without the causes and effects of racism. Although the general framework can be universally applied, my primary focus in this book is on the most embedded and long-standing form of racism in the West and arguably the most dominant form of racism in modern human society: antiblackness. Antiblackness is the process by which some people of more recent African descent get racialized as black, a historical proxy designating an inferiorly human, subhuman, or nonhuman status.[1] Even today, the dehumanizing process of conjuring and assigning "races" or, more specifically, "blackness" in contrast to "whiteness," results in material consequences that plague all people who get so racialized. Whereas "blackness" is a so-called racial term most often assigned to people of more recent African descent, "whiteness" is a so-called racial term most often assigned to people of more recent European descent.

Both "blackness" and "whiteness" refer not just to groups deemed "races" but also to corresponding ideologies,[2] cultures, ethnicities, and hierarchies (classes), including social, political, and economic ones. So long as both terms are also attached to "races," we need a lens that can help people better interpret racializing language into other socially constructed phenomena because we cannot effectively address the dehumanization of some "races" where racialization and the belief in human "races" exist and persist. Once we expand our conceptualizations of humanity and its attendant constructions and hierarchies, we can better imagine and create a future without destructive conceptualizations, practices, and hierarchies. In other words, more people can rightly turn their attention to collectively contending with the centers of power whose existences depend on the continued mass colonization of minds and imaginations.

While phenotype and genetic essence are often attached to so-called racial categories, the collapsing of essence, ideology, culture, ethnicity, and presumed or assigned access to power via humanness or sub/nonhumanness into "racial" terms from within racializing frameworks, lenses, and practices allows the ideology and practice of antiblack racism—what I also call "white" supremacy and racial/st ideology more broadly—to fester and persist. As the philosopher Charles Mills writes, "[R]ace has functioned as a marker differentiating the humans from the seeming humans who are really, in one way or another, inhuman—if not literally then at least in a weaker sense nonetheless undermining any presumption of their unqualified equality."[3]

Everything in our entire American system—from our educational and governmental institutions to our corporations, technology companies, religious institutions, and media platforms—participates in the machinery of this black-and-white racializing matrix. Escaping it is almost impossible—and least not without effective tools and lenses. Antiblack racism is a form of racism that gets solidified by virtually all other types of racism and systems of oppression, which is just one reason why I focus on and center antiblack racism in the development of what I call the togetherness wayfinder. As a *wayfinder*, the navigational framework I present is meant to lead to a future without today's causes and effects of racism. As a *framework*, the wayfinder includes tenets, tools, philosophies, historical and scientific information, definitions, and linguistic components that together compose a toolkit. While I center and propose the togetherness wayfinder from within the context of the United States, as a collection of tools and ideas, it can be used to analyze other places and times where there is a belief in human "races" and the practice of racialization (including practices of ethnicization that resemble that of racialization). What changes in other contexts include the corresponding historical information, like the names of groups, for example. But the bones of the deracializing lens and its potential impacts remain.

Formerly called the *theory of racelessness* and alternatively dubbed *raceless antiracism*,[4] this togetherness wayfinder helps people free themselves from binary modes of thought as it pertains to social identities and overlapping and interlocking systems of oppression. That freedom translates into

1. a clearer understanding and identification of economic and social systems of oppression;
2. an expanded conception of the human, culture, ethnicity, social class, economic class, and racism;
3. a mode of seeing and being that lessens the internalization of racism-induced traumas;
4. an internalized method of ending the causes and effects of racism that manifest from within individuals and that inspires the desire to contribute toward ending the causes and effects of racism that exist outside of the individual.

Ending racism will require ending the belief in what people call "race" and the practice of assigning "races" to the human species. "Race" is caught up with how one thinks about the human and who gets dehumanized and why. In places like the United States, "race" often gets conflated with ethnicity, culture, social and economic class, and even racism itself. Thus, the togetherness wayfinder culminates in, reflects, and includes a philosophy of "race" that is also a philosophy of the human that provides a pathway for ending racism. If we let it, the togetherness wayfinder can lead us toward a future where everyone is rightly humanized and humans are seen as commonly biological alongside all other species. We can then better "facilitate sustaining the conditions for our survival and the survival of all biological life on the earth."[5] How the "human" has been constructed has been to distinguish humans from animals. But if we cut through the racist imaginings of how the supposedly "nonhuman" human behaves, etc., we see that all of what makes us human includes all of what we tend to assign to "monsters," "animals," and other "nonhumans." So long as we continue to lie to ourselves, we will also continue to endanger all biological life on earth.

Over my twenty years and counting study of all things "human," the following writers, abolitionists, philosophers, educators, scholars, etc., have all given me life over the years: Martin Delany, Phillis Wheatley, Williams Wells Brown, Harriet Jacobs, Frederick Douglass, Charles Chesnutt, James Weldon Johnson, Zora Neale Hurston, Frances E. W. Harper, Jessie Redmon Fauset, Alain Locke, George Schuyler, Langston Hughes, Frank Yerby, W. E. B. Du Bois, Richard Wright, Ralph Ellison, Angela Davis, James Baldwin, Toni Morrison, Martin Luther King Jr., Nettie Jones, bell hooks, Malcolm X, Gayl Jones, Lucille Clifton, Frantz Fanon, Paul Gilroy, Achille Mbembe, Barbara Smith, Sylvia Winter, Kwame Ture, Percival Everett, Jacoby Adeshei Carter, Dana Williams, Greg Hampton, W. Lawrence Hogue, Leonard Harris, Édouard Glissant, Audre Lorde, Octavia Butler, Sonia Sanchez, Amiri Baraka, Stuart Hall, Adrienne Kennedy, Tade Souiaiaia, Valethia Watkins, Alice Walker, Ibram X. Kendi, Barbara Fields, Karen Fields, Carlos Hoyt, Angélica Dass, M. Jacqui Alexander, Nikole Hannah-Jones, Kimberlé Crenshaw, Gene Jarrett, Arthur Jafa, Henry Louis Gates, Jr., Rev. Dr. Starlette Thomas, and far too many more to name or count. Their range of politics, ideas, analyses, lenses, genres, times, disciplines, and experiences have brought me through and to intellectual, emotional, and spiritual journeys and destinations that I could never have imagined even just five years ago. They have informed not only my professional work but also helped me better understand my own personal experiences with antiblack racism. I have learned much from them and taken their calls to create a better and freer society without the interlocking systems that compose racism to heart.

Again, the togetherness wayfinder is a navigational framework that when put into practice—first within ourselves and then externally—provides us with the necessary rules, philosophies, information, tools, and language to become clear-eyed about what racism is and, just as importantly, to know how to stop racism in its tracks. In reorienting our methods of ending racism, I also present a method for expanding how we conceive of and practice humanness, culture, ethnicity, nationality, social class, and economic class. These expansions are intentional since the very idea of "race" and practice of having "races" assigned to humans remain intertwined with these other categories and our ways of creating or preventing belonging and inclusivity. Like Martinican writer Édouard Glissant's concept of relation, the togetherness wayfinder is "a sharp departure from *all* [emphasis added] currently fashionable obligations to celebrate incommensurability and cheerlead for absolute identity,"[6] including those "obligations" almost always upheld across the identity/anti-identity, woke/anti-woke, and antiracist/anti-antiracist spectrum. In the end, these alleged binaries reflect two sides of the same coin.

At times, my language about racism's causes and effects seems broad even though I remain hyperfocused on centering the causes and effects of antiblack racism. In those moments, it might be tempting to interpret my message through worldviews that you know, lenses that are familiar and comfortable to you. In actuality, what I present here in this book is undoubtedly unfamiliar to almost everyone. While various components will feel right to some readers and while the history I present should be familiar to many readers, I invite you to reorient yourself to genuinely new terrain, a world that has not yet existed in modern times but that can and must be realized to end antiblack racism.

The end of our belief in "races," as popularly conceived, and our practice of racialization, along with a paradigm shift away from more traditionally tried and accepted forms of antiracism and colorblindness and toward the togetherness wayfinder, will construct a future that not only acknowledges the reality of history and science but will also bring about the end of antiblack racism itself. Unfortunately, we can't simply ignore or jump over problems and skip to the good part to achieve such an end. That means that banning the study of that which can help us imagine and then create such a future (for example, everything that is categorized as diversity, equity, inclusion, and belonging or Black or queer studies) is off of the metaphorical table, too.

Experience shows us that when we free ourselves from the black-and-white confines caused by racism's effects, we open the door to seeing ourselves in full color. Everything else is a distraction, a deflection—and not the generative type. Stay with me, reader, this is not your typical antiracist book nor is it a book about colorblindness. Again, this is new terrain for almost all. Feel the excitement of exploring something at once seemingly familiar and entirely new.

The RACELESS Antiracist

TOGETHERNESS *Wayfinder*

Concepts
Architecture, the walking negative, renewing, creolization, opacity, warriorage, maternal energy, consolation, nation, diaspora, madness, twilight, invisible ink, and home

Philosophy
Ubuntu and philosophy of "race" (i.e., hereditary believer, synthetic believer, imaginary nonbeliever, preservationist, reformer, and abolitionist) with emphasis on abolitionism

Language
Race/ism, race/ist, antirace/ist, antirace/ism, racial/st, erase, erasure, erasing, a person who gets racialized as XYZ, and so-called

Information
Historical context and quantitative and qualitative data

The Racelessness Translator
Includes identifying philosophy of "race" and what appears to be "race" or "racial" into something about ethnicity, culture, social class, economic class, and/or evidence of the causes and effects of racism itself

Tenet #1
Race/ism (i.e., racism) is a socially constructed system of economic and social oppression that requires the belief in human "races" and the practice of racialization to reinforce various power imbalances.

Tenet #2
"Race" is an imaginary component of the socially constructed reality of racism (i.e., race/ism).

Tenet #3
Racialization is the process of applying an inescapable economic and social class hierarchy to humans that creates or reinforces power imbalances.

Tenet #4
The belief in human "races" and practice of racialization affect people differently. These differences serve to uphold the machinery of racism, acting as obstacles to unification, healing, and reconciliation.

Tenet #5
Translation of what one means by "race," including the presumed absence of "race" in any context, can lead to understanding and bridge-making. The racelessness translator helps people interpret "race" into something being said about the causes/effects of racism, culture, ethnicity, social class, economic class, or some combination thereof.

Tenet #6
Race/ism does not exist everywhere in the same way. We can end it.

Introduction: The Togetherness Wayfinder

It is becoming even more—what should I call it—current to insist on thinking in these terms whether we can call this the product of racism or a hate crime and not deal with it as what it is. I think that is an indication of leaning away from conceiving of justice in a way that would befit a human society.

—Barbara Fields, COMIT Panel, 2022

So that there is no confusion, I want to stress that *racelessness* is not a post-racial vision. The term *post-racial*, when taken alone, suggests an era in which society is free of all or most "race"-based discord. Rather, my focus is on the logical endpoint of antiracism—the *undoing* of our belief in human "races" and our practice of assigning "races" to humans. Only by doing so can we ever end racism, particularly antiblack racism. Only through the abolition of our belief in human "races" and the discontinuation of assigning "races" to humans can we ever hope to complete the work of antiracism and inaugurate not merely a post-racial era but a *post-racist* one. Further, in initiating a post-racist future, we must create vehicles for fostering true belonging and inclusion on the other side of the belief in human "races" and assignment of so-called racial identities. That is why we also have to reorient how we think about and practice humanity, culture, ethnicity, and economic and social class, too. The togetherness wayfinder helps us do that effectively and in ways that

1

are true to complex and opaque realities. This means we need to transform how we think about, talk about, and teach "race," not just across primary and secondary schools but also in universities, in media, and across society.

The continued belief in human "races" and the practice of assigning "racial" identities to humans, rendering some of us somewhat human (if human at all) and others fully human, causes all of us, including those who sincerely want to end racism, to remain within the machinery of the very racism we seek to abolish. We can achieve liberation from racism and end the dehumanization that is based on the systems of power that exist and that many of us are locked within. Although I am an Afrofuturist-inspired thinker, I don't imagine a utopic future. After all, religion, nationality, ethnicity, economic and social class, criminalization, militarization, politics, you name it, would all continue to offer us what we perceive to be justification for writing the "other" off as the inferior enemy, or as subhuman or nonhuman. But I do imagine a future distinctly different and better than today as it pertains to racism, particularly antiblackness. This raises the question: how can we bring such a future to fruition or, more specifically, how can we create a future without racism?

The togetherness wayfinder provides a roadmap for how to identify, discuss, and teach about racism, culture, ethnicity, social and economic class, and humanity, and how to stop racism in its tracks. Consider this book an invitation to wayfind and create a better future for all of us together starting today. No matter the context, the togetherness wayfinder enables us to teach about racism and, by extension, the realities of humanity properly and truthfully in a way that doesn't require any of us to forever suffer from, maintain, or perpetuate the causes and effects of racism. Although it charts a final path that we must begin to forge together, the starting line is already well behind us. The journey began centuries ago, thanks to the efforts of earlier human rights antiracist trailblazers.

While we live in a time where many people still feel too comfortable discounting, devaluing, and dehumanizing each other, the togetherness wayfinder, a staunchly nonpartisan framework, helps people see them-selves and others through a lens of compassion, understanding, love, and growth. That is true regardless of one's politics, how one is racialized, what one has experienced, what knowledge one has, and all that makes us simultaneously similar and different. As scholars such as Dorothy Roberts and Alain Locke note, "race," though a fiction, operates as a po-litical system and comes with real-world consequences. As a result, the fictional is reified. The fiction of "race" and the existence and persistence of racism not only continue to negatively impact those who get racial-ized as black (i.e., dehumanized) but also contribute to the overall di-visiveness and destructiveness of our predominantly two-party politics. People often say they wish for more from our political system—for more unification and less division—but that's not how politics work, not in practice anyway. Some level of dysfunction and unproductiveness will be part of any political system, but the perpetuation of our belief in human "races" and our practice of assigning "races" to humans makes otherwise tractable problems intractable, as does trying to jump over problems or ignoring the reality of problems altogether.

To step outside of the apparatus of antiblack racism means we also need to pay attention to how and why our society and politics uphold the belief in and practice of assigning "races." To make my own political alle-giances clear, I come to this work as a registered independent voter who is not a Democrat or Republican. Though most people will recognize that I am as far to the left as you can be without being completely off of the spectrum, I remain very skeptical and critical of our primarily two-party system, a system that reinforces black-and-white—pun intended—ways of seeing ourselves and each other and all of the corresponding detri-mental impacts that come with black-and-white worldviews. In the end, I advocate for the 99 percent, something neither party wants to do nor does outside of rhetoric, of course. That feeling of outsiderness often gets reflected through my ideas. And since I am solutions-oriented, I observe commonplace discourse about "race," racism, diversity, equity, inclusion, and belonging, and the like with fatigue, heartache, and frustration. The American political system is one that primes us as individuals to accept everything that is embraced by our in-group and to reject everything that's embraced by the out-group. The truths we all hold aren't always facts, as Toni Morrison once said. We need bridges between all truths and facts. Somewhere in the twilight—simultaneously in the gray and in-between yet entirely outside of the black-and-white space—is where our healing and unification happens. Our "my-way-or-the-highway" mindsets might allow us to feel self-righteous, but this approach often comes at the expense of justice and freedom.

Think of it this way: we are in a fishbowl. Therefore, we believe that we need to stay in water to breathe, to live. Our entire environment conditions us to just *know* that we need to stay in the water. We notice that some aspects of the fish tank could be improved for the betterment of all of us and the fish tank itself. Our collective truths keep us in the tank with corresponding ideological worldviews that affirm our beliefs and reinforce the fish tank system. Meanwhile, outer space, not even land, is on the outside of the tank. That is where the most economically and politically powerful people live. In fact, they alternate between inhabiting the fish tank and living in outer space. Unlike most people, they know that we don't need to live in water to breathe. They also know that there are multiple universes, not just the one with the fish tank in it. There are a multitude of ways of seeing and being, in reality, but our truths restrict and constrict us to the known fish tank, whether we revile or revere it.

How can any of us recognize the multiplicity of possibilities within human life? How can we free ourselves and help others get free from the fish tank without experiencing the placebo effect of death, not from being a "fish out of water" but from just knowing that to leave the water is to die. The causes and effects of antiblack racism are the water, fish tank, and miscellaneous fixtures and decals that cover all the walls of the tank that occlude from view everything outside of the tank. History shows us that we cannot confront the reality of racism, every facet of the fish tank, from within the very system of racism, the entire fish tank. Instead, we must find ourselves examining the fish tank from outer space. With increased clarity, precision, and imagination, truths can increasingly come to match facts and reality. Reality contradicts the underpinning ideology of "white" supremacy vis-à-vis antiblack racism: humans are humans, a single species. Humans are not monolithic or homogenous, and neither is culture. A person's assigned or inherited social or economic class standing doesn't make that person inferior or superior to another person. Freedom and belonging start from within and are magnified from without.

It's not enough to simply say there's no such thing as "race" and end the point there. We cannot shrug off the reality and impact of antiblack racism with "race-shouldn't-and-doesn't-matter" mantras or the misuse of figures like Martin Luther King Jr. While I agree that "race," as a proxy for color, isn't real, *racism*—which has real-world causes and effects—is. The reality of racism means we must actively and intentionally confront the illusion of "race" and practice of assigning "races" to humans. Both are foundational to and prerequisites of racism. The cruel irony is that so long as the belief in human "races" and the practice of racialization continue to be the status quo, the reality of racism will remain. That is so whether one actively opposes racism or passively allows it to persist.

That we are all human should be clear. Our shared humanity ensures that our minds select, sort, attribute, and essentialize.[1] More specifically, our minds select things to differentiate, sort them based on select criteria, attribute qualities to them based on surface-level information, and then essentialize them. We then act on this faulty process of "logic" while pointing to our construction (such as racism) as proof of the soundness of our supposed reasoning and our needed action. This process helps explain not only the belief in human "races" and practice of racialization but also the stubborn persistence of racism—that is, how we moved from seeing or presuming differences and sorting based on economic and social power to attributing qualities based on economic and social power and essentializing based on economic and social power. In short, early modern Europeans of higher economic and social status invented the illusion of "race" to maintain and reflect the economic and social systems that were on the ground during chattel enslavement, which in turn fed the belief and practice of "race" and racialization in a now centuries-long feedback loop. It was with their belief in human "races" and practice of assigning "races" to humans that the social and economic hierarchies that already existed were at once reflected and maintained in those newly invented so-called racial hierarchies—with "white" at the top and "black" at the bottom and all others similarly beneath "white."

When discussing the togetherness wayfinder, I am often asked one or more of the following questions: "Does 'race' not matter?" "What about Black Lives Matter?" "Do black lives matter?" All individuals who get racialized as black matter. The existence of racism does not mean that "race" is real or that our belief in human "races" and practice of racialization should persist if we are sincere about ending said racism. What's really being asked, of course, is this: "What about my color? Does the racism I experience matter?" or "What about the racism you—a black person—experiences? Are you saying that racism doesn't exist?" The implication here is clear: if you don't see or accept color (i.e., "race"), then you are ignoring the reality of the racism they've experienced or witnessed.

Ultimately, *racism*—particularly antiblack racism—is the concern. It is what matters—not "race"—yet we maintain the causes and effects of racism when we misdirect our language and efforts away from the roots of racism by adopting the language of its roots and centering that in paradoxical ways. Importantly, the togetherness wayfinder is concerned with the social, psychological, and physical wellness of people who might otherwise have a semblance of liberation and agency were it not for how the causes and effects of racism take hold. Part of how racism works is by keeping people in their respective or perceived places of the hierarchy. We all remain in the fish tank as long as we submit to it and fail to demand accountability and correction from our institutions. Ultimately, we can leave the tank and discover that we don't actually need water to breathe.

Importantly, as I am interested in ending antiblackness and continue to be sustained by my study of "blackness," I center what people call "blackness" in my discussion of effective antiracism. As many Black Studies scholars will rightly point out, "blackness" to some people who get racialized as black does not reflect only "race" or that which is "racial." The question is about how "blackness" continues to be translated and understood as "race" and how that fact consistently designates people who get racialized as black to a subhuman or nonhuman status in American society. It can be easy to miss that I am also advocating for the end of the belief in and practice of "whiteness," too. This is not a matter of alignment with people who deny their so-called whiteness and thereby sidetrack or stop conversations about initiatives to end antiblack racism, often while promoting antiblack racial/st ideology in their denials. This should also not be confused as a call for genocide or the end of *beneficial* aspects of culture. No, I am clear about the causes and effects of racism. As such, the togetherness wayfinder creates pathways between the continued obstacle of so-called whiteness and the desired outcome of ending antiblack racism.

The illusion of "race" and presence of the causes and effects of racism are so powerful that no matter where we are born in the world today, racism and our role in it gets attached to us whether we want the attachment or not. We not only inherit it but we also internalize it and attach it to others and remain in its cycle. Although we've made efforts to reconstruct racism by trying to reform our belief in human "races" and practice of racialization, we cannot ignore the continued harmful impact *or* ongoing salience of "race" or our belief in and practice of it. In other words, we must not ignore the continued harmful impact and ongoing salience of antiblack racism. As a result, the machinery of racism persists without us being the wiser or better. Our belief in and practice (i.e., production) of "race" remains the dehumanizing (i.e., antiblack) apparatus across the globe, precisely because it allows for continued social and economic power imbalances. And our use of "race" language to describe culture and ethnicity also serves to maintain the dehumanizing apparatus of race/ism. If we want to work toward a future without racism—if we want to create a post-racist world—we must today commit to the fullness of the togetherness wayfinder.

The core argument behind the togetherness wayfinder is that the undoing of racism requires the undoing of the belief in human "races"—the idea that humans can be divided into different "races"—and the practice of racialization to undo various social and economic power imbalances. Put another way, only by ceasing to maintain "race" ideology, which includes articulations of colorblindness and more explicitly "race"-centered discourse, and its corresponding language can we stop how society upholds racism, sometimes unintentionally. Listen. *Rather than center "race," I contend that we should center race/ism. The express purpose of the togetherness wayfinder is to disrupt and destroy racism. To do so, we must embrace and put into practice certain rules, philosophies, tools, information, and language to end racism, which is a socially constructed system of economic and social oppression that requires the belief in human "races" and the practice of racialization to reinforce various power imbalances.* Interpretations of the togetherness wayfinder that suggest that what I am advocating is that we should "not teach about race" or the like are blatantly false and missing the entire point of the wayfinder. Rather, we should not teach people to be in and maintain the fishbowl of "white" supremacy and antiblackness, a very different call to action.

While the togetherness wayfinder is a framework in theory and practice, it is also a philosophy of "race" that not only extends the boundaries of racial skepticism and delineates precise paths toward racial eliminativism but also extends philosophies of humanity, culture, ethnicity, social class, and economic class. This would free us from antiblack racism, in particular, and its harmful causes and effects and allow us to recognize our individual *and* collective cultural and ethnic pluralism—a prerequisite for a society based on cosmopolitanism in which every human is rightly humanized (i.e., not racialized or ethnicized). There are ways that we can honor and bridge how any of us think about "race" toward the goal of unification, healing, and reconciliation and the ending of antiblack and other types of racism.[2] Each aspect of the togetherness wayfinder can help us get closer to those goals.

To avoid the unintentional upholding of power imbalances and to signify that I see the illusion of "race" and how racialization manifests in practice as integral parts of "racism," I put the word "race" and associated descriptors like "black" and "white" in scare quotes or modify them with the adjective "so-called." I also use terms such as "race/ism," "race/ist," and "racial/st" throughout. The point of these hybrid terms is to highlight the deep reciprocal connections between the apparition of "race" and racism and to make clear that the illusion of "race" itself is a symptom—an effect—of racism. As an effect of racism, racialized worldviews serve to keep certain groups in the subhuman or even nonhuman category—the bottom of the social and economic hierarchies— and others in the human category—the top of the social and economic hierarchies.

In the context of the United States, as in much of the world, the dehumanizing "race" category is "black." The humanizing "race" category is "white." All other "race" categories fall between the two, sometimes aligned with the assigned subhumanity—inferiority—of so-called black people and other times aligned with the assigned humanity—superiority—of so-called white people. That alignment is often determined by one's willingness and success in assimilating or integrating into cultural norms that get associated with so-called whiteness. Notice how the collapsing of culture with "races" serves to allow the causes and effects of racism to hide and persist.

The illusion of "race" and practice of assigning it to humans serves to maintain—or cause—the continuance of racism. Most individuals tacitly believe that *"race"* exists independently of *racism* or *racist* systems, attitudes, and actions. They presuppose that there are inherent "racial" features of humans and that racism and racist beliefs and actions are biased against these so-called racial features or that antiblack racism has magically already ended, rendering "race" a nonfactor for people who get racialized as black, or that we must ignore "race" to end racism. Thus, by using nonstandard terms and spellings like "race/ism," I aim to disabuse such notions and emphasize the connection between what we call "race" and what is indicative of the causes and effects of racism.

The core tenets of the togetherness wayfinder are as follows:

1. *Race/ism* (i.e., racism) is a socially constructed system of economic and social oppression that requires the belief in human "races" and the practice of racialization to reinforce various power imbalances.

2. *"Race"* is an imaginary component of the socially constructed reality of racism (i.e., race/ism).

3. *Racialization* is the process of applying an inescapable economic and social class hierarchy to humans that creates or reinforces power imbalances.

4. The belief in human "races" and practice of racialization affect people differently. These differences serve to uphold the machinery of racism, acting as obstacles to unification, healing, and reconciliation.

5. Translation of what one means by "race," including the presumed absence of "race," can lead to understanding and bridge-making. The racelessness translator helps people interpret "race" into something being said about culture, ethnicity, social class, economic class, the causes/effects of racism, or some combination thereof.

6. Race/ism does not exist everywhere in the same way. We can end it.

The primary tool of the wayfinder is the racelessness translator, which allows us to translate that which is perceived or presumed to be "race" or "racial" into more apt and precise language. Specifically, when we talk about "race," we are really actually talking about one of five other things—culture, ethnicity, social class, economic class, or racism itself—or some combination thereof. By properly translating "race," we expose the reality of what we really mean. That then lends to increased shared understanding and clarity about racism and other aspects of humanity. It lays bare the reality of racism and enables us to imagine and create a different and far better future. This is not a matter of mere semantics or rhetoric. It is a matter of recognizing human-made systems of oppression and choosing to forge a better path forward for all of us without race/ism.[3]

Part of why we continue to stay within the cycle of race/ism comes down to how some people are programmed to believe that "race" is not a factor or should not be one and others are programmed to believe that "race" is always a factor but that it need not have a negative impact and should be embraced as a positive aspect of society. Others are programmed to fall somewhere between what I just described. We rarely get taught to think about race/ism in ways that effectively invite us to counter and question how we think about it and what we do about it. Typically, we all feel correct and even righteous. We all believe that we think critically about this one topic. In that way, we are all "heterodox" or, at least, on the "right" side of the argument or history.

When we listen to others speak about "race," we receive that information in ways that, more often than not, help to cement how we think about it. That means that both the rightness conveyed within how any of us think about "race" and the wrongness conveyed within how any of us think about "race" frequently get missed by others and keep us all going around in circles. Because of the design of race/ism in particular, we stay in our respective beliefs about the value of the specific versus the universal, the individual versus the collective, with little recognition of how both ways of seeing come into being from within the machinery of race/ism and both operate to uphold it. That cycle of poor or lack of translation—along with the meshing of binaries—enables the architecture of race/ism to remain largely unchecked and in place. Accurate translation is therefore needed.

The effects of race/ism remain significant on all working class and poor people in the United States and on those within the middle to upper classes but for different social and environmental factors than those impacting the lower class. Economic and social oppression—or "down-pression," as Bob Marley called it—seem particularly down-pressing in a time when the rich are getting richer and the gulf between the middle class and upper class is widening while the gap between the working and middle class is shortening. Add to that the complexity of social class oppression and, of course, some people want easy explanations and solutions. But that often works against solving anything. Historically, the social and economic class battles among people who get racialized as white and people who get racialized as black have remained constant to the detriment of the vast majority of people. We must add into our conversations and efforts the decentering of "whiteness," the psychological and physical aspects of unwellness that the environmental factors of something like race/ism contribute to or cause outright, the benefits of embracing the individual *and* collectives, and the power of having more expansive views of power and liberation (especially pertaining to people who get racialized as black). We must also consider how seeing oneself from outside of the paradigm of race/ism is helpful, not hurtful, and preferred for the wellness of individuals and communities, as is the disentangling of valuable aspects of humanity, like positive parts of culture and ethnicity—whereas there's nothing positive about race/ism.

What would happen if, instead of solidifying my own beliefs of agreement or disagreement when I hear someone speak about "race," I had the knowledge and know-how to translate what was being communicated in a way that was accurate and that fostered understanding rather than anger and madness and more binary thinking that keeps us all in the matrix? In a blog post titled "Discovering Theory of Racelessness," Anika Prather says it aptly:

Do not let the term *racelessness* scare you away into the fallacy of colorblindness, but the term *racelessness* is a realization of MLK's Dream for the Beloved Community, where all of our human experiences are welcomed into the conversation, seen, listened to, and embraced, but minus judgement or anger because the human experiences that others have contradict our view of the world. Instead, we welcome diverse perspectives and human experiences to expand our minds beyond our own human experiences.[4]

If you hear someone talk about "race" through the language of "whiteness" or "blackness," and you fail to understand that they are really speaking about culture, ethnicity, social class, economic class, racism itself, or some combination thereof, then you are not translating racelessness. There's a fundamental gap between what you believe and how you think and what that person believes and how they think. The responsibility of closing that gap is on you as the only person you have control over. (More on that in the last chapter.)

This book and the wayfinder are one of translation. I translate for you the most common and often misunderstood ways that the most commonly heard voices think about "race." What do they mean and why? This book is one of twilight that I invite you into. My aim is to give voice to why you might feel as you do and to challenge your thoughts and feelings about the topic of race/ism, especially race/ism in the context of the United States. To put a finer point on it, let this book and wayfinder act as a bridge. Shame on anyone who wishes to use the wayfinder to deepen any divide, which would be a fundamental misuse and abuse of everything I offer. We cannot move forward productively together if we do not understand and largely agree on the root causes and effects of race/ism. We also should not stay stuck in a loop of discussion, which is what the language we have used and the ideologies behind that language have helped to maintain. There remain inefficiencies and attendant barriers within our antiracist and colorblind methods and other methods, including in our language and actions.

One of the greatest benefits of the racelessness translator is that it strengthens our ability to witness and testify to how racism masquerades and gets carried as "race," which is what makes fighting racism from within by using racial/st ideology so cyclical and even regressive. And it also empowers us to see through each other's eyes, a vital aspect of solving such gargantuan and persistent problems. The other tools of the togetherness wayfinder include what I refer to as architecture, the walking negative, rememory, *Ubuntu*, creolization, opacity, marronage, maternal energy, invisible ink, twilight, madness, consolation, nation, diaspora, and home.[5] When best understood, the wayfinder allows for more astute identifications of what racism is and isn't. It also allows us to determine what will and won't work to stop racism and its ill effects in their tracks. Further, the togetherness wayfinder opens the door to a better understanding of culture, ethnicity, nation, humanity, etc. How we perceive a problem not only influences how we strive to solve the problem but also determines whether we choose to solve the problem at all. Philosophy of "race" is another vital component of the togetherness wayfinder, with special focus on the seldom taught and often misunderstood ways of seeing "race" and what to do with it.

Philosophers recognize six ways of thinking about "race." They are often dubbed naturalism, constructionism, skepticism, conservationism, reconstructionism, and eliminativism, but for the nonphilosopher, there's a simpler way to identify and discuss them. They can be divided into two categories. The first three answer the question "What is race?": "race" is either (1) hereditary, (2) synthetic, or (3) imaginary. The second three answer the question "What should we do about race?": we should either (4) preserve, (5) reform, or (6) abolish "race." We each hold two ways of thinking about "race"—one from each category—even if we don't always have the language to name them. And sometimes our way of thinking about "race" reflects slippage between one way and another.

If you believe that "race" is hereditary, you believe that it is biological. If you hold that "race" is synthetic, you believe that "race" is a real phenomenon that is human-made. If you contend that "race" is imaginary, like me, you know that "race" isn't biological and, therefore, believe that it doesn't exist. My view of "race" as imaginary takes me further, though. I hold that what people identify as "race" are other misidentified human-made constructions, such as ethnicity, culture, social class, economic class, and race/ism itself. In other words, I recognize the realness of other social constructions and am not an antirealist about all human-made concepts like some other skeptics. For me and the wayfinder, racism is the human-made construction, not "race." Preservationists, often believers in the hereditary philosophy of "race," want to keep "race." Reformers, typically believers in the synthetic philosophy of "race," work to refashion how "race" is conceived and how it operates in any given society. Finally, abolitionists, like me, whether believers in the imaginary nature of "race" or in the synthetic nature of "race," work to abolish the belief in human "races" and the practice of racialization. In this context, "raceless" and "racelessness" imply an imaginary-abolitionist or synthetic-abolitionist philosophy.

When I was younger, I believed that "race" was biological because that's what I was taught. After all, skin color, hair texture, and ancestry are all biological. I thought that those things were all also "race." I didn't conjure those ideas. I was taught that there are five biological "races" of humans in school. Media and socialization supported such beliefs, amplifying the idea that human "races" reflected a biological reality. Still, I gradually shifted to seeing it through a combination of hereditary (naturalist) and synthetic (constructionist) ways of thinking about "race" because I saw how physical markers and ancestry were often used to determine one's "race" but that one's "race" could be fluid or even change depending on the context. This compelled me to stop seeing the categorization as fixed and laid the seeds of my racelessness translator.

In thinking about how to contribute to solving the causes and effects of antiblack racism, I only ever imagined reconstructing or reforming "race" as possible solutions because that's how I learned to resist and fight against it. Indeed, the United States has never tried anything besides preserving and trying to reform "race" as it pertains to race/ism. This includes the idea of deemphasizing what people call "race." But simply deemphasizing "race" causes us to miss the reality of racism and thus solves nothing.

As a teen and young adult, I assigned everything I loved about myself—my resilience, tenacity, intellect, beauty, empathy, compassion, patience, all of it—to my "blackness." In other words, I attached all of my goodness with my so-called race just as easily as some people attach everything they detest to their so-called race or to someone else's so-called race. I conflated "race" with characteristics, culture, and ethnicity and felt I had an expanded view of humanity through which the prism of "blackness" blessed me. The prism of "blackness" has, in fact, blessed me. But that is not and has never been a "racial" statement even as I responded directly to racism itself. My humanity and that of others was magnified through my study of all things dubbed "black." The togetherness wayfinder was born out of that study, after all.

At the same time, I was constantly grappling with how I and other like-minded people conceived of "blackness" *and how non-like-minded people thought of and treated "blackness."* Intuitively, I recognized that the ongoing struggle for human rights was trying to affirm and assert humanity into the "race" category of "black." That was a failed effort because of all that lurked behind and stayed with said category. I saw that subhumanity—if not a complete lack of humanity—marked the category of "blackness" within systems that deemed some people "white" and others "black" or at least not "white." And I recognized that mark of supposed inferiority tracked with the racial/st language that had been assigned to so-called black people and has existed throughout the decades and centuries: Colored, Negro, Black, African American, mixed, mulatto, octoroon, slave, enslaved, biracial, multiracial, transracial, and so on. The reason I attached everything I love about myself to my so-called blackness and saw that as a "racial" statement wasn't because I despised people who don't get racialized as black but because I needed to fortify myself against some of the harms of antiblack race/ism that I had experienced.

I saw and honored the human rights efforts of those who came before me. The project of fighting against race/ism in the United States always required the reformation of "blackness" from the category of chattel to that of fully human. In a context of being treated as inferior, the people I remain most inspired by had to at least try valiantly to imbue positivity into "race" via "blackness" and render visible and clear the necrotizing impact of the invention and illusion of "whiteness."

During my undergraduate education, I felt a gravitational pull to study psychology and then literature with a focus on "race," racism, and what is now increasingly called *antiracism*.[6] I couldn't learn enough about this thing called "race" and think enough about how to address or even help to stop racism. During those years, I was a hereditary reformer and then a synthetic reformer. I wanted to understand all I could because, in countless and sometimes inexplicable ways, I felt connected with a body of literature that is often defined by *a priori* assumptions about "race." I just knew that my life's purpose was interconnected with the greater purpose of helping to imagine and create a better world, a world which I had come to see as designed to obscure, hinder, annihilate, or crush one's humanity, a powerful echo of the racism and abuse I had experienced as a child.

It took a lot of time to put language to the ironies I saw regarding racial/st ideology even as an undergraduate, but I didn't yet know what I was identifying. My extensive research empowered me to stop talking about race/ism in the language of "race," which misdirects solutions away from the root cause of racism—or, more correctly, race/ism. Further, I was able to get outside of the strictures caused by race/ism to see that we must undo our belief in human "races" and practice of racialization to undo racism itself. We cannot simply skip to the good part, which is where the wayfinder comes into play. The togetherness wayfinder is a bridge between how any of us thinks about "race" and what we aspire to do with it.

When I began my doctoral studies, I was advised by a professor to temper my hopes of trying to help to "end" race/ism. The professor viscerally flinched when I expressed confidence that this could be done, replying that the existing literature already shows us that "to end racism we must undo race." That was as far as my thinking had gotten at that time. I was still a constructionist about "race," even if I had finally come around to being an abolitionist about it. I recognized that I must've sounded alien talking about antiblack race/ism as if it were solvable—and as if any one person could be a catalyst for such a positive and radical change, especially given the disadvantaged position of power that I had inherited. Yet, I also recognized that I was following a very long line of people who knew that race/ism would never be stopped from within racial/st ideology and its language.

I am not against my antiracist contemporaries, such as Ibram X. Kendi, nor am I "against" any critical race theorist. In fact, I see many of the same problems they do and agree wholeheartedly with much of what they argue. Rather, I see myself and my work as pushing their core goal of actively identifying and opposing racism to the furthest logical conclusion. For example, I agree with Kendi that "the very heartbeat of [antiblack] racism is denial."[7] I also agree that the opposite of racism isn't not being racist, but I disagree that the opposite of racism is antiracism in its seemingly traditional sense, as he famously argues. The opposite of racism (or, more correctly, race/ism) is antirace/ism or, as Starlette Thomas puts it, antirace, both synonyms for racelessness. Put another way, to be antiracist in the truest and fullest sense, we must be antirace. In this regard, the togetherness wayfinder aligns with past and present antiracist discourse that seeks to disrupt and dismantle racism.

There are also obvious differences between my work and the work of some other antiracists and colorblind enthusiasts, especially those who insist on the permanence of race/ism, meaning the permanence of the belief in "races," practice of racialization, and related hierarchies. Unlike some antiracist or colorblind approaches, my approach offers an effective methodology for addressing racializing frameworks without upholding the practice of racialization and its consequential barriers in the process. In that regard, the togetherness wayfinder might be best seen as a bridge between contemporary antiracism and colorblindness and those who are opposed to racism but who, in good faith, do not subscribe to the ideas underlying today's more popular versions of colorblindness or antiracism.

The practice of racialization assaults people's ethnic, class, and cultural distinctions *and* similarities by sometimes obliterating or often obscuring how culture, social class, economic class, and ethnicity exist and how humans exist outside of race/ism. The outcome of the practice of racialization for each of us is what I refer to as *eracesure*.[8] If "erasure" is defined as an act or instance of erasing, an obliteration, or a removal of writing, recorded material, or data, then examples of eracesure would include the dismissal of the tradition of thinking and expressing oneself beyond race/ism, the history of obscuring such examples of thought from every canon, and the general practice of upholding racialization and the belief in human "races," which all determine how race/ism and antiracism are taught, learned, read, defined, and included or excluded from conversations.

These types of eracesure are widespread. Public discourse generally accepted as either "white," "black," *or* "colorless" confirms my conviction that racial/st language outside of and within antiracist and colorblind efforts—extending to earlier civil rights movements—often perpetuates the very imbalances of power and agency some people seek to change or ignore. Indeed, colorblind and antiracist initiatives typically assume "race"—that is, they rely on racial/st language and ideology, which means any solution they might propose will have the opposite of the intended effect. Note the current backlash against justice, diversity, equity, inclusion, and belonging efforts in the United States, for example.[9] In short, generally accepted approaches will ensure the continuation of the causes and effects of racism by raising or burying the salience of our belief in "races," practice of racialization, and subsequent power imbalances. This, in turn, leads to continued *eracesure*. "Eracesure" is just one significant outcome of race/ism. And it ensures the permanence of race/ism.

Seeing our fellow humans in racial/st terms—seeing them as "raced" without more effective language to discuss the illusion of "race" and practice of racialization—actually maintains the dehumanization that is the core of race/ism and does nothing toward increasing the acknowledgment or end of its causes and effects. Yet, if we see our fellow humans *only* in traditionally "raceless" terms without a nuanced acknowledgment and recognition of race/ism, we also drive racialization and dehumanization. That is, understanding human differences (which are attributable to culture, ethnicity, class, and other factors) in either benignly "racial" or malignantly racist ways create and maintain the causes and effects of race/ism. Hence *race/ism* and my other spellings keep before our eyes the fact that race/ism (i.e., racism) is a socially constructed system of economic and social oppression that requires the belief in human "races" and the practice of racialization to reinforce various power imbalances.

Ending racism requires eliminating the belief in human "races" and the practice of racialization toward the goal of ending specific social and economic hierarchies. While a number of different racializations happen throughout the world, I focus on the black/white dichotomy because grappling with this dyad is central to the existence of race/ism in many places and contexts. I center "blackness" not because there is something wrong with being "black" or because race/ism is the fault of people seen as "black," but because centering and translating "blackness" makes the reality of race/ism (i.e., antiblackness via "white" supremacy) clearer. Also, we must decenter so-called whiteness to end this particular type of racism. Further, translating "blackness" and "whiteness" is crucial to the objectives of the togetherness wayfinder: to be clear-eyed about race/ism's causes and effects and to effectively center the humanity of all—

needed steps for generating positive material impacts. In so doing, I'm indicting the practice of all racialization and the continued belief in human "races" as a component of the machinery of racism.

Racialization works primarily to the benefit of people who are at the top of the hierarchy, meaning those with the most political and economic power. (Note: from here on, when I mention the "elite" or "those in power," I am referring primarily to these individuals—the so-called 1 percent that holds or controls more wealth than the middle and lower classes combined.) *Racialization* is the process of applying an inescapable economic and social class hierarchy to humans that creates or reinforces power imbalances. It is the process that renders the causes and effects of racism real. "Black" as a so-called race was intentionally written outside of the human species to justify the enslavement of certain human beings and the reduction of those humans to beasts, to chattel.

I get racialized as black by those who see me from within an antiblack paradigm. I'm fully aware that society insists on racializing me. But how one's "race" is perceived and self-asserted has not always aligned. In that way, there's nothing new to see here. I consider myself raceless, whether anyone else acknowledges, likes, or approves this fact. In other words, I see myself as fully human and know the limitations of "racial" language and ideology in describing myself and others. That is not the same thing as denying past or present racism. If anything, my identification as raceless stems from my recognition and understanding of what racism is and isn't. I will not give my power away to racism nor will I define myself from the outside. While "racelessness" implies a sort of absence or denial of being, it should be understood as signifying the desired absence of the causes and some of the effects of race/ism. It is at once present *and* aspirational. It is not a fixed state of being but one always in progress, always in process against deeply entrenched race/ism.

As I recognize that racism operates through the belief in human "races" and the practice of racialization that creates and strengthens power imbalances, I embrace my agency, reject racial/st categorization, and acknowledge how others racialize me. I encourage others to do the same, no matter how they get presently racialized, while acknowledging, of course, how others racialize them and why. That acknowledgment is central to the togetherness wayfinder. As Toni Morrison told talk-show host Stephen Colbert,

> There is no such thing as race. There's just the human race, scientifically, anthropologically. *Racism* [emphasis hers] is a construct, a social construct. And it has benefits. . . . So, it has a social function: *Racism* [emphasis hers]. But race can only be defined as a human being.[10]

What Morrison says here should not be confused with simple clichés like "We are all the same," and she certainly isn't saying that we are all treated the same either. Notice the "it" with benefits is "[antiblack] racism." That is the social construct for Morrison, not "race." But because we live in a society that privileges the belief in human "races" and the practice of racialization, racism, which includes the constructed power imbalances, masquerades itself as the presupposed reality of "race." This distinction matters because to undo racism, we must first undo our belief in human "races" and our practice of racialization. And we need tools to effectively and actually do so. The illusion and application of "race" within the human species helps to maintain the causes and effects of race/ism—including the hierarchies. Our belief in it and practice of assigning and inheriting its assignment must finally come to an end. Reparations are due and should include the end of how society maintains race/ism.[11] In particular, we must hold politicians and governments accountable and responsible for the continuation of race/ism through their institutions, including in their education systems, while at the same time pointing out the culpability of the media, corporations, and religious organizations.

Just as my racialization does not dictate my cultural, social, interiority, or political identity, neither does my deracialization, but unlike my assigned "race," my racelessness emphasizes and elevates the complexity of who I am, who we all are. I rebuke the idea that any of us is or should be defined by the reality of racism (i.e., "race") and hope that more people will recognize their fullness and shared humanity by acknowledging their existence outside and separate from racism, too. Moreover, I invite others to acknowledge my humanity outside of racism. As it stands, too many people feel comfortable telling me who and how I am or who and how I should be without regard for how that type of thinking is itself an effect of racist thought. In her foreword to *Paradise*, Morrison writes,

> I was eager to manipulate, mutate and control imagistic, metaphoric language to produce something that could be called race-specific/race-free prose, language that deactivated the power of racially inflected strategies—transform them from the straitjacket a race-conscious society can, and frequently does, buckle us into—a refusal to "know" characters or people by the color of their skin [how they get racialized]. One of the most malevolent characteristics of racist thought is that it never produces new knowledge.[12]

If racist thought doesn't create *new* knowledge, by extension, neither does racialized thought. This means that we can never fully know ourselves or each other with racialized or racializing worldviews. That is the byproduct of racialized worldviews, whether explicitly or implicitly racist. That also means that colorblindness cannot lead us to a freer or more just future since it maintains both the belief in human "races" and practice of racialization. "Race" is not real, not in nature, and not as a construction. *Racism* is real as are the power imbalances that come with it. The difference matters if we remain serious about ending race/ism. So long as race/ism continues to camouflage itself as what people believe is "race," too many people will see racism as the same everywhere they imagine "race." And too many people will remain racist and okay with the systemic results of this racism. How can we subvert and dismantle the seemingly permanent imbalance of power, practice of racialization, and belief in human "races?"

It is deeply misguided to mistake "race," embrace "race," or teach "race" *separate* from a consequence of race/ism. The belief in human "races" and the practice of racialization are consequences of racism turned causes and consequences for racism. Racism is both a cause and effect of the illusion of "race" and the practice of racialization. One needn't internalize or otherwise embrace "race" and the practice of racialization—thereby internalizing or embracing the causes and effects of racism—to acknowledge or uproot racism. That is a standard error that works to keep people confined within race/ism. The power imbalance is permanent only so long as the belief in human "races" and practice of racialization are upheld. The application of "races" to humans results in the dehumanization of some humans and the seeming justification for social and economic hierarchies. The presumed presence of "race" signifies the dehumanizing process that is in progress. Thus, we need a paradigm shift: racelessness as conceived of within the togetherness wayfinder. We needn't wait for other people, especially those in political and economic power, for example, to liberate and heal ourselves. We needn't wait to create the vehicles we need to get to the imaginative and emancipatory future we desire and deserve. Race(ism)lessness—the togetherness wayfinder—is a necessary therapy not just for those already open to different ways of seeing, being, and moving forward but also for society writ large.

If we examine human society within the framework of the togetherness wayfinder, we not only gain greater understanding about what racism is and isn't but also can chart a clearer path for stopping the causes and effects of racism in their tracks. Throughout this book, I map out the key concepts of the togetherness wayfinder and rely heavily on the racelessness translator. My aim is to show how the togetherness wayfinder works in application. Only by translating what presents itself as "race" into more precise language can we begin to extricate ourselves from race/ism and solve our human-made problems. But the translator by itself is incomplete unless we also fully understand history, ethnicity, culture, nation, economic class, social class, race/ism, and what it is to be human—the things that make us who we are. We must rely on other concepts and approaches to fine-tune our translations and tease out this knowledge in order to begin to see and experience the world without the causes and effects of race/ism. I often draw on philosophy and literary criticism for this purpose. While many of the terms I use are specific to my academic fields—literary studies, Africana studies, and philosophy—and thus their particular meanings might be unfamiliar to you now, they are crucial for understanding and applying the togetherness wayfinder. Therefore, you will come to understand terms such as twilight, the walking negative, rememory, *Ubuntu*, creolization, opacity, marronage, invisible ink, etc. Each chapter builds on one another, as each element of the togetherness wayfinder interrelates and interconnects.

We use almost any excuse to divide ourselves from ourselves and dehumanize one another, whether for reasons of religion, economic class, social class, nation, ethnicity, proximity, profit, and so on. We also show a resiliency and tenacity, an ability to unify and love, that proves to be an unbreakable aspect of humanity, too. The togetherness wayfinder will help us all move beyond black-and-white thinking (pun intended) and begin to inhabit the gray—the just and rightful state of humankind. Undoubtedly, this book will challenge your beliefs and knowledge systems, as it should. I invite you to stay the course and consider the truth, facts, and merits of the togetherness wayfinder, not only for your own benefit but also for our collective benefit.

Let us once and for all end the illusion of "race" and practice of racialization—and with it, particular social and economic hierarchies. Racelessness is the only path forward for genuine human reconciliation, unification, and connection. As I noted earlier, we don't get there by skipping to the good part. Consider this book a corrective map and also just the beginning. It is an invitation.

The cruelness of how the most dominant form of race/ism works in places like the United States means that my very specification of race/ism or racial/st ideology will feel like a door closing for some readers who are approaching this book from a particular way of seeing race/ism. Add to that the fact that other types of racism and prejudice that happen in the United States all serve to maintain the most dominant form of racism—antiblackness—and you will find me always privileging the topic of antiblack race/ism. The irony here is that our focus on the particular results in our opening up of the universal—humanity—to all. However, how I propose to help us get there differs from how people have tried to achieve the same goal: "black liberation" or, in part, the end of antiblack racism. When properly translated, if we achieve such a goal, *all* people will be liberated from some of the primary effects of race/ism because we will finally have uprooted that which causes or obscures various forms of oppression and wretchedness, as Cornel West would call it. In a system where "white" is made to seem at the top and "black" is made to seem inferior and people are treated as such, my focus is and remains on antiblack racism. As with all forms of racism, this is not only to the detriment of all those humans deemed subhuman if at all human but also to all other humans not part of the "elite." In other contexts where the social and economic hierarchies differ, the focus should rightly be on whatever specific type of race/ism exists.

The cruelness of antiblack racism leads anyone expressing a focus on problack or antiblack anything to be misinterpreted or mischaracterized in ways that, again, only serve to maintain the broader system of "white" supremacy. That is why we need effective nonpartisan bridges between how anyone thinks about "race" and what to do about it with the expressed purpose of disrupting and dismantling racism. And whether anyone else changes how they see and address the problem or not, other people can, will, and do benefit from engaging in the togetherness wayfinder since it helps people free themselves from internalizing the reality of race/ism, which is a thoroughly pernicious aspect of racism that gets largely ignored when it comes to solutions and future-making.

The togetherness wayfinder is the primary way for us all to have our humanity recognized by ourselves and others—and for each of us to be viewed and treated as fully human. We are at a watershed moment. We can choose to forge a path forward for all of us or accept and encourage the persistence of race/ism by doing what we've always done: maintaining our belief in human "races" and our practice of racialization.

1

Architecture
Understanding Race/ism

*The historic associations of blackness with infrahumanity,
brutality, crime, idleness, excessive threatening fertility,
and so on remain undisturbed.*

—Paul Gilroy, *Against Race*, 2000

*Nearly all emphasized fixity, or extreme difficulty of change, arguing
that the races have "a predetermined ability or natural disposition"
that was most obviously manifest in external traits but also had
an inner dimension that affected the moral, mental,
and political trajectories of racial groups.*

—Eram Alam, *Ordering the Human*, 2024

Race/ism requires racialization for its spread and survival. In every context, racialization arises out of the interaction of groups of humans, whereby one group of humans assigns a "racial" identity to another group of humans for the purpose of dominating, marginalizing, or excluding the other group. Such us-versus-them dynamics, defined by in-group favoritism and out-group discrimination, have occurred throughout human history, but in the sixteenth century, a unique confluence of factors gave birth to the illusion of "race" and practice of racialization as largely imagined and practiced, respectively, today. These factors included the development of certain pseudoscientific and scientific language and ideas, the rise of sailing ships used for global trade, including the slave trade, and distant warfare, and the "discovery" and colonization of "new" lands to be exploited for resources and profit.

In this context, the idea of "race," as we now tend to think of it, and the practice of assigning "races" to humans—designed to reflect and maintain existing or desired divisions and to justify the subjugation and oppression of "others"—was born. In time, most racialized groups came to embrace or reject their racialization for a variety of reasons, both conscious and subconscious, even and especially in attempts to self-define and resist the effects of racism. Today, almost four centuries after the inception of race/ism as we now know it (increasingly after the 1670s), we still each inherit and get assigned a "racial" identity that we then must navigate and reconcile with who we actually are, especially in relation to each other. Infrequently, people push back against their racialization and, particularly, how racialization works to create and maintain divisions that we would all do well to remove. People who have consistently pushed back against their racialization—namely, people who get racialized as white—often mistakenly reject, ignore, or erase the reality of racism, which lends to certain types of resistance to what is often misperceived as racelessness. If some people who get racialized as white perceive themselves to be raceless and, in various ways, ensure that racism persists by their denial, then it would seem that racelessness is a proxy for "whiteness" and, by extension, continued race/ism.

As a result, people from nondominant racialized groups often accept their racialization as a strategy for resistance even as they reject the negative effects of their racialization. Allies—people who purport to be against racism who get racialized as white—embrace the same racial/st ideology. Typically, anyone suggesting "race" is imaginary or should be abolished is seen as an exception to the rule. As an outsider who invites

others into the unknown, they are reflexively ignored, discredited, deval-
ued, criticized, or otherwise silenced and dismissed out of a deep sense
of fear of the unknown. Our human minds love easy and straightforward
ways to view the world.

Consequently, we have transformed a fiction into a phenomenon
that most people believe exists in some helpful, immutable, or otherwise significant way. Whether we count ourselves as "colorblind," "race"
practitioners, or simply a person who is proud to be of fill-in-the-blank
"race," we've all inherited a framework, a worldview, a way of seeing, being, and acting that doesn't benefit or render apparent everyone's humanity—no matter how much we think it might. From chattel enslavement to
the Holocaust to countless other genocides and exploitations of people
and land, the horrors that racializing and thereby dehumanizing frameworks have led to are too numerous to count. People who seek to mar-
ginalize, exploit, or annihilate other people are well served by the illusion
and practice of "race," if not morally speaking then certainly materially
speaking. While it's true that some might receive a level of material gain
and social "prestige" from such a framework, it comes with a price that
inevitably must be paid. And not all that glitters is gold. Plenty of people
get tricked into seeing their interests as more aligned with people who
get racialized similarly instead of with those of the same or similar social and economic classes. That inevitably means that someone is going
against their own interests—for example, when the working class fights
each other instead of the people, policies, and institutions that benefit
financially and politically from their misalignment.

There is nothing positive about being racialized. Human history
shows us that. Racialization by design is meant to bring misery, angst, anger, fear, death, and division. In the case of American descendants of chattel enslavement, it also means some separation from ancestral languages and cultures. Given how the enslaved were stolen from their homes,
transported across the ocean and intermixed with people from other
backgrounds, and prevented from maintaining their mother tongues in

favor of English, their descendants today are often disconnected from traditional African frameworks for identification (e.g., Akan, Bambara, Igbo, etc.) and have inherited an identity specific to American soil. Collective heritage in the United States includes the racial/st ideology and language that was used to try to justify chattel enslavement and create a new ethnicity—American. "American" in actuality doesn't transpose onto any former country of origin, whether elsewhere in the Americas or Europe, Africa, or Asia. Even though a new ethnicity has been created in the United States, we learn to racialize even that. The United States always finds a way to keep the notion of "America" "white," and everyone else must hyphenate or add some sort of qualifier. That type of eracesure isn't accidental. Those who live in the United States must accept narratives with gaping holes or blatant lies from not only the government, media, and tech industry but also religious organizations and educational institutions. We must accept the practice of some people belonging and others not. Further, we must embrace the fact that nothing can or should change. Unbelonging and belonging are rendered permanent.

In much of the West, we get co-opted into racializing ourselves and racializing each other. We aren't born "white," "black," "mixed," "biracial," "transracial," "Asian," or any other racial/st designator. We are born human. Yet, we each, at various stages, get taught and learn about our so-called race. I learn your so-called race. You learn mine. Some goodhearted people might teach us how to embrace each other's "races" and not let our "natural" biases creep into how we treat each other. Others might teach us how important our "races" are or how our particular country's strength is reflected in the many "races" of people that populate the nation. Others might say they maintain blindness toward their "race" and that of others, even as they inevitably racialize others and themselves by operating within a racial/st paradigm. With very few and infrequent exceptions, we continue to be taught how to name and define ourselves through a relatively young but pernicious ideological framework of "white" supremacy that was created to "justify" enslavement through dehumanization and that we continue to pass on to the next generation.

This is by design. Race/ism is a technology used to maintain and fortify existing power structures. Consider briefly how closely race/ism is used to uphold economic and social class divisions. For example, in the United States, there were four economic classes prior to emancipation: the enslaved, the working class, the middle class, and the upper class, with the wealthiest "whites" at the top of the hierarchy and the enslaved "blacks" at the bottom. During this same period, the social hierarchy comprised three classes, with enslaved people at the bottom, free "people of color" (including people indigenous to the Americas, free people of more recent African descent, and immigrants from Asia) in the middle, and free people descended from Europeans at the top. After emancipation, the upper classes were able to ensure the maintenance of this basic hierarchy through the continuation of race/ism; they attached the racialized social class hierarchy to the economic class hierarchy to make both seem to be one and the same, an outcome that has resulted in a frozen-in-time way of thinking about our social and economic problems, a mindset that limits our ability to find possible solutions and reifies the social effects of race/ism. The United States keeps trying to wed poverty with "blackness." But by extension and as described above, poor and working-class people who get seen as white also suffer under an anti-black regime and can be rendered invisible within the discourse about poverty and "race." On one hand, so-called whiteness carries with it certain privileges, like getting seen and treated as fully human and superior. On the other hand, so-called whiteness encourages too many people to uphold the causes and effects of race/ism while also maintaining other economic and social hierarchies that would otherwise be addressed with more clarity, imagination, and willingness.

In other words, "black," not "white, became synonymous with poor, the material reality that the elite desired. That we live in a mostly economically and socially segregated society does give the impression that people who get racialized as black are still mostly poor, in part because poverty and racialization tend to overlap in many urban and rural areas of the country. The media and our overall national discourse contribute to this perception by often equating impoverishment with nonwhite racialization. As a result, when we focus on race/ism as opposed to economic class when thinking about how to uplift the poor, we fool ourselves into thinking that we are solving poverty in ways we aren't at all. The machinery of race/ism is so ingrained that even the suggestion that, here and now, we should address economic issues based on economic class—centering economic class power imbalances, not social class aspects of racism—is deemed antiblack by some people. In certain circumstances, such a charge might be true, but what if the quest for "racial" justice negates the probability of ever solving social and economic class issues? What if seeking a conceptualization of justice through the lens of "white" supremacy helps to maintain the status quo, the changing same, and what bell hooks called interlocking systems of oppression: transnational white supremacist capitalist patriarchy.[1]

While it's true that economic and social divisions are maintained through the privileging of one perceived social class over another, economic classes don't necessarily align with social classes. Today, the racial/st aspect of social class has been largely compressed into two primary and overarching categories: "white" people and everyone else—namely, "black," indigenous, and "people of color" ("BIPOC"). Yet, the economic hierarchy ostensibly reflects more than a binary: lower, middle, and upper. As a result, the rich and poor categories get conflated (often subconsciously) into "white" and everyone else (i.e., "BIPOC"), respectively. In turn, people who thrive economically are generally viewed as being in close proximity to "whiteness," no matter how they get racialized. Consider how "white" once referred only to Anglo-Saxons but this self-assignment gradually came to refer to ever-larger numbers of ethnic and national groups with roots inside and even outside of Europe. In today's United States, people of East Asian and South Asian descent are not only often referred to as "white adjacent" but sometimes get categorized as "white."[2] This is based, in part, on perceived and sometimes actual economic success and social standing,[3] demonstrating how racial/st categories overlay economic and social ones. It is also based on a desire to increase the number of people who get called white or white adjacent to maintain the status quo of power imbalances with "whiteness" at the top. Further, the process of increasing the reach of "whiteness" often signifies the assimilation or integration some groups undergo to better reflect the generally accepted norms and values of a country.

The United States is often described as a "melting pot," but there remain parameters to what is considered and upheld as acceptable and standard. Just as there are expectations imposed onto so-called black people about what it means to be "black," there are opposite expectations imposed onto people who get racialized as white or, at least, not black, that remain attached to a place on the social and economic hierarchies. For example, rather than create a culture that accepts the different ways that people speak English, American institutions treat "Standard English" as the prerequisite for success and class. Rather than create a culture that embraces different hairstyles, certain textures, styles, and lengths are banned in various contexts even in states that passed the CROWN Act. Consider how "whiteness" or "Europeanness" is imposed as normal and acceptable (i.e., human), and "blackness" or "Africanness" is imposed as abnormal and unacceptable (i.e., subhuman or nonhuman). Thus, what we call "race" actually reflects the biased, homogenous, and singular standards of a society that punishes people who do not get racialized as white in favor of packaging liberation and power with the category of white and gatekeeping everyone else's ability to access that seeming liberation and power. I say "seeming" since the category is still part of an oppressive system that renders even whiteness constraining, one-sided, and a critical part of the problem of race/ism.

This antiblack racial/st framework is further buttressed by and intertwined with how data is filtered and analyzed. Specifically, economic data is itself often racialized (i.e., organized according to "race"). As a result, racialized data leads to racialized interpretations of data. The data itself is frequently cited as proof of race/ism or an inferior racialized culture (i.e., cultural racism).[4] The othering "BIPOC" individuals experience due to the effects of these types of racializing lenses is only elevated further rather than ameliorated, while the problem of racism as a social and economic hierarchy not only remains unsolved but also becomes further fortified. Race/ism results in the continued acceptance of the illogic practice that to be socially and economically successful in the United States is to adopt a form of "whiteness." And that is how it will forever be to the detriment of all who don't get racialized as white or who refuse to culturally assimilate or integrate. Only through the machinery of race/ism can we conclude that "whiteness" and everything assigned to it will always remain at the top of social and economic hierarchies. Of course, it will always remain there if we do not radically change how we operate and create pathways of belonging instead of sustaining the unbelonging too many people inherit.

My reference to social *and* economic hierarchies and not to a *socioeconomic* hierarchy is intentional. The term *socioeconomic* itself reflects the presumed sameness of social and economic class hierarchies. Yet, those within each economic class often share more in common with each other than they do with some people within their respective social classes. Many current policy initiatives ostensibly favor social class dynamics over economic class ones, which hinders our ability to solve issues related to things like poverty, child welfare, the militarization of policing, and a failing education system in meaningful and substantive ways. As a teenager, I was subject to homelessness, neglect, and severe abuse. A love for reading and education and an inordinate amount of resilience enabled me to overcome tremendous adversity. Today, we maintain racial/st ideas about who has what and who values what, while doing less to address elitist and dehumanizing ideas about poor people or the working class, who may not be functioning much above the government-ascribed poverty line. This creates superficial economic class divisions that keep us all pandering to or against social identifications, all while still operating from within our assigned designations, and prevent us from identifying with each other in ways that would benefit all of us.

As long as antiblack race/ism persists, we will never be able to improve conditions for all, including those people at the bottom of the economic and social class hierarchies. Racial/st ideology guarantees that we will remain in lockstep "against" each other because black/white (binary) discourse will never help us unify. Our shared belief in human "races" and practice of racialization across the political spectrum remain our downfall, as our belief in human "races" encourages a black-and-white way of looking at ourselves and each other. We can recognize racialization without upholding it. We know that humans are tribal. We needn't be tribal because of race/ism and the attending racial/st ideology that we inherit. We can choose to forge a better future together today.

Nowadays, race/ism might look different than it did in past centuries, but the framework is as rotten today as it was at its inception. We continue to uphold race/ism by continuing to believe in "race" and assign races to the human species, which in turn supports the race/ist (i.e., "white" supremacist) power structures that were erected centuries ago. Our most impactful public and private institutions, from our governments, universities, and schools to our corporations, religious organizations, and media companies, continue to play significant roles in upholding racialization and reinforcing racialized identifications to the detriment of everyone. In many cases, they continue to benefit and profit from race/ism itself, even as they pretend to care about or participate in solving the problems that plague us.

We have made significant progress against antiblack race/ism. This progress has been hard-earned. It has also been hindered because of how racial/st ideology works. As long as we as a society operate within the ideology and framework that the early, wealthy, and primarily Anglo-Saxon colonialists crafted, any progress we make will be forever bounded within a race/ist system. Ibram X. Kendi is right about the following: to get racialized as black in the United States is to be stamped from the beginning.[5] Racialization is a stamp that a ruling class or an aspiring ruling class practices to dehumanize and dominate other groups, and it serves to alienate the poor, working class, and arguably the middle class from itself in favor of continued domination by the elite. That's how race/ism works, even if some racializations themselves have changed across time and space. That is why, in the context of the United States, I focus primarily on antiblack racism. Unlike other racializations, the racialization of people who get assigned "blackness" has been largely fixed since before the country's creation. This stamp need not be permanent, but it will never be erased or reformed so long as the type of race/ism that manifests in the United States is upheld.

The typical antiracist reconstructing or reforming of "race" and the continuing of racialization is not the answer. Despite what others say, colorblindness is also not the answer. We've been reconstructing the idea of "race," addressing the impact of racialization, and trying to change how we see ourselves for centuries. Many people have tried to espouse or live out a colorblind ethos, especially following the end of the official Civil Rights Movement and Martin Luther King Jr.'s assassination. Indeed, the United States has been reconstructing the meaning of "race" since before the American Revolutionary War—in other words, since before the United States even came into being as an independent country.[6] Yet, even with the variety of "racial" categories that have been added to and deleted from the U.S. Census since emancipation, "White" and "Black" (formerly "Slave," "Colored," "Negro," etc.) continue to be presented as constants—distinct "races," separate and unequal—even though this consistency wasn't exactly the case in the early colonial period. Largely influenced by longstanding and ever-fluid European class systems, "race" in the early colonies reflected an economic and social class system that, at its most complex, included not only free "whites" and free "blacks" but also "white," "black," and "brown" indentured servants, who, for all intents and purposes, were enslaved indigenous or African people. Notably, enslavement and freedom were not initially racialized—in the way typically understood—until approximately 1660, when various states began outlawing "miscegenation," calculating "blackness," and passing laws that allowed for the capture and return of runaways from enslavement.

As indentured servitude was formally phased out, "black" and "Negro" came to describe people of African descent who were considered, by law and practice, to be enslaved and chattel. "People of color" primarily described free "black" or "brown" people, including those of mixed African and European ancestry. People who got racialized as white became free of all forms of enslavement in the United States, with "white" describing all free people of seemingly visible and traceable European (at first primarily Anglo-Saxon) descent. "Whiteness" was coded within laws and policies to represent political, social, and cultural freedom and entitlement to the ideals that would become associated with the United States (democracy, rights, liberty, opportunity, individualism, mobility, and equality, to name a few). Put another way, "whiteness," as it was tied to racialization, was conflated with the absence of color or "race" (i.e., racelessness), a grave conceptual error that persists today.

"Blackness," on the other hand, conjured as a counter to "whiteness," meant being enslaved or being fit to be enslaved, lacking freedom and upward mobility even outside of enslavement, and being outside of citizenship and humanity (i.e., chattel). Importantly, collectivism, immobility, and inequality were written into the concept of "blackness," which was presupposed to be *racial*. The black/white binary was crafted to mirror other binaries—for example, individual/collective, free/enslaved, good/bad, American/hyphenated American, saint/criminal, victim/victor, etc. The presupposed differences between people who get racialized as black or white as reflected in these various binaries play out today in complex ways that can confound. More than anything, racial/st ideology continues to encourage the type of living death caused by race/ism, requiring fewer and fewer influences to exact its detrimental outcomes. It forces and reinforces a binary—a black-and-white way of seeing the world that is contrary to the grayness of it.[7]

Racial/st ideology, as society teaches it in various ways, keeps us believing in the mythology of "race" and practicing racialization. That precludes us from knowing that the belief in human "races" and practice of racialization themselves must be stopped to achieve better ends—that is, to end the attending social and economic hierarchies of race/ism. Other mythologies of "race" and practices of racialization inspired the Nazis to support and carry out the genocide and attempted annihilation of the Jews (1939–45) and the Dominican Party to support and carry out the genocide and attempted annihilation of Haitians (1937). From serfdom (Europe and Russia) and debt enslavement (Africa and Europe) to prisoner-of-war labor camps (global) and human-trafficking (global), humans across the globe have demonstrated their ability and willingness to do the inexcusable and unspeakable to out-group "others" even as they do wondrous things for those in their conjured in-groups.

From the inception of the word "race" and the frequent reconstruction of what the word meant in much of the Americas, especially in what came to be the United States, "race" was class, but class was never "race." Part of what gets upheld by the maintenance and propagation of race/ism via racial/st ideology is the continued masquerading of economic and social class as "race," which, in turn, produces and perpetuates a particular cultural identity that is misconceived as "racial." The cultural identity that has predominantly been understood to represent "blackness"—that is, the "authentic" "black" experience, culture, and so on—is that of the working class or poor Americans who get racialized as "black." While there is a substantial wealth gap between people who get racialized as white and people who get racialized as black in the United States, a gap that is largely a product of chattel enslavement, segregation, Jim Crow, redlining, mass incarceration, massacres, the burning down of towns, prejudice in hiring practices, the loss of opportunity and income across generations, and the compounding effects of wealth,[8] the washing over of entire populations with so-called racial identities fails to account for the wide disparity in wealth among so-called black households.[9] Today, we should recognize the reality and plurality of cultural creation and expression. Our continued insistence on maintaining and making sense of culture through racializing frameworks obscures the fact that humans create and keep race/ism through culture. "Race" does not create or come from culture. It is the other way around.

In truth, the economic and cultural divide among people who get racialized as black is wide. Here, as elsewhere, much of what we encounter regarding "race" can be translated—in this case, as partly an economic class issue, which is part of race/ism, that can be approached through economic class–based data and policy solutions. Indeed, as People's Policy Project founder Matt Bruenig states, "nearly all white wealth is owned by the top 10 percent of white households just as nearly all black wealth is owned by the top 10 percent of black households. The lower and middle deciles of each racial group own virtually none of their racial group's wealth." While the median so-called white household has roughly seven times more accumulated wealth than the median so-called black household,[10] 97 percent of that difference, according to Bruenig, is attributable to the top half of so-called white and black households. As Bruenig continues, "the overall racial wealth disparity is being driven almost entirely by the disparity between the wealthiest 10 percent of white people and the wealthiest 10 percent of black people."[11] The increasing gap between the top 10 percent of all households and the remaining 90 percent strikes me as relevant in our analysis of the economic landscape and how to address these disparities.

While the culture of the working class has always been far-reaching and impactful, the creators of the culture that most people identify as authentically "black" are, in reality, a statistical minority within another statistical minority. Notably, the poverty rate for people who get racialized as black was 17.1 percent in 2022.[12] (As a point of comparison, the poverty rate for those who get racialized as white was 8.6 percent.) That population has an outsized and unmatched positive impact on global culture, even though credit is not often given to the creators in favor of "racial" views of culture that collapse social and economic class. As Paul Gilroy says in *Against Race: Imagining Political Culture Beyond the Color Line* (2000), contemporary processes and attempts to maintain the alleged coherence of the idea of "race" "have added a conspicuous premium to today's planetary traffic in the imagery of blackness."[13] So-called black representation in media and different mediums often centers and upholds the "historic associations of blackness with infrahumanity, brutality, crime, idleness, excessive threatening fertility, and so on remain undisturbed."[14] Time and again, artists and writers alike get accused of being antiblack when such viciously racist caricatures of so-called black people get expanded or countered through media and mediums with other types of "representation" (i.e., images and stories).

While some people insist that there is no singular way to be "black," in practice and in theory, the nation has not caught up with that reality. The machinery of race/ism requires the homogenization of all who get most adversely racialized. When almost half of Americans who got racialized as black were poor, the conflation of racialization and economic class could be forgiven—if for no other reason than this association helped advance civil rights. But today, the context is different. This continued conflation leads to a skewed perception about the lives and experiences of the majority of Americans of more recent African descent, their contribution to and place in American society, and everyone's understanding of culture, ethnicity, nation, diaspora, and humanity.

By conflating racialization with essence and conflating racialization with social and economic class, Americans continue to assign impoverishment to "blackness," which helps maintain the economic and social class hierarchies that existed during enslavement, when only "whiteness" was afforded access to power. By locking up lower economic class status with "black" racialization, people unintentionally reinforce social class tensions and problems (i.e., impacts of race/ism). Just as "white," in reality, never meant all or only rich and wealthy and "black" has never meant, in reality, all or only poor, the ways people continue to racialize themselves and others remain incoherent and not reflective of reality now or even historically (admittedly, the conflation of social and economic class was closer to reality then than now). By masquerading as social and economic class, our belief in human "races" hinders clarity about the true causes of social, cultural, economic, and political problems and thus prevents us from identifying solutions that will optimally address these problems. An ineffective focus on race/ism will make us less likely to meaningfully address poverty, as poverty constantly gets racialized and misinterpreted as indicative of "black" essence or reflective of the alleged inferiority of "black" culture. When the problems are misidentified, any solution will be incoherent at best and damaging at worst. And both the economic and social hierarchies impacted by race/ism will persist. In practice, intersectionality falls short largely because "race" does not also get translated as ethnicity, culture, economic class, social class, and racism itself. Instead, all of these categories get collapsed and conflated into a point of indiscernibility.

While ideas about "race" continue to undergo reconstruction in the public and private spheres, the racial/st hierarchy created by once legal and now illegal practices remains embedded in society. The ways that race/ism has been studied, discussed, and taught from its outset have allowed the problem to persist. Too often, the focus is on the symptom of "race," not the cause, which is race/ism—as defined within the togetherness wayfinder. The belief in human "races" and practice of racialization are *the* prerequisites for specific power imbalances; both serve to demarcate subjugated and dominant populations. While reconstructing racial/st language and its corresponding ideology proved an expedient strategy for advancing human rights in earlier periods, the practical utility of this strategy has run out if we want to undo the causes and effects of race/ism once and for all.

People from a variety of political ideologies and educational backgrounds continue to strive to reform the meaning of "race" and how the belief in human "races" and practice of racialization manifest materially. They often do this by either ignoring or recognizing America's violent history of race/ism and striving to maintain or remove the violence of race/ism from racial/st ideology. As it pertains to philosophies of "race," the default positions continue to be hereditary (naturalism) or synthetic (constructionism) and reformationist (reconstructionism) or preservationist (conservationism). Ironically, most colorblind or antiracist literature and activism today help reify antiblack race/ism because they inhabit and promote these positionalities of racialization and belief in "races." Most traditionally accepted forms of antiracism and appeals to colorblindness both hold that "race" is real, either as a biological fact or human-made phenomenon, and want to refashion the idea of "race" and practice of racialization—which is the same as trying to reform racism, which means that we will ultimately keep it.

"Race," according to philosopher Charles Mills, "puts into question the full humanity of the stigmatized racial group(s)."[15] When best understood, our imposition and presumption of "race" result in our (sometimes) unintentional maintenance of a social and economic hierarchy. Race/ism is the social construction that necessitates our continued belief in and upholding of racial/st ideology and its correlated language and practices. We continue to convince ourselves that "race" *is* skin color, phenotype, and DNA—inescapable aspects of humanity—or ethnicity and culture—inescapable aspects of society that have value. Race/ism hides behind the illusion of "race," which is why misunderstanding "race" and talking about race/ism in the language of "race" contributes to the causes and effects of race/ism. The machinery of race/ism requires the persistent belief in and assignment of "race" in the first place. Dehumanization is unavoidable whenever "race" is imposed because "race" and the assigned/inherited racialization of humans *is* reflective of the presence of dehumanization in the first place. In this way, many traditionally antiracist and colorblind approaches to antiracism—no matter how well intended—are part of the machinery of perpetuating the causes and effects of race/ism.

The whole assigning of "race" to people (i.e., racialization) as indicative of one's *fixed* status in society is indicative of what too many people are convinced is true. The hierarchy is built into the apparition of "race," as race/ism created and continues to perpetuate the idea of "race" and the practice of racialization in the first place. There has never been a neutral way to racialize people. There will never be an unbiased or beneficial way to do so. To undo race/ism, we must undo our belief in human "races" and practice of assigning "race" to the human species. We need to redirect antiracist and good-faith colorblind efforts away from "race" to that of race/ism, thereby targeting the real roots of race/ism without upholding the thoroughly pernicious roots of the problem. This topic is not merely a matter of rhetoric. If we are serious about forcing a complete reckoning with race/ism in the United States and across the world, the solution is not to further reform "race:" "race" can never be saved nor can it save us. It is within us as humans to end race/ism. After all, humans invented it, and humans maintain its madness.

2

Madness
Identifying Systemic Race/ism

What is demanded in this country, I think, it's very important, and it
probably won't be done, is that we surrender the notion, surrender the
notion of being a white nation. It is an absolutely useless idea, anyway.
And with 22 million Negroes here, occupying the peculiar
and dangerous position that they do, we cannot be called
a white nation anymore.

—James Baldwin, in conversation with Studs Terkel, 1962

Race/ism is systemic but not always or only in the ways some people think. It is an ingrained part of our practices, knowledge, and beliefs. From an early age, our entire sociocultural system programs us to believe in "race" and racialize ourselves and each other, thereby upholding the causes and effects of antiblack race/ism. That is, of course, by design at this stage. We then get told that to fight race/ism, a perpetual battle, we must reform it—that is, we are asked to believe in "race" in a way that will simultaneously inflict less harm and recognize and embrace human diversity. But maintaining a belief in human "races" and practice of racialization will never eliminate all the harm each cause. Ultimately, we must hold our governments, media, corporations, religious organizations, technology companies, and education systems responsible and demand substantive change. To continue to reinforce racial/st ideology is to reinforce the material consequences of the hierarchy and the madness that ensues via race/ism. Here, I mean madness to reflect anger, chaos, disorder, excitement, ecstasy, rage, and insanity. One result of race/ism is madness in all of its meanings. The togetherness wayfinder helps us to recognize and better interpret all forms of madness, which is a necessary step toward unification, healing, and reconciliation.

If you believe in the power and agency of the individual or talk about interpersonal race/ism too much, you've missed the *systemic* part of race/ism, how racism has tangible impacts, say some antiracists. If you believe in the power and agency of the collective over that of the individual, you've missed the strides made by individuals against racism and the American values of personal agency and tangible upward mobility, say those who are critical of antiracist discourse and initiatives. Both views are right and wrong. It is a marvelous and impactful thing to see our individual selves as part of humanity, a collective that is bigger and greater than any single one of us. And every person also benefits from being seen and seeing themselves as beautifully made individuals. We can and should hold both ways of seeing at once. Although "whiteness" is often associated with "individuality" and "blackness" with "collectivity," for reasons consistent with human rights efforts and advances and traditional African modes of thought that uplift communal aspects of life,[1] no single association is unique to any racial/st group in the United States, nor should any association be. As discussed in the last chapter, racial/st ideology imposes expectations of authenticity and representation onto people, especially those who get seen as part of a collective (i.e., those who get racialized as black), to the detriment of everyone in a place where people who get racialized differently coexist. Race/ism creates a lose-lose sociocultural environment.

No single person has or ever will represent any single racialization in reality. But believing that there is an essence to humans and that thus there are "right" and "wrong" ways for individuals to represent their "race" serves to stigmatize and dehumanize. This is what racial/st ideology does. It limits our humanity. For example, individuals who get racialized as black but who don't fit the "white" supremacist narrative of "blackness" are often deemed "inauthentic." In other words, there's a way to be politically black, ideologically black, culturally black, ethnically black, and so on. And there is, if one understands what is meant by such terms. However, none of that is "racial." The racelessness translator can help more people understand what is meant by such assertions. Understanding is foundational to growth and healing. Humans are complex, even—and perhaps especially—when part of a collective. Let the collective be something outside of race/ism. Stop mistranslating "race" to receive what people mean when they use it. That is the work of the togetherness wayfinder.

To be clear, the togetherness wayfinder or raceless antiracism owes significant debts to what can be called an antiracist tradition and the tradition of opposing antiracism. I'm not opposed to nor am I blaming other antiracists for antiblack race/ism. Rather, the togetherness wayfinder helps to bridge the gap between various strategies of resistance and nonresistance toward the betterment of all of us. The problem isn't and has never been people who get racialized as black, which I know some readers will make synonymous with antiracism. The problem is the human-made system through which race/ism is maintained in which almost everyone participates, intentionally or otherwise, and experiences the effects of it. Solutions rest in addressing the social and economic class aspects of race/ism. The goal is for individuals who get racialized as black or as nonwhite to see themselves from outside the bounds of race/ism while still being clear-eyed about the reality and impacts of said racism, which is one reason I center my discussion on the category of "blackness." Let us not fool ourselves into thinking that individuals don't have any choice or agency. Let us not fool ourselves into thinking that self-liberation from the strictures of antiblack race/

ism or any other type of racism doesn't benefit the individual. And let's acknowledge the role of the broader systems in maintaining the causes and effects of race/ism.

Different cultures have different ways of giving voice to the power and agency of the individual while simultaneously acknowledging the individual's place in a vast, boundless, and interconnected world. Consider the philosophy of *Ubuntu*, a Nguni Bantu term and a central component of the togetherness wayfinder. The best one-word translation might be "humanity" or "humanness," but a better translation would be "I am because we (or you) are." Social work practitioners and scholars Rugare Mugumbate and Admire Chereni define *Ubuntu* as

> A collection of values and practices that people of Africa or of African origin view as making people authentic human beings. While the nuances of these values and practices vary across different ethnic groups, they all point to one thing—an authentic individual human being is part of a larger and more significant relational, communal, societal, environmental and spiritual world.[2]

In other words, *Ubuntu* ways of seeing and being center the acknowledgment that none of us exists within a vacuum. Hyperindividualism exists in antithesis to reality. Who we are as individuals is shaped and informed by who we are as a community, and who we are as a community is shaped and informed by who we are as a community among and within other communities. Who we are as a species is shaped and informed by who we are as one of many species and biological beings. In these ways, the reciprocal nature of identity formation of individuals and communities—the multidimensional and multidirectional nature of you, I, they/them, and we/us—remain central to the wellness of both individuals and communities. African studies and comparative philosophy scholar Michael Onyebuchi Eze says that the core of *Ubuntu* is best summarized as follows:

A person is a person through other people strikes an affirmation of one's humanity through recognition of an "other" in his or her uniqueness and difference. It is a demand for a creative intersubjective formation in which the "other" becomes a mirror (but only a mirror) for my subjectivity. This idealism suggests to us that humanity is not embedded in my person solely as an individual; my humanity is co-substantively bestowed upon the other and me. Humanity is a quality we owe to each other. We create each other and need to sustain this *otherness* creation. And if we belong to each other, we participate in our creations: *we are because you are, and since you are, definitely I am.* The "I am" is not a rigid subject, but a dynamic self-constitution dependent on this *otherness* creation of relation and distance.[3]

The philosophy of *Ubuntu* underscores how culture humanizes (or dehumanizes) its participants. It also points to the fact that each person's humanity is cocreated by their community. There's a simultaneous acknowledgment of everyone's humanity and the human practices that shape it, the existence of unique individuals even within potentially homogenizing contexts, and the human practice of othering with emphasis on the benefits of owing each other humanity. Humanity, at its best, is a process of generative reciprocation, in which we as individuals engage in community action and collectively create something larger than the sum of our individual impacts. The philosophy of *Ubuntu* also implies the inverse: if communities help shape our individual humanity, then we as individuals can also be dehumanized based on the expectations and rules of our communities.

Indeed, our upholding of racial/st ideology obscures our shared humanity more than it illuminates it. By design, the ideology predisposes us to see each other as insiders or outsiders, as human or nonhuman, as separate, distinct, and unequal. If we hyperfocus on the individual to the detriment of the collective or continue to assign individuality only to a particular racialization, we place limits on ourselves and others. We all deserve the benefits of seeing ourselves as part of something bigger than ourselves, part of a national and global society. At the same time, if we hyperfocus on the collective to the detriment of the individual and if we racialize that collective and the desire for collectivity, we limit ourselves. We all deserve the benefits of seeing ourselves as complex and rich individuals who are also in relationship with other complex and rich individuals. Our belief in human "races" and practice of racialization causes individuals to be seen as avatars of their so-called race but only when the image conforms to the explicitly race/ist ideology about what it is to get racialized as black, which diminishes if not "eraces" our shared humanity. We must recognize and stop reinforcing this bifurcation, which neither strengthens nor serves us. It places liberation just outside of reach for too many people.

A nation's practices, knowledge, and belief systems remain a critical part of how racial/st ideology perpetuates systemic race/ism. Thus, if the United States and other countries seem more divided now than before, that is, in part, caused by our inheritance and continuation of racial/st ideology via race/ism.[4] Individuals compose any collective, so to solve any problem we need enough individuals to bring to fruition positive changes in their respective fields, industries, networks, and so on. We need individuals in government, education, technology, religious institutions, and media to change course. That requires a profound level of knowledge that is unhindered by race/ism of any kind and especially antiblack race/ism. It also requires imagination and courage. We need individuals who are willing and able to dream bigger than Martin Luther King Jr. and Malcolm X and act accordingly.

When enough individuals embrace and harness their power and agency, the system will come to reflect what the collective believes and knows. Yet, collectives cannot change a system, truly and sustainably, without addressing the root causes of the system's problem. In the context of the United States, the root causes of the system's race/ism are the maintenance and practice of racial/st ideology by the country's main political parties, religious organizations, media, corporations and tech companies, and educational institutions. Although people are increasingly speaking out across the political spectrum about how racialization (i.e., race/ism) negatively impacts them and their children, rarely do they strategically cite the apparition of "race" itself and the practice of racialization as that which simultaneously upholds and reflects social and economic power imbalances. Even more rarely do people conclude that to undo race/ism we must undo our belief in human "races" and cease our individual and collective practices of racialization. As I see it, that rarely happens largely because there hasn't been any viable and truthful alternatives or pathways to avoid trying to "skip to the good part," which would inevitably increase harm and allow open wounds to fester.

Before we can undo our belief in human "races" and practice of assigning it to humans, we have to have an agreed-upon and clear idea of what any of us means by "race" and its attending language. Nowadays, people tend to discuss "race" in the language of skin color, ancestry, culture, ethnicity, or some combination thereof. Complexion and parentage are viewed as surrogates for "race," but "race" isn't skin color, ancestry, culture, or ethnicity. "Race" is the dehumanizing apparatus that we inherit and pass on to future generations. Historian Barbara Fields and sociologist Karen Fields define "race" as the term that "stands for the conception or the doctrine that nature produced humankind in distinct groups, each defined by inborn traits that its members share and that differentiate them from the members of other distinct groups of the same kind but of unequal rank."[5] This definition is connected, in part, with the one given by philosopher and cultural theorist Kwame Anthony Appiah in his seminal work *In My Father's House*. Appiah's definition similarly refers to the ranking/hierarchy/power imbalances that pertain to the presumed belief in human "races" and the assignment of it to humans.[6] In both cases, "race" depends on biological and ontological presumptions about human beings that then sorts different "races" into a predetermined hierarchy that humans uphold. Such a definition doesn't, of course, infer that "race" is biologically real—rather, it suggests that "race" is either a "social construction" that can include biological features of humans or that "race" is presumed to be biological by believers.

Even if social constructions are inventions (i.e., synthetic), they are still real and have material impacts. Money is a made-up thing. Yet, it's also real and has real material impacts. Marriage is a made-up thing. Yet, it's still real and has material impacts. Nations, borders, language, culture, norms are all made-up by humans. And yet, all are still real and have material impacts. My shirt is synthetic. I cannot find it anywhere in nature ready-made. However, it is still real. It has parameters and qualities to it of which we could mostly agree. Although made in a factory, it's still real.

Similarly, ethnicity is a social construction (that includes language, religion, politics, customs, etc.), even as it typically involves a biological reality in most people's minds. Ethnicization (as opposed to racialization) tends to dominate in societies where seemingly homogenously racialized groups of people live. That interpretation of people in other places as being similarly racialized, of course, centers a Western view of the world. Within various contexts, people see themselves differently and, in fact, might not see themselves as the same "race." Remember that within the togetherness wayfinder framework, "race" does not travel because race/ism is not the same everywhere. In some instances, the language of ethnicity correlates with how the language of "race" manifests in places like the United States. Sometimes the dehumanization elsewhere is influenced or caused by Western influences and racial/st ideology.

Consider, for example, the Twas, Hutus, and Tutsis in Rwanda or the Greeks and Turks on Cyprus. Racialization and ethnicization look different depending on the context (i.e., time and place) and on the biases of the person examining history and contemporary events. But each works toward the same ends of creating and maintaining a hierarchy that dehumanizes. More often than not, that dehumanization is intended to "justify" violence and subjugation of a particular group or groups. In some cases, racialization and ethnicization happen simultaneously. In the United States, for example, many people argue that the designation "black" is not just a "race" but also an ethnicity that applies to Americans of more recent African descent. This argument is seen in the recent trend to capitalize "Black," because, as the argument goes, "Black" serves as an ethnic and cultural designation just like "Hispanic" or "Asian."[7] Some people make similar arguments about capitalizing "White." But "white" and "black" cannot and should not be the linguistic choice to reflect a particular ethnicity for Americans for two principle reasons.

First, the terms "white" and "black," in the context of the United States, derive from antiblack race/ism (i.e., "white" supremacy) through racial/st ideology, with "white" being supposedly superior and "black" being allegedly inferior. As such, what gets attached to "black" culture are archetypes, vicious caricatures, and all that is thought to be immoral and, therefore, inferior—for example, criminality, violence, hypersexuality, laziness, ignorance, self-victimization, etc. Such attachments took hold not because they reflect something truthful about the nature of so-called black people but because the very idea of "black" people, especially in the context of the United States, was created to reflect and maintain the power imbalance that was on the ground—the one between the civilized enslaver and the nonhuman and therefore uncivilized enslaved person. Regardless of how positively people who get racialized as black have striven to transform the language of race/ism, such associations get carried through language, thoughts, behaviors, and systems. For example, you needn't look far to find people spouting the importance of colorblindness, while, in the same breath, promoting what they think is representative of "black" culture: immorality, illiteracy, violence, criminality, hypersexuality, and the like. Mills calls this phenomenon cultural racism. As long as culture is considered part of an ethnicity that is inevitably tied to the belief in human "races" and practice of racialization via the language used to describe it, then that (cultural) race/ism will persist with the same language being used to describe "ethnicity."

Second, there is no monolithic "black" or "white" culture that could imply a single ethnicity for either group, even within the context of the United States. "Black" as an ethnic term could equally apply to any number of groups of more recent African descent. But the music culture, hair culture, fashion culture, food culture, language culture, and religious culture of these groups needn't be racialized or ethnicized, no matter how local or how widespread. And although some people seek to unify all people who experience racism under the language and banner of "blackness" because there is, typically, strength in numbers, such a collective categorization does not undo the causes and effects of antiblack racism (i.e., race/ism). We need ways to address and stop both the causes and effects. Just as there's nothing inherently positive about being racialized, there is nothing inherently positive about being ethnicized, especially when the ethnicization is created or enforced by a dominant group to uphold preexisting or desired power structures. Both processes inevitably keep societies divided and lead to false beliefs about who and how people are or who and how people should be.

Some people fail to see racialization and ethnicization as stemming from the same process, which often lends to blanket statements and simplistic—even if seemingly logical—thinking that restrict race/ism to a narrow temporal and spatial conceptualization. When actress and talk show host Whoopi Goldberg said that the Holocaust was "not about race, but about man's inhumanity to man,"[8] for example, she exposed the limiting nature of how race/ism via racial/st ideology works to keep people within black-and-white paradigms. While most people jumped at the chance to tell her how wrong she was, not enough people saw the truth in what she said within the context of the United States, where beliefs about race/ism often only include the "black"/"white" or the "white"/"nonwhite" binaries. After all, if you believe that people who get racialized as white are incapable of experiencing race/ism anywhere and that racialization is fixed and not subject to change based on geography or time, saying that the Holocaust had nothing to do with race/ism makes perfect sense. By that understanding of race/ism, Goldberg was right to say what she did. People who get racialized as white can and do experience the effects of *antiblack* race/ism. They do not experience antiwhite race/ism since in any paradigm with so-called whiteness, "whiteness" is presupposed to be at the top of the social and economic hierarchies. Unfortunately, Goldberg's statements perpetuated the very misconceptions about race/ism that serve to maintain the antiblack racial/st matrix.

Even if race/ism is rigid due to its self-reinforcing nature, particularly the American variety of it, there is nothing static about race/ism itself. As Roland Dixon wrote in *The Racial History of Man*, "If by the term 'race' we mean to describe actually existing groups of people, as I think we should, then our types are certainly not races, since, with few exceptions, there are no groups of men who actually represent them."[9] He goes on to say that these "types" are

> but scantily represented among the world's peoples, the vast majority of whom present not the characteristics of our pure types, but of blends between them. . . . [W]e cannot point to any group of criteria and say these are inherently connected and form a true racial standard. . . . Moreover, from this point of view a race is not a permanent entity, something static; on the contrary, it is dynamic, and is slowly developing and changing as the result of fresh increments of one or another of its original constituents or of some new one.[10]

But Dixon, writing in the early twentieth century, falls into the trap that people even today rarely sidestep. As philosopher and educator Alain Locke argued, Dixon, at once, points to the fallacy of racial/st ideology while going on to treat these "types as 'real' races, blithely confident that they have played recognizable historical roles and exhibited characteristic cultural capacities."[11]

"Race" either is or isn't real. It is or isn't fixed. To apply the racelessness translator, race/ism either is or isn't real. It is or isn't fixed. Or culture is or isn't real or fixed. Culture does or doesn't stem from one's so-called race. Race/ism does or doesn't stem from one's culture. Try as they might, anthropologists, scientists, social scientists, and scholars across multiple disciplines continue to fail to answer Locke's century-ago call-to-action: discover "some criteria of true race, of finding some clue to the inter-connection between physical character, and group-behavior, psychological and cultural traits."[12] He understood that "race" was not reflective of a biological reality and that culture dictates one's "race" or, more aptly, how one is racialized, how one racializes oneself, and how race/ism manifests in one's context.

After all, social constructions have the meaning humans give them. That is true even if there isn't a consensus about what a construction is or isn't. The meaning of the construction might change from person to person, but it is no less real. In this regard, social constructions are not fixed. This truth is what informs the position of "race" reformers. Indeed, the fact that constructions change and get revised over time would seem to strengthen their position about "race." After all, if something is created, it can, in theory and practice, be reformed. But inserting positivity into the conception of "race" and practice of racialization doesn't change the substrate—that is, it doesn't address the issue at its core.

If "race" is a human-made concept that is used to oppress or uplift people based on their racialization and assigned place in the social and economic hierarchies, why would we continue to require people to racialize themselves? Why would we continue to accept that mistreatment from our governments, corporations, tech companies, religious institutions, media, and education systems? Those who call for reconstructing "race," including by promoting colorblindness, would have us continue an inherently nefarious practice. Countless scholars and activists have tried to position synthetic reformation as the solution to race/ism. But trying to reform or reconstruct race/ism is like trying to fix a house with a rotten structure by throwing a new coat of paint over it. Attempts to reform or reconstruct the illusion of "race" only obscures and hides problems and solutions. It incarcerates our imaginations and hearts. It keeps us divided and unhealed. It keeps us within the architecture and machinery of race/ism.

Racism is generally defined as the belief that groups of humans possess different behavioral traits corresponding to inherited attributes and can be divided based on the superiority of one "race" over another. Baked into this definition is not only the prejudice, discrimination, and antagonism that inevitably accompany the apparition of "race" but also the presupposed reality of "race," whether hereditary or synthetic. In the context of the United States, scholars and activists often define racism as power plus prejudice. Here, the definition presupposes the existence of more than one "race" and the inescapable practice of racializing humans by leaving out any explicit mention of "race" or racialization being the impetus for the constructed "superiority" or "inferiority" of people in the first place. Importantly, how some people translate that definition results in unintentionally locking up freedom from race/ism—racelessness—with whoever holds the most power, which can often be discerned by acknowledging who assigns "racial" identities. By the definition's logic, only so-called white people or people "wanting to be white" or "in close proximity to whiteness" can be freed from the effects of race/ism, even if some people's "freedom" comes at the cost of assimilation or who a person *really* is, as dictated by one's racialization. Why is freedom from the negative effects of race/ism forever locked up with any single "racial" category? Because if the hereditary or synthetic reality of "race" is baked into the definition of racism without any disclaimers or red flags, then the very questioning of "race" in ways much like what the togetherness wayfinder invites becomes viewed as antagonistic to the project of resisting racism.

Other scholars take a slightly different approach. In *How to Be an Antiracist*, for example, Ibram X. Kendi defines a *racist idea* as "any idea that suggests one racial group is inferior or superior to another racial group in any way. Racist ideas argue that the inferiorities and superiorities of racial groups explain racial inequities in society."[13] To be racist, then, according to Kendi, is to have ideas about the superiority or inferiority of racial groups relative to other racial groups. Inherent in his definition of *racism*, like the commonly accepted definition among other scholars and activists, is the idea and practice of power. Notice that power is also at the core of my definition within the wayfinder. After all, inferiorities, superiorities, and racial inequities all point to power imbalances. He gives the same definition of a racist idea in *Stamped from the Beginning*.[14] My analysis of his consistent definition of racism, which presumes rather than interrogates the reality of "race," overlaps with what Barbara and Karen Fields say about racism in their book *Racecraft: The Soul of Inequality in American Life*. For them, *racism* is "first and foremost a social practice, which means it is an action and a rationale for action, or both at once. *Racism* always takes for granted the objective reality of *race*. . . . The shorthand transforms *racism*, something an aggressor does, into race, something the target *is*."[15] As demonstrated in Kendi's definition, many people take for granted the objective reality of "race" even as they work to define racism (i.e., race/ism). When they discuss racism, they talk about it in the language of something the target is rather than as something an aggressor upholds, does, or believes.

In layperson's terms, that misdirection results in the continued causes and effects of race/ism. However well-intended, Kendi is no exception to falling into this trap, which Barbara and Karen Fields refer to as *racecraft*. In addition to obscuring the causes and effects of race/ism, Kendi also creates a false dichotomy between "a *dual* and *dueling* history of racial progress and the simultaneous progression of racism."[16] As important, he misses how the maintenance of the belief in human "races" and practice of racialization on both sides of the not-so-tidy dichotomy (really a spectrum) of antiblack racial/st beliefs and practices has been the primary reason race/ism—racist ideas, rhetoric, tactics, and policies, to borrow his language—has marched forward with a seemingly inescapable strength and consistency.

No matter how similar or different the definition of race/ism, all commonly used definitions presuppose the existence of "race." We are, therefore, forced into a conception of "race" that is biological, a construction, or some combination thereof. This forces us then into an unending cycle: when we accept "race" as a permanent fact—either implicitly or explicitly—we guarantee the persistence of the causes and effects of race/ism, even as we fight to destroy its causes and effects.

Given these definitions, how do we *know* our "race?" At some point, people in countries like the United States learn it. Our media, government, religious organizations, corporations, tech companies, and education systems teach us to be perpetual believers and practitioners. All of our first encounters with racialization are directly tied to race/ism. Whether we learn about our "blackness" because of the imposition of "whiteness" or our "whiteness" because of the imposition of "blackness," race/ism is always at work. From an early age, we learn to believe in "race" and to practice racialization. For example, in *Black Skin, White Masks*,[17] psychiatrist, philosopher, and writer Frantz Fanon illustrates how "blackness" is not a "race" or subsequent culture intent on breaching cultural norms but one on being free, on being liberated, on being embraced and encouraged to live authentically without reprisal or violence. He theorizes that the identity of so-called black people is not something that can be self-created, despite gargantuan and long-standing efforts, but is something that is imposed by society based on their expected position of power in the social and economic class hierarchies.

Much of what we think of as "race" or race/ism is specific to a time and place, which means its face has changed and suggests it can be overcome. As one of the tenets of the togetherness wayfinder explicitly states, race/ism does not exist everywhere in the same way. Under the framework of "white" supremacy, "race," as an identity, washes away who a person actually is in favor of a presupposed and imposed identity via race/ism or cultural race/ism. While I care most about antiblack race/ism, whether reinforced through a so-called cultural framing or a "racial" one, the type of race/ism that still dominates much of the globe and most directly impacts my family and me, "white" supremacy, is very young when compared with the entirety of human history. People who immigrate to places like the United States often become racialized as white, black, Asian, etc., whereas they may not be racialized in the same way before immigration and certainly were not racialized in the same way before the 2000s, 1900s, 1800s, 1700s, or 1600s, depending on the racialization. People whose families have been in the United States for generations might also find that their family members were not racialized during their lifetimes in the way that they would be now (e.g., the Irish or Italians). People who get racialized as indigenous now would not have been racializing themselves and each other as indigenous before the context of European colonization, and those who would get racialized as black today were not *racializing* themselves as black before the Middle Passage.

In the context of a time and place in which race/ism is defined by "white" supremacy, people who get racialized as white cannot experience race/ism that is "against whites" because the logic of that particular form of race/ism denies that possibility. After all, "white" is intended to be supreme. Yet, antiblack racism negatively impacts everyone who gets racialized, whether they get racialized as black, white, Asian, Hispanic, indigenous, mixed, etc., especially the working class and poor. "White" supremacist or antiblack race/ism keeps us fighting each other rather than keenly aware of our shared interests and shared oppressors. In other contexts, people who Americans racialize as white but who are not racialized the same way elsewhere in the world can experience other types of race/ism. Whether they can experience race/ism while also being racialized as white often has to do with whether they hold more power than other racialized groups in a given context. Racism and prejudice are not the same. Race/ism is fundamentally about power imbalances that require the illusion and practice of "race." Prejudice is about bias. Almost everyone in the United States can experience the consequences of antiblack race/ism. But antiwhite race/ism in the context of "white" supremacy is impossible by history and definition. A person can experience the social ramifications of race/ism even if not the economic ones. Just as with antiblack race/ism, though, we should not collapse or conflate the similarities and differences of social racism and economic racism.

Similarly, people who Americans racialize as black but who get racialized differently elsewhere can experience different forms of race/ism elsewhere. For example, Tyla Laura Seethal—known as Tyla—is a South African singer and songwriter. In the context of South Africa, race/ism requires that Tyla gets racialized as colored, a term reserved for people of multiple "races" and ethnicities (i.e., African, Asian, European, etc.). In the United States, some people refuse to refer to her as "colored" because of that term's history in the context of American race/ism. Instead, some people want to call her "black," even if that term is similarly rooted in antiblack race/ism. Despite the pressures, however, Tyla has refused to bend to other types of racial/st designations. She is aware that the history and treatment of people who get racialized in South Africa differs from the history and treatment of people who have been racialized as colored in the United States. She has expressed that she does not want to offend people by coopting the category of "blackness." Yet, one can recognize that when she isn't in South Africa and is, instead, performing in the United States, people will racialize her as "black." Her racialization then shifts when she's home in South Africa. Our context dictates how we get racialized and how we see the world through our own racialized and racializing perspectives. Race/ism has the same dehumanizing and oppressing effects everywhere even if the types of racializations and the specific histories and contexts change. Acknowledging the universalism of race/ism while understanding the particularities of it can help us stop its causes and effects. But if we pretend or believe that it's all the same everywhere and anyone can experience it anywhere, it becomes impossible to stop. Liberation becomes impossible. And that has tragic consequences.

In the United States, we have tried many times to reform "race"—
to make it self-fashioned, self-understood, and self-imposed—even as
"race" has been and continues to be dictated by every major system and
institution, from education and government to media and technology.
Although we see efforts in today's antiracism movement to remake "race"
by remaking "blackness," such as by capitalizing "Black," this effort and
these strategies aren't a new phenomenon. As part of the (re)construc-
tion of race/ism outlined earlier, reconstructing "race" for the purpose of
advancing human rights in the United States has a storied history. The
Abolition Movement, the Harlem Renaissance, the Civil Rights Movement, the Black Power Movement, and the Black Lives Matter Movement
all represent moments in time when courageous people sought to transform what "race" meant in an effort to simultaneously undo and illustrate the reality of race/ism. Their efforts bore important fruit. They did
so by inspiring more people to change their minds about what it meant
to be racialized as black. More than that, they did so by inspiring more
people to take action against race/ism via the government, technology,
religion, media, and education. In other words, they reframed "race" via
"blackness" to signify humanity rather than nonhumanity for more people. Despite these positive developments and hard-earned advances, the
rotten architecture of race/ism, specifically antiblackness, remains.

The writing of Harriet Jacobs, an American who freed herself from
enslavement, sheds light on this dynamic. In *Incidents in the Life of a
Slave Girl*,[18] she bared her humanity to her then mostly so-called white
women readers. She showed how she, a formerly enslaved woman who
got racialized as black, was more similar to her so-called white readers
than dissimilar to them. At the time, conceptions about people who got
racialized as black were such that far too many people felt comfortable
with chattel enslavement. People seen and codified as "black" were believed to be outside the bounds of humanity, as race/ism dictates. Even
though Jacobs, like Frederick Douglass and other abolitionists, understood this, she undertook the impossible task of writing humanity into

her presupposed "race," a racialization that ensured the tenuousness of such an effort. So long as the belief in human "races" and the practice of racialization remain, the stamp of race/ism via "blackness" is permanent. Race/ism ensures this by constantly adding stain. No matter the time or era, as long as the belief in human "races" and practice of racialization persist, people who get racialized as black will continue to be identified as such, with all of the attending supposed inferiority and dehumanization that is baked into the categorization. It doesn't matter whether that imagined group is called "free people of color," "colored," "Negro," "African-American," "Afro-American," "African American," "black," "Black American," or "Black." Similarly, people who get racialized as white will continue to be seen as such, with all of the attending supposed superiority that is baked into the categorization. Make no mistake: we should abolish "whiteness" and its material impacts first. But it can't go until more people actually grapple with what "whiteness" is and what it represents in contexts of "white" supremacy. To invite more people to participate in honest dialogue about "whiteness," we need an effective wayfinding toolkit.

The very categorization of "black" sprang out of a need to solidify the material realities of race/ism and a desire to "justify" the inhumanity of what was dubbed the *peculiar system* of chattel enslavement. The entire system depends on us learning to maintain race/ism and its supporting ideology from an early age and then teaching it to future generations. Even as people fought against the blatant injustices and violence caused by race/ism, they did so from within the framework, trying to reform the entire thing without reckoning with the immovable foundation upon which they continued building. We make the same mistake today. We fight to end or ignore race/ism and its effects from within the philosophies of race/ism—primarily through what are now called colorblindness or antiracism—that we've inherited. This speaks to the insidious nature of racial/st ideology and systemic race/ism. It is so ingrained in our system that it is almost impossible to peer beyond its limits—or to even recognize and see all the damaging aspects of it. It is less and less possible to see how neither path of resistance is desirable or viable and that there are and must be alternatives. The world really isn't black and white.

As a social species, humans are especially prone to following established paths. It is reflected in our entrenched views toward race/ism and what each side of the black-and-white binary means. If "blackness" has traditionally represented the subhuman or nonhuman, then "whiteness" has represented the human if not superhuman. If "blackness" has represented dehumanization, then "whiteness" has represented dehumanizing. Yet, unlike "blackness," "whiteness" remains largely invisible. It remains invisible when those who get racialized as white deny their own racialization. The invisibility of so-called whiteness remains reflected in the absence of racialized language when talking about a person who gets racialized as white, unless in direct relation with someone who gets racialized differently. Although discussions about "whiteness" have markedly increased in some circles in recent years and has consistently been discussed in other circles, especially in the wake of the death of George Floyd and ensuing protests, this relative invisibility explains why people often misunderstand and mischaracterize what it is to be raceless with the category "white," as if "white" isn't a racialization and a distinct aspect of race/ism.

Ironically, the barriers commonly caused by the designation of "whiteness" also explain why talking about the need to abolish "whiteness" is, unfortunately, misinterpreted as annihilating so-called white people, as opposed to eliminating the roots of race/ism in particular contexts. People are so entrenched in the causes and effects of race/ism that they have a hard time imagining a world without it that still includes them. Whereas many people who get racialized as black readily assert and embrace their presupposed "race" when asked about their identity, many people who get racialized as white do not acknowledge their "race" at all when asked about their identity. We must not address that gap that is caused by the machinery of race/ism by going in the exact opposite direction of forcing, a strong word, everyone to see "race" as part of their identity. Instead, we should provide tools that highlight the reality of race/ism without reinforcing its causes and effects.

The resistance of some people who get racialized as white against the elevation and privileging of their racialization as part of their identity results partly from the implications of "whiteness" and how "whiteness" has become codified in equally restricting ways that promote and uphold race/ism to the detriment of everyone's humanity. But instead of lambasting people who get racialized as white for not embracing the inherited and assigned significance of their "white" identity, we might do well to learn from what scholars across disciplines have taught us about the imposition of identities born from violence. It isn't that one should want so-called white people to embrace their "whiteness." Instead, one should want so-called white people to recognize and acknowledge the reality of race/ism and simultaneously work toward a future without it.

Race/ism "eraces" in other visible and invisible ways. Take, for example, African American literature and studies. From its inception as a distinct field of study, these areas of study were identified, formulated, and presumed to be a distinct field of study outside of American studies for race/ist reasons. With rare exceptions, their canons uphold the illusion that most or even all people who get racialized as black agree on certain fundamental truths. Yet, this canon formation doesn't account for thinkers like me. Other historical voices along with newer and other often misunderstood voices are left out of classrooms. I point out these exclusions not because I don't recognize that we always have to choose what to include and exclude when making such decisions, but because I want to highlight the cruel irony of this exclusion.

For centuries, people have tried to make "blackness" and what it is to get racialized as black be one thing and something that is situated safely within the confines of the human. Though, in any given period, there is often an imagined consensus about what it means to be "black" or "Black," the agreement has never been and will never be unanimous.

How can there be when the category itself and the invention of an entire group was born from antiblack race/ism aka "white" supremacy? There will never be unanimous consensus about what is it to get racialized as white either. What most people today agree on, though, even without having the proper knowledge, imagination, understanding, or tools to do anything about it, is the pernicious effect and nature of race/ism via racial/st ideology. Because even if that one thing that has been imagined into "blackness" today is all encompassing and expansive and primarily positive, nothing can overcome or undo the nature of "blackness" in its foundational form and how it is understood as being both outside of that which is human and lesser in every regard—violent, criminal, hypersexual, illiterate, etc.

The underpinnings of "race," whether "whiteness," "blackness," or any other racialization, when fully examined and understood within the context of the United States, is the exact opposite of anything positive, which is the primary reason scholars and thinkers have theorized "blackness" and "whiteness," as a specific attempt to undo, understand, confront, or counter racism, to the extent that they have. By illustrating the complexity and humanity of people who get racialized as black and confronting the reality of race/ism via "whiteness," they aim to undo the race/ism that gets carried with the racialization and its attending language and racial/st ideology. But this is a Sisyphean task. Similarly, even if positive things have been imagined into "whiteness," such as individualism, freedom, and all that is supposedly right in the world, "whiteness" is often understood and theorized as callous, unethical, limited in charity and goodwill toward people who don't get racialized as white, etc. Given how "whiteness" operates in a racial/st society, the machinery of race/ism requires "whiteness" to operate in those ways to the detriment of even those who get racialized as white and especially poor or working-class folks. How people define each racial/st category and racialized humans will be influenced by their worldview and whether the causes and effects of race/ism dominate their imaginations, that is, whether they are able to see culture, ethnicity, themselves, and others outside of race/ism—that is, outside of the strictures imposed by the system of race/ism.

Governments impose these strictures when they define "racial" categories for their populations—or at least determine the "racial" categories based on what the public is programmed to demand. Although the internal logic and mechanics of race/ism do not change, the racial/st framework allows for the drawing of ever-changing lines and the use of ever-new racial/st language to uphold race/ism. For example, the first U.S. Census, taken in 1790, had only three "racial" categories: "Slave," "Free White Females and Males," and "All Other Free Persons," and the first U.S. Census after the Civil War, taken in 1870, had only four: "Indian," "Chinese," "Black; Mulatto," or "White."[19] The most recent U.S. Census (2020), meanwhile, asked individuals to identify themselves as one or more of the following: "White," "Black or African American," "American Indian or Alaska Native," "Chinese," "Filipino," "Asian Indian," "Vietnamese," "Korean," "Japanese," "Native Hawaiian," "Samoan," "Chamorro," "Other Asian" (e.g., Pakistani, Cambodian, Hmong, etc.), "Other Pacific Islander" (e.g., Tongan, Fijian, Marshallese, etc.), or "Some other race." It also asked those individuals who identify as "Latino, Hispanic, and Spanish origin" to choose from the following subcategories: "Mexican, Mexican American, Chicano," "Puerto Rican," "Cuban," and "Another Latino, Hispanic, and Spanish origin."[20] Although "White" (including "Free White") and "Black" (including "Slaves," "Free Colored Persons," "Negro," "African American," etc.) have been the most stable categories across U.S. government classification standards, the U.S. Census now even includes a dedicated write-in response area where respondents who identify as "White" or "Black" can add their point of origin (e.g., German, Irish, English, Italian, Lebanese, Egyptian, etc., for "White" and African American, Jamaican, Haitian, Nigerian, Ethiopian, Somali, etc., for "Black"). The closeness of "race," ethnicity, and even nationality is there for all to see in the evolution of this framework. What are arguably ethnicities or nationalities get labeled as or lumped in with "race" via race/ism. Meanwhile, the umbrella categories "White" and "Black" subsume ever more ethnic or national groups under the racial/st ideological framework of the U.S. government. Race/ism would fundamentally shift if the primary categories of antiblack race/ism ("White" and "Black") were disrupted by shrinkage. The only way to maintain antiblack power imbalances is to ensure that the category of "White" and "Nonwhite" keep growing at relatively similar rates.

The U.S. Census Bureau's website reveals the nature of its categories:

> The racial categories included in the census questionnaire generally reflect a social definition of race recognized in this country and not an attempt to define race biologically, anthropologically, or genetically. In addition, it is recognized that the categories of the race item include racial and national origin or sociocultural groups. People may choose to report more than one race to indicate their racial mixture, such as "American Indian" and "White." People who identify their origin as Hispanic, Latino, or Spanish may be of any race.[21]

This disclosure underscores the fictional nature of "race" and the constructed reality of race/ism that racial/st ideology and language maintain and that the U.S. government advances. How could the elite remain so if its citizens stopped fighting each other? Here, the hereditary realness of "race" is presupposed, and the language used upholds the realness of that which is presupposed or perceived to be "racial." Note the doublespeak of going along with socially defined conceptions of "race" while "not" defining "race biologically, anthropologically, or genetically." If the U.S. Census Bureau does not want to socially define "race" or participate in how "race" gets defined, then it would do well to recognize how collecting data that it racializes and weaponizes defies and refutes its supposed neutrality and indifference. Let's not continue to pretend that the government cares about people it *most* adversely racializes (or any of us), including those it dupes into thinking that their interests are most aligned with people in a higher economic class.

Under frameworks derived from the roots of race/ism, the number of potential changes and categories to come are limitless, all designed to maintain the status quo of race/ism. Indeed, the Biden administration has announced that it is adding a Middle East and North African (MENA) category to the U.S. Census and reframing "Hispanic or Latino" to be not only an "ethnic" identification but also a "racial" one.[22] "This will help ensure the Standards better reflect the diversity of the American people."[23]

Oh, joy! More racializations. More upholding of antiblack race/ism!

Our belief in human "races" and practice of racialization cause harm, not just because race/ism hides its face as "race" but also because it conflates culture, ethnicity, social class, and economic class with what we call "race." If "race" was simply reflected in or determined by a person's skin color, it wouldn't also be used to dictate a person's culture or ethnicity (for example, "Black" American or "white" American or American "of color"). People who get racialized as Asian also wouldn't be accused of trying to be "white" or being in close proximity to "whiteness" or wanting to be "black" when they don't conform to racial/st "Asian" standards. Phenotype also doesn't dictate a person's class or politics. There's a very long list of metaphors used against those who are perceived to betray how they get racialized: banana, egg, Oreo, Twinkie, apple, coconut, etc.[24] If "race" was simply reducible to one's skin color, phenotype, or DNA, there would not be a way to so easily betray one's immutable and arbitrary characteristics. That wouldn't make logical sense. There also wouldn't be a way to escape or end race/ism. But "race" has never been any of those things. "Race," as noted, is neither arbitrary nor skin color. It is fundamentally a reflection of social and economic hierarchies and power imbalances. The causes and effects of race/ism hide behind the language of "race." What one communicates through the use of "racial" language in the above instances is not "racial." Instead, it is about the continued impact of cultural race/ism, something that gets continued by many largely due to the barriers racial/st language reinforces and requires. Remember:

we are supposed to remain in the cycle of divided and conquered.

That people who get racialized as black in the United States have been "stamped from the beginning" proves the very point I'm underscoring: the definitions of "race" and race/ism that people have given both in the past and now serve to uphold a false distinction between the two that doesn't always match reality but that does create and exacerbate the madness caused by race/ism. Racism, culture, ethnicity, and social and economic class hide their faces behind the veil of "race"—or as that which is perceived to be "racial." Intersectionality, in practice, encourages us to collapse, combine, and obscure systems of oppression, not distinguish between them, which hinders the chance of any further sustainable positive change. Until intersectional analyses translate "race" and become more clear-eyed about racism, we will continue to overlook, ignore, or collapse various aspects of society to the detriment of the poor and working class and the lower brackets of the middle class.

The continued belief in human "races" and the practice of sorting humans into different "races," which requires presumptions of inferiority and superiority between "races," makes redundant any definition of "race" that presupposes the existence of "race" and does not excise that belief and the practice of racialization in the first place. A better definition is needed. The togetherness wayfinder or raceless antiracism defines "race" (or, more correctly, race/ism) as a socially constructed system of economic and social oppression that requires the belief in human "races" and the practice of racialization to reinforce various power imbalances. Under this definition, "race" doesn't exist outside of our belief in it and practice of racialization, but racism (or race/ism) in the form of hierarchical power structures does. Under this definition and in practice, race/ism is systemic. If we are to breach what Charles Mills calls the "racial contract," we must also breach the limitations of our so-called knowledge systems that constantly produce and reproduce, create and reinforce, the fiction of "race," the practice of racialization, and the subsequent power imbalances.[25]

Ultimately, how we have been taught to think about what it is to be human (i.e., humanity) upholds the existing hierarchical power structures and the processes that enable such structures. Thus, to imagine and construct a future without race/ism, we must first unlearn what we think we know about the human species.

3

Human Relation
Embracing Our Rhizomatic Origins

by Tade Souiaiaia and Sheena Michele Mason

Biology is a metaphor for the destiny imposed on the other.

—Albert Memmi, *Racism*, 1999

Today, virtually every aspect of American culture teaches us that "race" is a social construction, a tragically flawed European invention based on existing and desired social and economic power imbalances that required pseudoscientific ideas designed to "justify" the mass capture and enslavement of other humans for profit. Yet, more than 150 years after emancipation and despite an unequivocal consensus across every modern scientific discipline that humans represent a single species, the belief in "races," the practice of applying "race" to humans, and the upholding of power imbalances remain. Although today fewer people might believe in the biological reality of "race" than during the height of the Atlantic slave trade, the weight and strength of centuries of hereditary beliefs in "race" and practices of racialization have led to ongoing misconceptions and misinformation about "race" that people hold onto for both logical and illogical reasons.

William Montague Cobb, an American board-certified physician, physical anthropologist, and professor at Howard University, studied the belief in biological "race," its assignment, and negative impacts, especially on people racialized as black. During his career, which lasted through much of the twentieth century, Cobb wrote and presented hundreds of papers and conducted research that demonstrated "race" is a firmly pseudoscientific notion while also showing the adverse effects of the continued belief in biological "race." He refused to maintain the status quo—belief in human "races"—and wanted to dismantle the racial/st hierarchy via the associated power imbalances. In other words, he sought to end antiblack race/ism. He was a raceless antiracist who got racialized as black. Cobb knew these basic truths based on his deep understanding of anatomy and physiology, even without the benefit of the greater scientific knowledge we have today. Indeed, he died in 1990, the same year the Human Genome Project was launched. An international scientific research project that completed its mission in 2003, it identified, mapped, and sequenced the more than 20,000 genes of the human genome. Providing fundamental information about the human blueprint from a physical and functional standpoint, the completion of the project confirmed that humans are 99.9 percent identical at the DNA level and that there is no genetic basis for "race."

While there are important genetic differences among human populations, it is futile to attempt to describe human populations as "subspecies" or "races." As the genome has shown us, there is more diversity within these genetic "races" than between them, which renders them not only flawed but also incoherent. Still, the biological idea of "race" is often justified through appeals to genetic ancestry groups and attempts to tie together recent genetic ancestry to shared genes and shared physical traits (phenotypes). We can investigate such appeals through an examination of two important ways that humans share genetic identity: identity by descent (IBD), where an identical gene or DNA variant in two or more individuals is due to a common ancestor and thus the same ancestral origin, and identity by state (IBS), where an individual's genetic state refers to DNA that is literally or functionally the same despite not being due to common ancestry and thus not implying a genealogical connection.

This means that people who have an identical phenotypic trait—say, brown eyes—either share a common ancestor from whom they inherited the relevant genes (i.e., IBD) or inherited an allele from unrelated individuals who independently acquired the genetics that result in the same phenotype (i.e., IBS). Shared traits that are due to IBS undermine the proposed utility of "race" because they break the relationship between ancestry and phenotype. One popular example of this is blond hair. If a person in Micronesia and a person in Northern Europe (both regions where blond hair is prevalent) share some aspect of genetically mediated physical appearance, this implies only similar functional genetics; it does not imply shared ancestry.

A popular example of a widespread IBD trait is sickle cell anemia, which is caused by a single genetic variant that can be traced to a single genetic ancestor from over seven thousand years ago who lived in central Africa. If four people—one each in Nigeria, Greece, Qatar, and India—all have sickle cell anemia, this indicates that they share a recent great-great-great . . . great-grandparent (hereafter called GGG) from whom they all inherited the mutation. Because IBD traits do provide a concrete link between traits and ancestry, it follows that this quartet who share both a trait and common ancestor are all members of the same subgroup or "race." However, when we look more closely at this hypothetical quartet, we notice that despite being spread all over the world and sharing a specific genetic variant inherited from a single shared ancestor some seven thousand years ago, they also all have recent ancestors from geographic regions where malaria is or was recently present, which include Central and West Africa (but not South or East Africa), Greece, and the Arabian Peninsula, as well as parts of South Asia and India. In reality, this environmental commonality is what drives them to share this variant. It turns out that GGG is a genetic ancestor of everyone in the Old World,[1] but that the portion of his (or her) genome containing the variant for sickle cell anemia has stuck around only among individuals where it remains advantageous due to the presence of malaria. Thus, it turns out that the four members of this "race" can easily be expanded to include everyone in the world—even those who no longer carry the sickle cell disease–causing variant. In short, premodern humans who are ancestors to at least one human living today are ancestors to everyone living today,[2] meaning that concepts of "race" cannot be informative about who your ancient ancestors were.

But what happens when we look at more recent ancestry? Do conceptions about "race" make sense using this model? The first thing we notice when we study recent IBD relatedness is that the portion of genes inherited from a common ancestor that one individual shares with another diminishes rapidly over successive generations. While siblings share matching ancestry (making them invariably the same "race" in popular understanding), they share only 50 percent of their IBD ancestry, meaning a genetic test might well label them *different* "races" (think, for example, of siblings of a father who gets racialized as black and a mother who gets racialized as white, with one child having a skin color typically associated with individuals who get racialized as black and another having a skin color typically associated with individuals who get racialized as white). In fact, two siblings that have the same parents—one who gets racialized as black and one who gets racialized as white—can be born such that one child "looks black" and the other "looks white," but their genetic tests label the "black-looking" child "whiter" and the "white-looking" child "blacker."

More importantly, IBD relatedness drops off quickly and exponentially because we share far more DNA with our recent ancestors than with our relatives. A second cousin once removed (someone who shares a single great-grandparent with you) may seem like an especially significant genetic relationship to you, because you have a shared ancestor

Table 1. Expected Shared Genetics with Ancestors and by Shared Ancestry

Ancestor	Expected Genetics Transmitted per Ancestor	Expected Shared Genetics for Descendents Sharing K Ancestors							
		K=1	2	3	4	8	16	32	64
Parent	50%	25%	50% (Siblings)						
Grandparent	25%	6.25%	12.5% (First Cousins)	18.75%	25% (Double Cousins)				
Great Grandparent	12.5%	1.56%	3.13%	4.69%	6.25%	12.5%			
Great-Great-Grandparent	6.25%	0.39%	0.78%	1.17%	1.56%	3.13%	6.25%		
Great-Great-Great-Grandparent	3.13%	0.1%	0.2%	0.29%	0.39%	0.78%	1.56%	3.13%	
Great-Great-Great-Great-Grandparent	1.56%	0.02%	0.05%	0.07%	0.1%	0.2%	0.39%	0.78%	1.56%

from whom you each inherited roughly 12.5 percent of your genome, but you likely share only 1.6 percent of your genome with each other (see table 1). Heritage, then, must mean more than DNA, and popular conceptions of "race" that inevitably include ancestry only help to uphold the inescapability of "race" and, therefore, the inescapability of race/ism.

To get an idea of how quickly DNA relatedness among relatives diverges, imagine a scenario in which someone shares all of their ancestors with another person who is not their sibling. For example, if two brothers marry two sisters, the children of each couple will share the same set of four grandparents. Even though these "double" first cousins will share 100 percent of their ancestry (at the level of grandparent and beyond), they will share only 25 percent of their DNA with each other on average. Nonfamilial relatives with whom you share many of the same ancestors and who intuitively seem to be of the same "race" as you share less of their DNA with you than your ancestors, so much so that a DNA test may put you and your relatives in a separate racial category. Heritage, then, must mean more than DNA, and popular conceptions of "race" that inevitably include ancestry only help to uphold the inescapability of "race" and, therefore, the inescapability of race/ism.

If a person cannot be sure that they are of the same "race" as their relatives, surely, they can at least be certain that they are of the same "race" as their ancestors, from whom they inherited their "race," right? The trouble here is that the transmission of DNA is nonlinear. At more than six generations, one begins to "lose" genetic ancestors through the randomness of recombination. This means, for example, that after twelve generations, an individual gets about 75 percent of their ancestry from 5 percent of their ancestors and that the vast majority of their ancestors are no longer represented in their DNA.[3] Therefore, an American whose ancestors all came from Europe before the Revolutionary War (at least twelve generations ago) who takes a DNA "ancestry" test to learn where their European ancestors lived is, at best, finding something out about approximately 8 percent of their ancestors (because the others simply did not contribute any DNA to their genome). Because modern humans share a starting point in Africa and only later spread to other parts of the earth beginning approximately 60,000–90,000 years ago, human variation is not constant across the globe. How related one's ancestors were can be assessed using "individual heterozygosity," which measures the genetic variance or diversity inherited from one's parents. The genetic difference between two random individuals in one population is often greater than the average group difference between populations. This means that two individuals who get racialized as black and are from South Africa can have greater genetic difference between them than a so-called black South African and a so-called white Swede. That is just one reason why even if "races" existed in nature, it wouldn't make much sense to compare the mean values of traits, like IQ or height, between these groups unless the goal is to maintain race/ism's causes and effects.

Additionally, where evidence exists for common genetic influences on traits like height and IQ, they are thought to be of polygenic (many genes) etiology. Thus, such traits would be expected to have far more variance in individuals with greater genetic diversity, such as among so-called black South African populations than among groups with much less diversity, such as those in the Americas. That is another reason comparison of means is uninformative between specific ethnolinguistic populations in South Africa or in the Americas. A comparison across a larger group (such as of "national IQ") is even less informative, and a comparison between groups of billions of people (such as of "racial IQ") is absolutely incoherent. The takeaway for biological "race" here is that vastly different amounts of genetic diversity within broad geographic populations and within individuals calls into question the notion of a stable and shared genetic basis for "race" that exists outside of the operating system of race/ism.

The final concept worth grappling with is that modern attempts to create a scientific concept of "racial" or "ancestral" identity requires an arbitrary time point be chosen to represent the starting time of one's ancestors. Indeed, if we choose a time point far enough back (e.g., 100,000 years ago), we will find that all of our ancestors lived in Africa, while a more distant time point (300,000 years ago) would tell us that all human ancestors were species other than *Homo sapiens*. If we go even further back (65 million years ago), we will find that the ancestors of all of us were likely the size of squirrels and roamed among the dinosaurs.

In much of the West, of course, we tend to focus on far more recent points in time. In the Americas, specifically, we choose timepoints just prior to when our ancestors arrived in the New World, whether tens of thousands of years ago in the case of those considered native to the Americas or a few hundred years ago in the case of those considered nonindigenous. For those who get racialized as black, one is taught to choose the start of the Middle Passage. In cases where groups have multiple choices, one point of origin is usually chosen—for example, French

Canadians are unlikely to give much consideration to the Roman conquest of Gaul when thinking about their identity relative to non-French-speaking Canadians.

For groups where the genealogical record is less well known, governments, media, religious institutions, and education systems have historically assigned an identity that reified and fortified existing power imbalances. That was the case with populations in Asia and Oceania, such as the Andamanese and the Semang, who were thought to have more recent African origin due to their darker complexions, facial structures, hair texture, and shorter stature, traits that resembled the pygmy peoples of central Africa. The machinery of antiblack racialization inspired missionaries and later researchers to consider them "Negritos." However, modern genetic studies have found that their phenotypic similarities are a result of positive evolution due to their common environments (i.e., tropical rainforests) and not due to common ancestry. Yet, they and other so-called black populations in the region like the Vanuatu and other groups in Melanesia ("islands of black people") have suffered from the same type of race/ism that plagues all those assigned "blackness" within or from a context that includes "whiteness" as a racialization: antiblackness.

As these examples suggest, racialization is not only an inaccurate proxy for ancestry but also inconsistent because it is rooted in maintaining social and economic power imbalances. It is about justifying and maintaining social, cultural, political, and economic power for some and keeping it from others. The process of racialization in the United States and elsewhere responds to the social needs and desires of those who hold the most power during any given timeframe and subscribe to the dominant historical narratives of the day; it does not describe something in the DNA of humans.

Although the complex relationship between ancestry, genetics, ethnicity, and identity makes so-called racial groups incoherent, this doesn't stop some from trying to salvage the idea that "race" has a biological basis. They might argue, for example, that "races" are imperfect representations of genetic clusters, which are a recognized part of human diversity. But no matter the clustering algorithm or parameters, global genetic data almost never produces a coherent "black"/African cluster, let alone a "Hispanic" one. As one science communicator writes, "We may intuitively think of Europeans, Africans, and East Asians as three circles that barely overlap, like the Olympic rings. Time and time again, however, genetic studies reveal the opposite. They are rings all right, but they almost completely overlap."[4]

As noted, individuals from Asia and Oceania who get racialized as black almost never cluster with individuals from Africa. Even when those who believe in the hereditary model of "race" concede these points, they argue that these inconsistencies are merely evidence that "race" should be improved rather than discarded. For example, they will argue that "Hispanic" is not a real "racial" group and that individuals from Asia and Oceania only look "black" but belong to a different "race." Given that genetic evidence shows little relation between the Andamanese and Vanuatu people means not only that looking "black" and being "black" are not equivalent but also that looking "black" while not being "black" does not imply a common ancestry. In other words, the Andamanese and Vanuatu people are also not of the same "race."

For many reasonable people, this incoherent set of rules is reason enough for them to let hereditary beliefs in "race" go, but many believers in biological "race" are not deterred. Their argument is that these small populations are rare exceptions and that individuals from populations who frequently "cluster outside of their race," including but not limited to individuals from much of Central and South America, parts of South, East, and North Africa, and Southern Europe, and Americans of more recent African descent in the United States, etc., are not exceptions to the ideology dictated by race/ism. Instead, they say that the "race(s)" of individuals with multiple "racial" ancestries can be determined by looking at the clustering of humans from more "stable" populations.

This reversion to stable or "pure" ancestries is necessary for those seeking evidence to maintain race/ism. After all, "whiteness," as applied to humans, is supposed to signify "racial purity," a lack of mixedness. Without purity, the subhuman or nonhuman cannot exist. But does "whiteness" really exist at all or, at least, outside of the system of antiblack race/ism? Does DNA clustering demonstrate definitive genetic evidence that there exists a "Caucasian or white race, Mongolian or yellow race, Malayan or brown race, Ethiopian or black race, and American, including all people who populated what became the Americas, or red race."[5] Is there any subtype of "human" that meaningfully and accurately describes any single human outside of the reality of race/ism, either through singular visual assignments (i.e., someone is *obviously* 100 percent "white") or through multiple assignments that can be difficult visually but validated through genetics (i.e., someone who is 25 percent "black" and 75 percent "Asian")? No.

When we compare modern DNA to ancient DNA from all over the world, genetic clustering shows that modern humans are all more similar to each other than they are to ancient humans who lived 10,000 or more years ago. That is another reason that there are no stable, identifiable human "races." Even though humans mate more with their nearby neighbors than faraway ones, and therefore humans confined to one continent can be more genetically related to others on the same continent than to those on a distant continent, this is not meaningful for the purposes of establishing "race." The genetic clustering that is purported to validate continental groupings involves only a fraction (15 percent) of very recent mutations. Further, a recent study provides evidence of "subcontinental admixture in individuals with European ancestry, which, if not properly accounted for, can produce spurious results in genetic epidemiology studies."[6] Humans have spent the last 10,000 years migrating, sharing DNA, killing each other, and reappearing far too fast and too incoherently for biological "race" to hold. A meaningful branching map of humans is impossible to create because humans just have too much ancient and recent admixture to determine origin even when analyzing a single continent. These facts are why the idea of "race" as something biological must be discarded. It isn't. Grouping humans into racial/st "subspecies" is futile except to uphold race/ism.

Only when we understand our ancient ancestors can we hope to understand a so-called racially diverse Sunday gathering in the park for what it really is: a multigenerational family reunion where our genetic differences don't represent who we are at some presupposed level but instead provide clues to the path we took to get where we are. Ancient DNA has steadily revealed why modern humans are as connected as we are because it shows how our ancient ancestors so frequently crossed geographic boundaries. In other words, the ancient ancestors of modern humans on one continent may have just as easily come from a different continent. That is especially true outside of the Americas. A common lineage is found in Africa, Eurasia, and Oceania, even for humans living outside those regions today. The case for racialization as it works in places like the United States often rests on the idea that those humans who migrated out of Africa separated and segregated into continental groups and started to speciate due to dramatically different climates and genetic drift. DNA shows us that this segregation occurred far too recently for any such "speciation" to occur and that migration patterns often changed, with some later migration occurring out of Eurasia and back to Africa.

If we go back 15,000 years, we find direct evidence of genetic interactions among modern humans throughout Africa and Eurasia.[7] For example, individuals who lived in the Taforalt caves of Morocco in that period most closely resembled three groups of sequenced people: less ancient (but still ancient) Natufians from the Middle East, modern West Africans, and modern members of the Hadza, a group in East Africa thought to have been genetically isolated for close to sixty thousand years.[8] The Natufians are the presumed ancestors of Neolithic inhabitants of the Middle East who built some of the world's earliest known settlements, such as Göbekli Tepe in modern-day Turkey. While this assumption is reasonable from a geographic standpoint, the genetic similarity between Natufians and modern Middle Eastern humans is not as strong as one might expect. Interestingly, the Natufian Y-chromosomal haplotype or pattern had an ancient presence in the Middle East but is today found mostly in Africa, having descended from an older pattern that originated in Africa.

That means that the most direct way to make sense of the West and East African signatures present in Late Pleistocene individuals from Taforalt is that modern human interaction across the whole of Africa and Eurasia was dynamic enough that the Natufians represent a group of humans that repeatedly left and returned to Africa. It also suggests migration from the Middle East to Africa. It could be just as likely that the Tarforalt only appear to have "mixed ancestry" and that, in reality, their ancestry appears mixed due to the mixing of their descendants—us. In South Africa, we find evidence that humans who once left the continent later returned to it. Studies there suggest a number of recent migrations to Africa by people whose DNA resembles that found in modern Europe and Western Asia.[9]

Among the variants brought back to Africa were a great many that cause fairer skin or lighter-colored hair. While researchers initially assumed that variants causing lighter skin invariably originated in Eurasia and those causing darker skin invariably originated in Africa, this turns out not to be the case. Variants that cause lighter or darker skin were not confined to any one continent. These variants followed one of four patterns:

1. Originated in Africa and spread to Europe, Asia, and the rest of the world.[10]
2. Originated in part of Africa, spread to Europe, and reintroduced back to Africa.[11]
3. Originated in Europe and introduced to Africa by migration back to Africa.

4. Originated in an unknown location and spread to both Europe and Africa.

This means brown or pale skin, blond or black hair, by themselves, tell us nothing about one's ancient ancestors, other than that they were human.

One of the most interesting examples of a variant known to impact skin complexion is that affecting the SLC24A5 gene, which is thought to have arisen in Europe and is, today, present in almost all Europeans as well as the lighter-complected San people of South Africa. Notably, this gene has not been found on ancient remains older than six thousand years. In fact, most of the ancient DNA thus far discovered in Europe does not have any mutations at all that would suggest that that population had fair complexions. It is thought that there was little evolutionary benefit to having lighter skin in Europe for hunter-gatherers who ate a diet high in vitamin D. The adaptation to lighter complexions came when the diet changed to agricultural starches, which provide almost no vitamin D. The introduction of agriculture and settlements also increased the time people spent indoors and led to the adoption of a diet dependent almost solely on staple foods. People's shift to farming, which inspired greater economic and social class disparities along with landowning, feudalism, and serfdom, is the source for the ironic and taboo assertion that "white people didn't create slavery; slavery created white people."

While today's scientific understanding of skin complexion dynamics subverts the mistaken conflation of skin color and "race" and corresponding taxonomies, advocates of functional racial/st designations often point to well-established disease associations with "race," including but not limited to Mendelian diseases (e.g., sickle cell disease and Tay-Sachs) and complex genetic traits (e.g., statistical differences in kidney disease, lung function, and lactase persistence). In the case of true Mendelian traits, the assumption that a genetic mutation remained confined to a single continent betrays everything we now know about ancient migrations. As humans spread out and migrated around the world, mutations followed them.

The sickle cell variant is regulated by environmental balancing selection, which means it has both negative impacts (sickle cell disease in those with two copies of the mutation) and positive impacts (protection against malaria in those with one copy of the mutation—carriers). Sometimes, however, it is unclear whether there is a positive impact to being a carrier of a risk variant for a disease, as is the case for the more recent variant causing Tay-Sachs disease. Tay-Sachs is thought to persist primarily due to genetic drift and recent population bottlenecks. Population bottlenecks, which can occur along with migration, reduce the size of populations and thus genetic diversity. This explains why Tay-Sachs is largely confined to a small migratory "racial group"—namely, Ashkenazi Jews—and how it came to be racialized as a "Jewish disease." The disease has also been identified in a French-Canadian population,[12] but in that case, it is caused by a slightly different mutation than what is observed in the Ashkenazi population and is thus referred to as "Non-Jewish Tay-Sachs" or "French Canadian Tay-Sachs." It also occurs in a Cajun population in Louisiana, where, despite the shared link to French language and colonization, it is caused by the Ashkenazi mutation,[13] meaning it is quite literally, according to those operating within a racial/st paradigm, an occurrence of "Jewish Non-Jewish Tay-Sachs."

The racialization of disease does not just lead to confusion with respect to naming; it also has a negative impact on genetic screening and, by extension, the individuals many scientists and people in medicine claim to want to help. In fact, while the majority of Americans that carry a copy of the Tay-Sachs allele are, in fact, Jewish, the vast majority of babies diagnosed with Tay-Sachs disease are not Jewish.[14] Racializing Tay-Sachs as a "Jewish disease" has hindered efforts to fund the cheap universal genetic screening necessary to prevent the infant paralysis and death Tay-Sachs can cause. As is the case with sickle cell, the racialization of this disease has caused stereotypes and fear as well as misdiagnosis and confusion—it negatively impacts both those in the presumed in-group and the presumed out-group.[15] That we would insist on the continued practice of racialization in medicine despite the cheapness of universal genetic screening is cruelly ironic in light of the billions of dollars in revenue earned by mail-in genetic testing companies that maintain the system of race/ism by giving estimations of one's "racial" makeup.

While it's patently obvious that genetics is more informative than racialization for well-understood genetic diseases, those in favor of upholding the belief in human "races" as something hereditary or synthetic point to complex and less understood diseases or processes to argue for its continued use.[16] In these more complicated cases, either genotype still outperforms "race" (for example, when identifying kidney donor risk[17]) or "race" outperforms genotype by acting as a proxy for culture, environment, and social and economic status for diseases that are under very little genetic influence at all and, instead, are all environmental in nature. In the latter case, the solution is simple: base the predictive models on the environmental—including social—variables that "race" currently serves as a proxy for. This will lead to better treatment and outcomes.

How we learn to think about the human story, which often includes stories about our own ancestry, remains skewed by the lens of antiblack race/ism and hinders us from freeing our imaginations as it pertains to ourselves and each other. The frequent correlation of DNA and its manifestations, like how a person looks, mustn't be confused as causation. People who are the most adversely racialized aren't the cause for their racialization or the race/ism that comes with it. Scientists, including social scientists, should be doubly skeptical of "race" and attuned to racialization and race/ism as social processes and systems that, for too many people, still render "race" biologically real and continue to have real material consequences.

"Race" isn't biologically real no matter how much any person or ideology may make it seem. The continued belief in the biological realness of "race" (i.e., nature) outside of the reality of race/ism (i.e., environmental) simultaneously creates and maintains the collective reality of race/ism, which includes pernicious material effects.

To uproot race/ism once and for all, identifying, diagnosing, and discrediting our belief in biological "race" is not enough; we must also treat it. The treatment is simple in principle, but it requires all of us to more effectively embrace and articulate our humanity through engaging and practicing the togetherness wayfinder and to be raceless antiracists—in theory and practice. As part of our wayfinding corrective process, we must be able to translate "race" (i.e., racelessness).

4

The Racelessness Translator
Translating the Meaning of "Race"

*Identity would seem to be the garment with which one covers the
nakedness of the self: in which case, it is best that the garment be loose,
a little like the robes of the desert, through which robes one's nakedness
can always be felt, and, sometimes, discerned. This trust in one's
nakedness is all that gives one the power to change one's robes.*

—James Baldwin, *The Price of the Ticket*

"Race" isn't and has never been arbitrary, skin color, phenotype, or any
other immutable characteristic. If it could be reduced in some meaningful and biological way, then "race" would have a true biological basis that inspires disdain, indifference, or adoration in people. Race/ism
wouldn't need to be taught and learned. Because it is taught and learned,
we must fundamentally change how we talk, think, address, and teach
about race/ism. To stop the causes and effects of race/ism in their tracks,
the solution is straightforward: we must start defining *race/ism* (i.e., racism) as a socially constructed system of economic and social oppression
that requires the belief in human "races" and the practice of racialization
to reinforce various power imbalances. Rather than defining "race" sepa-
rately, it must be recognized as a part and parcel of racism. In the United

States, the primary way to do this effectively without the barriers caused by "whiteness" and without unintentionally upholding the causes and effects of antiblack race/ism is through the togetherness wayfinder.

Some people assume that the solution of the togetherness wayfinder implies colorblindness, for better or worse, but racelessness via the togetherness wayfinder should not be mistaken for colorblindness. In its most basic form, colorblindness holds that a person's skin color, "race," or ethnicity—often conflated and used interchangeably—should not influence how people treat that person, whether socially, culturally, politically, interpersonally, or collectively. In good faith, colorblindness often operates on the assumption that "race" is real, that it should just be ignored, and that we should simply overlook this thing called "race" so that we might treat people with the humanity they deserve. This approach would be sound in theory if "race" was simply a proxy for immutable characteristics, but this is not what "race" is. In practice, colorblindness often falls into the trap of imagining that race/ism doesn't exist at all. Further, colorblindness promotes the continued biological belief in human "races" and reinforces the dehumanizing apparatus of race/ism by wanting to ignore it. These are all aspects of colorblindness that raceless antiracism contends with and operates to highlight and uproot.

The concept of colorblindness is often raised with respect to Martin Luther King Jr., a figure who often gets revered now in colorblind circles but who was widely feared and hated during his lifetime. His ostensibly colorblind vision is repeated by those professing to be colorblind. In his seventeen-minute "I Have a Dream" speech, delivered during the 1963 March on Washington, King said, "I have a dream that my four little children will one day live in a nation where they will not be judged by the color of their skin but by the content of their character."[1] Although this line is often quoted today in response to certain antiracist policies, practices, and proclamations that are increasingly being met with exasperation in the public imagination, these words, especially when paraphrased

as "Judge me not be the color of my skin but by the content of my character," do not communicate the entire radical framework of King's vision.

Dr. King didn't *really* mean don't judge me "based on my skin col-
or." He meant, "Don't judge me because of my 'race.'" *Translation:* "Don't
judge me because of my racialization." *Translation:* "How you racialize
me carries race/ism. My skin color is interpreted as 'race,' a dehumanizing apparatus." *Translation:* "To not 'judge' me, you mustn't racialize
me." If we push this translation to its logical end, the line will read, "Your
belief in 'race' and subsequent racialization of me is the problem, not
me or my skin color." This process of translation and inquiry rarely happens because most of us get defaulted into racializing worldviews. We
see the world through our own perspectives and can bastardize what we
think someone is saying by hearing them say what we want to hear. But
people during his lifetime intuitively translated King's words to mean
how I've translated his words, which is what made King so dangerous to
the status quo. As long as colorblindness both assumes "race" and tries
to overlook it, antiblack race/ism will persist. Colorblindness will continue to fall woefully short of helping people unify, heal, and reconcile,
because it does not address how intolerance, injustice, dehumanization,
and discrimination operate in practice. By implying that "race" is real but
that we should simply be "blind" to it, colorblindness, like other hereditary preservationist and synthetic reconstructionist views toward "race,"
maintains, promotes, and supports race/ism.

Just as most commonly practiced forms of antiracism under and
within the praxis of racializing frameworks fall short of helping us stop
race/ism and its harmful effects in its tracks, colorblindness does too,
because it operates from within race/ism and keeps the same beliefs in
"race" and practices of racialization, which simultaneously reflect and
maintain power imbalances. It really is the other side of the antiracist
coin. It requires folks to willfully and wrongly mistranslate "race" time
and again. People who profess to be colorblind but believe in "race" and
racialize people will fail to stop race/ism because they uphold the dehu-

manizing apparatus that they sometimes believe they are acting against. Most people who try in good faith to "not be racist" or to be antiracist, at least, try to not let their biases inform how they treat people. Yet, they still carry bias with them, not because humans are born to be racist but because they learn race/ism—an inescapable aspect of culture—from a very early age. That carrying of bias transfers into the continued upholding of the status quo of systemic race/ism. In other words, one remains complicit in the context of antiblack race/ism because of the internalized ideology of race/ism. For example, when we teach our youth to racialize themselves and others, and we applaud them for recognizing "racial" differences or insist that they needn't recognize "racial" differences, we uphold the very machinery of race/ism and the design of racialization, even when we then try to teach them that these differences are rooted in racism.

If colorblindness hasn't and won't work, what about humanism, a philosophical stance that emphasizes and embraces the individual and its social potential and agency over more collective philosophies of humanity? Surely advocating that every person be seen as human is *the* answer, right? To be sure, humanism does not reify race/ism in the way that colorblindness often does. But humanism itself—the very need for it—implies the existence of human "races," whether from a biological or synthetic standpoint. The construction of the "human" stemmed from the imagining of the sub or nonhuman. Western humanism, like colorblindness, is inherently limiting and has, in practice, been used by some to maintain antiblack race/ism, specifically. By pointing to the humanity and dignity of every person, some forms of humanism obscure and deny that which collectivizes entire swaths of humans—that is, race/ism—and often fails to acknowledge that those humans often have limited individual agency because they are inextricably linked primarily with the collective.

If I get racialized as white, for example, I might more readily embrace my humanity as an individual far more easily than if I get racialized as black. This is, in part, because a so-called white individual in a predominantly so-called white society need not rely on the collective for protection in a way that a so-called black individual in a predominantly so-called white society might need to. Further, anyone who gets racialized as white and embraces individualism will be conforming to societal racial/st expectations and thus will still be operating within the confines of preexisting antiblack race/ism. A person who gets racialized as black or is otherwise not white who expresses ideas of individualism, on the other hand, risks being labeled as "white," "white adjacent," "white supremacist," or "wannabe white," because the imposition of antiblack race/ism requires all so-called nonwhite people to agree that the collective, the community, is more important, salient, and necessary than the individual—particularly in the face of race/ism. This makes logical sense, considering that the pathway to significant change must include strength in numbers. As long as race/ism continues to place limits on who is seen as fully human, however, most forms of humanism can be pro-human for all only in theory, not in practice. Any humanist position that stems from within racial/st ideology—such as belief in "white" as a "race"—is a nonstarter since the imagined presence of "whiteness" and manifestation of "whiteness" within human contexts necessitate the existence of the imagined subhuman if human at all.

This does not mean that pro-freedom movements for those who identify as and are assigned the identity of "black" cannot simultaneously be pro-human movements, even if the movements themselves reference "race" (e.g., Black Power, Black Nationalism, Black Lives Matter, etc.). Writing about chattel enslavement, Frederick Douglass said, "The limits of tyrants are prescribed by the endurance of those whom they oppress. In the light of these ideas, Negroes will be hunted at the North, and held and flogged at the South so long as they submit to those devilish outrages, and make no resistance, either moral or physical."[2] It was those humans who got racialized as Negro (now understood primarily as "black") or colored (free people of more recent African descent depending on the state and year) or white (free people of more recent European descent) alike who understood how racialization worked and who sought freedom for enslaved people. Yet, those same people, including Douglass, were born into a society that believed in "race" as something biological, first and foremost.

Abolitionists' imaginations were limited to working against the travesties of enslavement in the United States from within antiblack racial/st ideology. Douglass and other abolitionists tried to abolish chattel enslavement, not the belief in human "races" or the dehumanizing and disempowering practice of racialization. Douglass and other abolitionists did so by reforming "blackness" and what it meant to be simultaneously part of the "Negro race" *and* human. Over time, this sentiment went from "the enslaved are human, too" to "the Negro is human, too" to "Black lives matter, too." Yet, any focus on so-called black lives inevitably leads some people to miss the pro-human point and to instead hear "*only* black lives matter" or "black lives matter more," etc. Those who hear this might then respond with the words "all lives matter." Yet, because the United States has not directly addressed the root causes and effects of race/ism, all lives don't matter.

To illustrate my point, consider Marcus Arbery's use of the phrase "all life [sic] matter" on the day that William Bryan and Travis and Gregory McMichael, three so-called white men, were found guilty of murdering his son, Ahmaud Arbery, a so-called black man, during a hate crime motivated by race/ism. Outside of the courtside, he responded to the verdict by passionately and emotionally proclaiming,

> We conquered that lynch mob. We got that lynch mob. This [is] history today, letting you know that black kids' lives don't matter. For real, all life matter, not just black children. We don't want to see nobody go through this. I wouldn't want to see no daddy watch their kid lynched and shot down like that. . . . So, hey, let's keep fighting, let's keep making this place a better place for all human beings. All human beings.[3]

In the context of the broader Black Lives Matter movement, including protests held in his son's name, his words were striking for some people who mistranslated their meaning. For years, anyone who responded to the phrase "black lives matter" with the words "all lives matter" or anything comparable to this had been dismissed by some as insensitive at best or race/ist at worst. Thus, some people held onto his assertion of "all life" mattering as the ultimate counter to the charge that "all lives matter" was a racist slogan. After all, if Marcus Arbery, a so-called black man whose so-called black son had been killed in an explicit example of race/ism, could say and believe it, anyone could. Indeed, Marcus Arbery's response appeared to be the antithesis to how many people respond to race/ism in places like the United States these days—by loudly asserting that "Black lives matter."

But what does "Black lives matter," the statement, not the movement, mean? What does it mean to respond to the phrase "Black lives matter" with "all lives matter"? Importantly, "Black lives matter" *means* "all lives matter." In saying that "all life matter," Marcus Arbery, of course, agreed that "black" lives matter. In fact, he emphasized the point that the outcome of the trial resulted in a guilty verdict, which proved, according to him, that all lives matter, *even* in the eyes of an imperfect community and American (in)justice system. He pointed to a history of race/ism with his repeated use of the term "lynch mob" and "lynched." Yet, in a moment of pain and passion, Marcus Arbery did the unimaginable for many: he acknowledged both the history and current problem of race/ism while avoiding rhetoric that often unintentionally upholds and inflames race/ism.

Arbery's humanity and words serve as an inspirational and aspirational model, but they aren't the slam-dunk *against* the assertion "Black lives matter" that many people imagine—or even for the assertion that "all lives matter." In the logic of colorblindness, saying that "all lives matter" in response to "Black lives matter" makes perfect sense, but proclamations of "all lives matter" imply blindness to the true issue of concern:

specifically, antiblack race/ism. Our goal should be to get to a genuine universal chorus that behaves as if "all lives matter," but not if it means diminishing or denying the reality of race/ism—or submitting to the terms of antiblack racial/st ideology, such as by implying that "all lives matter" no matter where those lives fall on the racial/st hierarchy. To get to a place where "all lives matter" in theory and practice, people replying with sentiments of "all lives matter" must first recognize that "blackness" has been and continues to be written and understood as being outside of humanity, whether in the context of enslaved people or Ahmaud Arbery, and that we humans are, in reality, raceless. Humanness and humanity have always been a given for people who get racialized as white, so without a recognition of the race/ism experienced by so-called black people and the truth of racelessness, "all lives matter" will continue to be a statement that diminishes race/ism and even inadvertently upholds racial/st ideology.

Similarly, those who say things like "race is meaningless" or "race shouldn't matter" are wrong because "race" signifies the presence of a type of race/ism. The causes and effects of race/ism matter. As philosopher Charles Mills posits, "Race, whether formally designated as such or not, generally comes to signify the fully human and the subhuman, whether genuinely within the human community or outside it (the subhuman as actually not human at all)."[4] "Race" often reflects and represents a society's process of creating and maintaining social and economic hierarchies. It reflects the attending power imbalances that get carried on by our continued belief in and upholding of "race" and practice of racialization. Just as racism does not exist everywhere in the same way, neither does the belief in human "races" and practice of racialization. Thus, when I say that "race" doesn't exist in nature or as a social construction, I literally mean that "races" do not exist outside of the construction of race/ism in the local context that requires the illusion of "race." This means that "race" in the United States is not imagined and practiced in the same way that "race" is imagined and practiced in the

United Kingdom, which is not the same way that "race" is imagined and practiced in Rwanda, which is not the same way that "race" is imagined and practiced in Japan, etc. Race/ism exists differently everywhere, but it *always* dehumanizes and subjugates one or more groups while elevating one or more groups. Still, racelessness is universal and the same everywhere. If we can hold both of these truths, we can better translate what presents as "race" or "racial" into more precise language and have a keener understanding of antiblack racial/st ideology to create a future without it.

When we shrug off the reality and impact of race/ism with simple appeals to colorblindness or humanism, "whiteness" itself also remains invisible, which can make racism invisible to some people. The denial of "whiteness" only amplifies racism because it represents, in effect, a denial of race/ism. This resistance to the idea of "whiteness" is, of course, understandable, if "whiteness" is understood as "white" people. But just as "blackness" is not a synonym for "black" people, "whiteness" is not a synonym for "white" people. It says nothing about the individual or the "essence" of the individual. Rather, "whiteness" represents the highest level of Western society's most dominant form of racial/st hierarchy, "white" supremacy or antiblack race/ism, which exists in practice whether anyone acknowledges it or not. And it serves to keep the average person blind to the overarching power structures that benefit from continuing and controlling the matrix and the masses. Although people who don't get racialized as white did not create the rules underpinning racial/st ideology, everyone participates in upholding the causes and effects of race/ism. To be clear, when I say that anyone can and often does uphold the causes and effects of racism, I mean the racial/st hierarchy of so-called white people at the top and so-called black people at the bottom (i.e., power imbalances). In other words, anyone can intentionally or otherwise uphold race/ism (i.e., "white" supremacy). Yet, everyone benefits from seeing themselves and others outside of race/ism.

I am because we are. Ubuntu.

Only racelessness via the togetherness wayfinder will truly allow us to see ourselves and others in this way. In practice, this means we must stop falling back on antiblack racial/st ideology and thought and use better language to discuss and solve our problems, whether on an individual, local, national, or global level. This might seem like a daunting challenge, but it needn't be. There are various tools and lenses we can use to see and interact with the world as raceless beings. To begin, we must all get comfortable using what I refer to as the racelessness translator, an intuitive tool that is based on a simple truth: when people use "race" to describe a person, they generally are actually saying something about that person's culture, ethnicity, social class, economic class, experience with or participation in racism, or some combination thereof. But if my worldview and role in the system of race/ism prevent me from knowing that or from properly translating and understanding what is being communicated, I might respond defensively or offensively to a person's use of "race" language. The goal is to stop confusing "race" for these other things and to translate "race" accordingly, so that we stop using imprecise and dehumanizing language and metaphors like "white" and "black" and begin to free ourselves from race/ism. The goal is also to stop allowing the barrier of "whiteness" and other barriers to constantly mistranslate everything under the sun into "race" without recognizing the nuance and reality of what is being communicated. It is only if we understand each other that we will be able to create a better future for all together.

Culture is a term that encompasses the social behavior, institutions, norms, language, knowledge, beliefs, arts, laws, customs, values, and politics in human societies. *Ethnicity* is a grouping of people who identify with each other on the basis of shared attributes that distinguish them from other groups. Those attributes can include common traditions, ancestry, language, history, culture, nation, biological features, phenotype, DNA, and religion. A *social class* is a grouping of people into a set of hierarchical social categories. Membership in a social class can be dependent on education, occupation, income, and family history. *Economic class* is a grouping of people into a set of hierarchical social categories based on income: lower, middle, and upper class. All of these things, along with racism itself, get confused for "race."

To further illustrate how the racelessness translator works in practice, let's consider how we might translate "race" in a news article titled "Race Plays Big Role in Whether Kids Learn to Swim."[5] We must first ask ourselves: what is meant by "race" in this headline, and why would "race" play a role in whether kids learn to swim? The presence of the word "race" implies the reason must be race/ism, but when we read the actual story, which focuses on "racial" disparities in childhood drownings, we see little explaination for why "black" kids drown at seven times the rate of "white" kids beyond the fact that the parents of "black" kids are much less likely to be comfortable with their own swimming than the parents of "white" kids. No mention is made of race/ism or other direct causes. While expanded access to pools and affordable, culturally tailored water safety programs are suggested as possible solutions to this disparity, no direct mention is made of how some people who get racialized as black have limited access to pools due to living in impoverished areas, how many "black" parents might have limited time to take their kids to pools or to pay for swimming lessons due to their work hours or low wages, and how many so-called black families have not adopted swimming as an activity even decades after President Lyndon B. Johnson signed the Civil Rights Act into law because of past race/ism that forbade "blacks" from swimming in certain pools. By focusing on and upholding the belief in human "races" and the practice of racialization without directly exploring the multiple variables that contribute to this disparity, including race/ism, the article unintentionally upholds and perpetuates race/ism by not applying a truly intersectional analysis and by not naming antiblack race/ism explicitly. Instead, it appears to make "race" the cause for the disparity rather than racism, a fine example of racecraft in action.

You've no doubt seen countless articles that frame a problem as if a person or group's so-called race is causing a poor outcome as opposed to how that person or group gets racialized. That distinction matters if we want more people to stop blaming victims of race/ism for racism. In other words, a person's "race"—meaning the person themselves—isn't the cause of a problem. That external factors make a person appear to be of a particular "race" is a reflection of the problem (i.e., race/ism). Again, Barbara and Karen Fields call such misdirection away from racism toward "race" *racecraft*. All instances of that which appears to be "race" or "racial" can be translated in this manner.

For example, the oft-cited studies that say that children notice "race" before age five lead us into thinking that children notice real biological differences between themselves and their peers and thus know "race" and understand the effects of racism—the environmental aspects of the racial/st hierarchy. But the idea that children know race/ism before society teaches it to them is false. Children aren't born knowing "race," the dehumanizing apparatus that is both evidence of and the cause for continued racism.[6] Rather, parents, families, daycare providers, schools, media, religious institutions, tech companies, and governments uphold the belief in human "races" and the practice of racialization, a process that in turn maintains and supports existing power imbalances. One such study, titled "Adults Delay Conversations about Race Because They Underestimate Children's Processing of Race," argues the following:

> [R]esearch has shown that 3-month-old babies prefer faces from certain racial groups, 9-month-olds use race to categorize faces, and 3-year-old children in the U.S. associate some racial groups with negative traits. By age 4, children in the U.S. associate whites with wealth and higher status, and race-based discrimination is already widespread when children start elementary school.[7]

Notice the language here. The authors underpin a biological belief in "races," which they then combine with the cause and some of the effects of racism. Describing racism in the language of "race"—"race-based discrimination"—without explicitly acknowledging the power structures that "race" reflects allows for, again, the naturalization of the category, which is itself unnatural, and the upholding of the very hierarchy many people, including the researchers themselves, seek to end. Infrequently do people acknowledge and interrogate the interconnectedness between racism itself—which includes social and economic power imbalances—and the belief in human "races" and practice of racialization. Further, people rarely distinguish between economic class, social class, ethnicity, culture, and race/ism, which only further inspires constrained and inaccurate beliefs about humanity and the continued traumas associated with experiencing race/ism.

Whereas the imposition of racial/st language "eraces" each of us, racelessness is something that should be accessible to everyone if we want to bring to fruition an equitable future. It is something we achieve not by maintaining the illusion of people's so-called race and "racial" identification but by turning a critical eye toward abolishing all of it. While translating "race" into racelessness is an important first step, racelessness per the togetherness wayfinder requires awareness and mindfulness in all aspects of our lives. That includes the recognition that most things—not even humans—should not and cannot be so easily dichotomized.

5

Twilight
Disconnecting Freedom from "Race"

As far as my identity is concerned, I will take care of it myself. That is,
I shall not allow it to become cornered in any essence; I shall also pay
attention to not mixing it into any amalgam. Rather, it does not disturb
me to accept that there are places where my identity is obscure to me,
and the fact that it amazes me does not mean I relinquish it.
Human behaviors are fractal in nature. If we become conscious
of this and give up trying to reduce such behaviors
to the obviousness of a transparency . . .

—Édouard Glissant, *Poetics of Relation*, 1990

Most of us like things to be simple and straightforward, to be black and white, and most of us see the world through a black-and-white lens. But we are limited when we are unwilling or unable to play in the twilight—the in-between space, the gray space, the place of initial and frequent confusion—the madness—that often comes before clarity. In the introduction to her one-woman play about the 1992 LA riots, *Twilight: Los Angeles 1992*, professor, playwright, and performer Anna Deavere Smith says, "Few people speak a language about race that is not their own. If more of us could actually speak from another point of view, like speaking another language, we could accelerate the flow of ideas."[1] By excavating the "twilight moments," the in-between moments, the universal moments found among those she interviewed for the project, Smith simultaneously and necessarily points out the similarities *and* differences found within the same racialized, cultural, and political groups. Her conception of twilight, a liminal space, a raceless space, a space for discourse and healing that otherwise might not occur, is precisely what is needed most to empower us to understand our black-and-white thinking and create pathways that no longer continue to enable and fortify the causes and effects of race/ism.

Like the bounty-hunter alien colonist from *The X-Files*, race/ism shapeshifts and camouflages itself as the idea of "race." That is why when people talk about the reality or argue the unreality of race/ism in the language of "race," they believe they are talking about race/ism appropriately. That is also why too many people think of race/ism as the same black-and-white dichotomy everywhere. They've learned to see "race," in black and white, everywhere. As a result, what one calls "race" is actually a mask. Imagine an episode of *Scooby-Doo* in which the gang catches and finally unmasks a villain named "Race," who is thought to be the cause of division and inequality and superiority and inferiority, on the one hand, and beauty and unification, on the other hand. Behind the mask, we see the true culprits: economic class, social class, ethnicity, culture, and race/ism, which requires the belief in human "races," the practice of racialization, and the subsequent reinforcement of social and economic class-based hierarchies. "Race" was a fiction all along—an illusion—that kept us entrenched in economic and social class–based quagmires and conflicts. We must recognize and stop our conflation of it with aspects of society that actually add value to our lives, unlike race/ism—a thoroughly pernicious system.

Indeed, humans are victims, enactors, and participants of race/ism, and we remain so because of how well the process of racialization and design of "race" keep us at each other's necks rather than together against the elite—a small group of people who hold a disproportionate amount of wealth and political power. None of us are victims of *only* one circumstance—or *only* victims. Life is much more complex than that. One can be a victim and a survivor and thriver. Yet, there is no way to justify or rightly uphold racialization—in theory or in practice—once we unmask the villain. Race/ism produces a fragmented and limited way of seeing oneself and others because it writes certain racialized groups outside of what it is to be human, outside of the grayness, and reinforces fragmented and false views of humanity.

The normative standpoint for all humans is and should be racelessness (human), not "whiteness" or any other racialization. Yet, one central barrier that we run into today continues to be the conflation of "whiteness" with racelessness. This conflation is understandable given the insidious and cyclical nature of antiblack racial/st ideology and the insidious practice of race/ism, which has impacted life and institutions for generations, especially in the United States. For example, Langston Hughes, in his seminal essay "The Negro Artist and the Racial Mountain," writes: "One of the most promising of the young Negro poets [Countee Cullen] said to me once, 'I want to be a poet—not a Negro poet,' meaning, I believe, 'I want to write like a white poet'; meaning subconsciously, 'I would like to be a white poet'; meaning behind that, 'I would like to be white.'"[2] In the time and era in which Hughes wrote, such a translation is not unexpected, but it reflects a problem we still grapple with today: only people who get racialized as white can be free from the effects of race/ism.

So, what does it take to achieve "black" liberation? We must free our conception of liberation from race/ism from "whiteness" and, more specifically, from people who get racialized as white. Hughes interprets Cullen's desire to be seen as a "poet" as a desire to be a "white poet." Because antiblack racial/st ideology is so invasive, he did not consider that perhaps Cullen wanted to be seen as a human who writes poetry. Time and again, those who strive to see themselves and to be seen clearly outside of the confines of race/ism and its attending racial/st ideology get misinterpreted as wanting to be "white."

We see this today, for example, in response to people like Neil deGrasse Tyson and Morgan Freeman, who want to be seen as an astrophysicist and actor, respectively, and not as a "black astrophysicist" and "black actor."[3] Sometimes these types of assertions—those that reject "blackness"—are rooted in antiblack sentiment. But sometimes these types of assertions are rooted in antiracist sentiment. It is important to recognize and embrace the difference for further antiracist progress. Governments, media, religious institutions, tech companies, and education systems teach so-called white people to see themselves as, yes, raceless. That is why many people who get racialized as white don't include "race" or "racial" language in their self-descriptions of identity. But that doesn't mean that "race" is not still central to their identity. In fact, it is evidence of how "race" *is* central to their identity. That's the design of racialization and race/ism via "whiteness." It is intended to keep us going 'round the white-versus-black mulberry bush. Some authors present it as truth that to be "white" is to be "raceless," an unfortunate misrepresentation and side effect of race/ism.

In *Raceless: In Search of Family, Identity, and the Truth About Where I Belong*, for example, Georgina Lawton, an Irish woman, shares her experiences with race/ism.[4] Her mother and father pretended as though she was the biological daughter of them both, telling her that her complexion was due to a "throwback gene" in the Irish population from shipwrecked sailors from the Spanish Armada, but after her father's death, Lawton took a DNA test to "put a name to the country responsible for my [her] appearance."[5] She learned that she was the product of a brief affair her mother had with a Nigerian man. She writes, "I'd only been trying to piece together my identity on my own for over two decades, straddling the borders of a racialized existence outside my family and a nonracialized one in their presence, all the while dealing with projected ideas from strangers about what I looked like, who I resembled, what I was."[6]

Lawton inherited the idea that to be racialized is to not be so-called white. Conversely, she learned that "whites" are a magical "race" that are somehow simultaneously (e)raced and raceless, free from the strictures of racialization, free from the confines of race/ism. Here, she conflates the lack of acknowledgment of her being on the receiving end of race/ism with racelessness and "whiteness." Notably, she ties her identity to her DNA (ancestry)—that is, to a man she, to a certain point, had never known. Much of her memoir focuses on her construction of her identity that stems from the outside and becomes internalized. In those descriptions, we gain insight into her understanding of "racelessness" and how, in her mind and in practice by the society in which she lives, it is inextricably intertwined with "whiteness."

> Because whiteness has functioned as the normative standpoint for most of humanity, white people, up until very recently perhaps, have not had to think about race in the same way as everyone else and in many ways have functioned as raceless individuals. This goes some way in explaining how I saw myself as white, or raceless, as a small child in a white world. Largely, I was not aware of what race meant or that I was in possession of any sort of racial identity, least of all one that was different from my parents'. I . . . [wondered] if my parents had hoped that our shared ethnicity—the bonds forged through British and Irish customs—would somehow mitigate my race. What was so bad about acknowledging my blackness? Had they meant to erase it?[7]

Notice her use of the word "functioned" when describing how some people who get racialized as white move through the world. Part of what lends to what Peggy McIntosh calls "white privilege" is "an invisible package of unearned assets."[8] One such unearned asset could easily include the privilege of racelessness, a privilege that benefits all who are able to radically see themselves as "raceless," not to be confused with "white." Some people hear "raceless" or "racelessness" and imagine the genocide of everyone who does not get racialized as white, often while proclaiming the socially constructed nature of "race." "If you dream of a raceless future, it goes hand in hand with the elimination of black people, and so we must learn to decenter and deconstruct whiteness and white supremacy instead," Lawton says.[9] But the terrible irony in how people have thought and have been taught about race/ism continues to be the way people have simultaneously seen "whiteness" both as a "race" *and* as racelessness and as inextricably linked with liberation from the effects of race/ism, making that same liberation impossible for anyone else.

In a context of achieved racelessness, so-called white people wouldn't exist even in our imaginations. In turn, future history books would depict so-called white people as having been believed to exist (along with so-called black people) during the racial/st era in which antiblack race/ism and its attendant belief system and practice of racialization caused and maintained material impacts. But people who would get racialized as white today would still exist in this future; they just wouldn't get racialized as white anymore and, therefore, wouldn't have a monopoly over the benefits associated with "whiteness." Similarly, people wouldn't get racialized as black, indigenous, or people of color either, which means that people who get racialized as subhuman if human at all today would finally reap the benefits of being recognized as fully human in practice and in theory. And the dehumanization that people in systems afflict onto other groups, whether via racialization, ethnicization, or any other process, would be rendered clearer, enabling us to strategize and dismantle those practices, too. The togetherness wayfinder won't lead us to utopia. It will, however, help us solve and resolve the causes and effects of race/ism and create a future without it. The exact type of race/ism that needs to be fully identified and expunged might vary according to a country's specific history and context, but the same tools—language, tenets, philosophies, concepts, etc.—of the togetherness wayfinder can be applied for that expressed purpose.

In the view of collapsing "race" with racelessness, "whiteness" is simultaneously a metaphor and a biological reality, making it inescapable, inevitable, and indestructible. The quagmire of fighting antiblack race/ism within a racial/st ideological framework is the continued packaging of "unearned assets," like the presumed "racelessness" of those seen as "white," with so-called white people, and accusations that some people who don't get racialized as white are "white adjacent" if not "white inside" (recall here epithets like Oreo, coconut, banana, Twinkie, apple, etc.). Of course, such accusations go in various directions. One can also be accused of being an egg or a snowball. If "race" were truly a social construction and one that stood apart from the machinery of race/ism, then one wouldn't actually have to "betray their race" and turn toward "whiteness" to succeed or be valued, seen, and treated as equal.

People should be encouraged to think outside of antiblack racial/st frameworks to see more clearly the framework of race/ism so that they will stop upholding its causes and effects. Instead, Lawton and countless others conclude that we all must embrace our "race" to be whole humans. In Lawton's case, this prescription is ironic; her entire memoir communicates her sense of brokenness and unbelonging created and perpetuated by the racial/st thinking of those around her, yet she embraces and perpetuates this same thinking within herself. "The painful consequences of engaging in racial masquerade have been documented for years in America, but the stories of those who have been passed off as something they are not remain layered, complex, and obscured by embarrassment and fear within families," says Lawton.[10] Here, she refers to "passing." There's a body of literature that explores through fiction and nonfiction the realities of people who "pass" or "masquerade" as a "race" that isn't their own. There's now a term for those who live in a race/ist society and who see themselves differently from the dictates of their society's race/ism: *transracial*. Transracial people identify as a different "race" than the one presumed to be associated with their biological ancestry. What does such a phenomenon tell us about race/ism?

Lawton's words are poignant and heartfelt. Ultimately, she sees the world—and herself—through an antiblack racial/st lens and, as a result, suffers some of the negative effects of race/ism that would otherwise be within her realm of control and impact. We shouldn't be ashamed of how others racialize us or how we racialize ourselves. Instead, we should hold accountable the systems and people who profit from race/ism—the top one percent more than anyone else—and try to remain outside of its harms and material impacts. Staying in the matrix of racialization and belief of "race" prevents us from recognizing and embracing our full identity—our full humanity, who we are, from outside of the confines of such unnecessarily limiting and trauma-inducing thinking. We must come to reject our dehumanization *wholly and effectively*, a necessary step toward liberation from race/ism. We also must recognize the humanity of people who do not get racialized in the same ways *wholly and effectively*, a necessary step toward stopping race/ism in its tracks.

I don't highlight such beliefs about "race" and racial/st identity to "other" Lawton, Hughes, or anyone else. Instead, I seek to illuminate the fullness of how we've come to where we are as it pertains to philosophies and practices of race/ism and antiracism and our lack of progress against antiblack racism, specifically. The differences between people who see "race" as synthetic and those who see it as hereditary remain too muddied, and neither belief offers a path forward, especially if the goal remains to preserve or reform it. If we are sincere about ending race/ism as we've now known it for centuries, we require a radical shift in our belief systems and systems of practice. For too long, we have stayed within a system that was designed to keep us from thinking and doing differently. But we needn't persist down this path of inescapable racism (i.e., race/ism).

"Assets," such as fully seeing the humanity of yourself and others, shouldn't be tacitly or explicitly accepted as a feature of so-called whiteness nor should "whiteness" be discussed simultaneously as metaphor *and* biology. Freedom from race/ism's causes and effects should be accessible to everyone. Individuals who claim that freedom for themselves, regardless of how others may misconstrue that freedom, should be lauded for being themselves, not for "wanting to be someone else." Race/ist ideas about people persist so long as people operate within racial/st ideology, regardless of one's politics or racialization. In the United States and other parts of the world, we've missed so many opportunities to embrace and create a reality outside of race/ism in favor of maintaining an antiblack racial/st ideology that would prefer to have people who get racialized outside of "whiteness" to be forever confined and enslaved in one capacity or another. As a result, literal and metaphorical racelessness gets encapsulated with the so-called white race rather than the human species outside of race/ism, a reality we must imagine and then create. This means that humanity and all of the positives generally assigned to what it is to be human remain locked up with the category of "white." How unfortunate and on brand for "white" supremacy.

Antiblack racial/st ideology has done nothing positive for humanity besides dehumanize, divide, and oppress. If that's not bad enough, it is also practically self-reinforcing and does not allow us to self-define or come to any semblance of consensus when defining ourselves as collectives. *Ubuntu.* This is especially true for those assigned a so-called black identity who are not given the freedom to unshackle themselves from race/ism, precisely because racelessness is said to be outside of and inaccessible to that particular racialization. Race/ism, after all, is believed to be inescapable, a permanent aspect of society. This forever locks those who get racialized as black and everyone else into the ideological remnants of chattel enslavement and its material and immaterial impacts.

Those individuals who get racialized as black who do ultimately free themselves from the strictures of racial/st ideology often get accused of wanting to be "white." Consider again how Hughes interprets Cullen rather than lauding him for wanting to be liberated—to be raceless, to be seen as human. Many people say they want this for themselves and others, but at the same time they accept as true that the only way of doing so is from within an antiblack racial/st ideological framework. This approach is paradoxical, because this lens starts with the conclusion that "race" is real outside of race/ism—and that race/ism is permanent and inescapable. In other words, the social and economic power imbalances that are part of how most people understand racism are permanent. The best one can do is try to positively impact such imbalances in the other direction toward justice, but justice can never be fully achieved. Under this lens, "black" lives will forever not matter in practice or theory. And there are innumerous reasons for one to believe that given the manifestations caused by imagining "whiteness" and the performance of power that results from the illusion of it. Black-and-white frameworks hinder our ability and willingness to see when we are wrong and when we are right and how or why we are right or wrong. They stop our ability to question everything. But we must question everything. Question all of it.

If we "see" race/ism everywhere without question, it becomes this omnipresent villain that we can never escape or end. The irony is that a black-and-white framework is self-fulfilling; it not only nourishes but also becomes part of the very machinery that it is ostensibly trying to eradicate. One need only look at the reactions those who get racialized as BIPOC receive when they speak or behave outside of the box that antiblack racial/st ideology mandates, a burden that is not generally assigned to people who get racialized as white. Simultaneously a symptom of race/ism and a cause of it, racial/st ideology, including the practice of racialization, must become history. Uproot all of it. Leave no crumbs except a clear-eyed understanding and acknowledgment of the lessons we've learned along the way toward creating and enabling a better future for all, one without antiblack race/ism.

Race/ism tricks many of us into seeing ourselves and each other through a racialized framework, a black-and-white framework that comes disguised as reality. It has led us to see social class, economic class, ethnicity, culture, etc. through the apparition of "race" and the framing of race/ism. By continuing to conflate these things with "race," we continue to perpetuate the same thing many people say they want to end or, at minimum, do not support: race/ism. The only thing we lose by undoing our belief in human "races" and by stopping our practice of racialization is the corresponding race/ism that often camouflages itself as "race." Everything else remains. Of course, we must avoid and condemn attempts to skip to the good part. The togetherness wayfinder, as a whole, helps to ensure that people who act in good faith won't skip to the good part. There's no hiding or erasing the truth here. Instead, the togetherness wayfinder reveals facts and truths while bridging and opening imaginations to a far more expansive future.[11] We cannot get to that future without recognizing and understanding each other and exploring the twilight together. The profound differences in meaning assigned to a person's racialization lead to vital misunderstandings and mischaracterizations of people's thoughts and beliefs today. But that needn't be how it works.

In a country like the United States, if we started to live more in the twilight—if we started to see and create more gray spaces and embrace opacity—we could quickly move from being a racializing country to one that embraces a shared and unified (but not homogeneous) ethnic identity. Beyond that, we could start to see ourselves as connected with all humans and all biological beings.[12] And we could rightfully start to see ourselves as especially connected with the continent of Africa where humans were born.

We must reject the dehumanization of any of us, which in effect dehumanizes all of us, and expand our origin stories that are more rhizomatic and interconnected than singular and linear. The togetherness wayfinder allows us to not only accept but also live in our natural state.

6

Walking Negatives
Defying Dehumanization

*We aim to excavate the different mechanisms by which global science
and racial reason are recruited to propel projects
of power and domination.*

—Eram Alam, *Ordering the Human*, 2024

Every human's "natural" or "normal" state is one of being "unraced" or, at least, part of the human species. The term "race," as a categorizing concept, didn't exist before the sixteenth century, making the idea but a blip in the long history of humankind. Between the sixteenth and nineteenth centuries, it was most often used to denote ethnic or national groupings. It shifted more to its contemporary meaning with the increase of scientific race/ism, which was common in the 1600s but rose significantly in the nineteenth century.[1] Like the negative of a photograph, we are colorless—that is, we are raceless.

So-called people of color with fair skin are, in many respects, living embodiments of colorlessness—walking negatives. They are often misraced or erased by society not only due to their atypical skin color but also due to other phenotypical identifiers and, with further speculation or inquiry, even their ancestry (consider here the nefarious and race/

ist one-drop rule). They are "colorless" because "color" is presumed to be absent from their skin, and their colorlessness simultaneously mirrors their racelessness, as all humans are, indeed, raceless. A person who gets racialized as black and who has very fair skin, in particular, visually and viscerally inverts how society, at large, views and conceives of "race." Even those so-called black individuals who "pass" as so-called white will likely always be identified with some degree of ambiguity, as they are neither fully "black" nor "white." Yet, even if they are phenotypically different from others of their presumed "race," they become erased by society despite their status at birth as noticeably unraced and "abnormal."

The concept of a walking negative, then, centers and highlights society's desire to categorize and claim people based on antiblack race/ism and illustrates how "race" does not, should not, and cannot exist in a world where all are rightly humanized and none are dehumanized or seen as fit for subjugation. Around the world, society's nuanced and often troubled engagement with people perceived as "racially ambiguous," including people with albinism, underscores that which the concept of the walking negative promotes or, at least, illustrates, which is, in part, that eliminating race/ism necessitates the undoing of our belief in human "races" and our practice of assigning "race" to humans.[2] Yet, antiblack racial/st ideology guarantees that we examine society from within an antiblack racial/st worldview that concludes that "race" is real and that race/ism is omnipresent and everywhere or, according to some, no longer present at all. In other words, we literally and metaphorically learn to see in black-and-white ways. This tendency is so strong that even those who loudly state that "race" is synthetic (aka human-made)—that "race" is not something in nature—often think that "race" is something that is readily obvious to most minds. Put another way, they themselves tend to have some underlying belief in the biological reality of "race"—and paradoxically so. As philosophy professor and dehumanization specialist David Livingstone Smith once tweeted,

Most of my students come to class dutifully mouthing that race is a social construct. A little bit of Socratic probing reveals that they say this because that's what they've learned they're supposed to say, and that they are actually closeted biological realists. As I like to put it, "Scratch a social constructionist, and a biological realist bleeds."[3]

Part of the philosophical tension among hereditary belief, synthetic belief, and imaginary nonbelief in human "races" derives from the muddiness of the three categories, certainly, but also from how people learn to think about, identify, and solve race/ism—particularly antiblack race/ism—in the first place. As Smith aptly observes, synthetic believers—constructionists—are often hereditary believers—naturalists—in disguise. How some synthetic believers help to perpetuate race/ism isn't often classified as helping to uphold antiblack race/ism by self-proclaimed constructionists, because one's political beliefs are thought to absolve or confirm one's complicity in race/ism. Indeed, synthetic views on "race" tend to be more dominant on the left side of the political spectrum, a side that is too often believed to be synonymous with "not being racist" or being antiracist—and thus openly hereditary believers are often associated with the right. But when one recognizes that race/ism is itself a political system, the black-and-white way that race/ism plays out in politics, especially in the United States, is just another binary that must be interrogated and dismantled. Antiblack race/ism infects both sides of the political spectrum, unfortunately, which is just one reason why I find myself staunchly outside of it.

Antiblack racial/st ideology is the vehicle for maintaining race/ism, even in its seemingly innocent forms, like belief in "authenticity" when it comes to "race" or, more specifically, when it comes to being "black." According to this logic, some people who get racialized or who racialize themselves as black are authentically "black" and others aren't. Yet, there's no one way to be "black,"[4] as there isn't one way to be human. To argue otherwise is to accept that to be "black" is to be outside of humanity—to bind the individual with the tentacles of race/ism. The imposition of racialization, by design, obstructs one's full humanity. Here, recall the words of the then Democratic presidential nominee Joe Biden to radio host Charlamagne The God, when he said in the context of the 2020 presidential race that "if you have a problem figuring out whether you're for me or [Donald] Trump, then you ain't Black."[5] Even with supposedly progressive but really moderate or even arguably conservative politics, Biden demonstrated his and many others' sincere belief that to be "black"—whether racially, ethnically, or culturally, including politically—is to be monolithic. It is to be on my side or theirs for both of the primary political parties in the United States.

In many ways, all of us humans defy how people think of us and what we think of ourselves and each other. We can't be captured in any one image or word, not even "human," nor can we be defined by how we get racialized. In truth, we are raceless. We are walking negatives who get sorted into color-coded boxes based on our society's systems of oppression. We then perform or act out our lives from within the confines of these racializing blueprints. The complex nature of our realities and selves means that almost none of us fit into the caricatures drawn by antiblack racial/st ideology. Yet, these caricatures are demanded so that we are all kept in our places—so that we remain seemingly separate and distinct as groups, thereby enabling and reinforcing the power imbalances on which race/ism relies.[6] Although some sociologists have argued that people who get racialized as biracial often transcend racial/st ideology owing to their "mixedness,"[7] even people who get racialized as mixed are forced into a box and labeled, for example, as either "black" or "white" depending on the decade and context. Consider, for example, how the media regularly refers to Barack Obama as "black" and not "white" or "biracial."[8] This is consistent with his own self-identity—a self-identity that is also firstly and largely an imposed identity.[9]

Our entire sociocultural and political system participates in the machinery required to keep us willingly in this matrix. Any idea that doesn't serve this system is hindered from reaching a broad audience. As a result, a rich body of work that provides an abolitionist vision of race/ism has remained uncanonized, untaught, and uncommunicated for over a century. One understudied and underappreciated thinker in this regard is George Schuyler, a twentieth-century American writer, journalist, and social commentator. Once a socialist, Schuyler shifted to conservatism later in his career, a shift that has been used, in part, as a justification to keep his work outside of classrooms. Even though Schuyler's philosophies about race/ism and his cultural critiques resonate many decades later, they are seldom taught and often misconstrued because of his radical, not conservative, ideas about "race" and racialized culture in the United States. Over the course of his lifetime, Schuyler grappled publicly with his and others' beliefs in "race" and practice of racialization and what ought to be done with that belief and practice given the persistence and nature of antiblack race/ism.[10]

In a 1944 essay titled "The Caucasian Problem," Schuyler points to the self-fulfilling nature of race/ism. He writes,

> Race, which began as an anthropological fiction, has become a socio-logical fact. Socio-economic biracialism advanced as a "solution" for the color question has brought about a psychological biracialism which may bring about an entirely different "solution." An antagonism has developed on both sides which is increasingly similar to that between two Balkan nations. From being regarded as something present in and yet apart from American life and institutions, the Negro is coming to regard himself in the same way.[11]

Biracialism, here, speaks to the advancing belief in separate and distinct "races," namely "white" and "black," and the correlated hierarchies that underpin such ideas. The fiction of "race" and practice of racialization has for too many people, according to Schuyler, been accepted as necessary and permanent realities outside of race/ism itself. Consequently, "Negro[es]," in Schuyler's words, or people who get racialized as black, have come to see themselves as simultaneously apart from and outside of that which is Americana.[12] Keeping in mind that people see themselves differently despite how racialization is *supposed* to work, it should trouble all of us who compose a single nation to know that within that same nation we maintain, inherit, and pass on belief systems and practices that encourage some people to see themselves or others as perpetual outsiders. Nowadays, "white" nationalist groups, like Patriot Front, argue that people who get racialized as black aren't part of "the American people, the American ethnicity which has descended from the European race who conquered and settled this land."[13]

Whether one gets racialized as black or white or something else altogether, far too many people who uphold the belief in human "races" and the practice of racialization help to uphold such views. One need not actually believe that only those people who get racialized as white belong and are American to be complicit in supporting the antiblack framework on which this more explicit and open race/ism rests. Power is not only externally given. Power also comes from within. That we have continued to promote racial/st ideology and achieve the same pernicious results since Schuyler wrote those words during the Jim Crow era only give them more power today. In short, we're doing something wrong. We need to begin to think, see, and talk about humans in radically different ways to end race/ism, both explicit and implicit.

American society continues to devolve into a place where social class warfare takes precedence over economic class warfare in ways that maintain limitations not only on the quality of life and lifespan but also on interpersonal connections and individual and collective agency, particularly for those in the lower class. In 2020, television personality and media mogul Oprah Winfrey was joined by former football player Emmanuel Acho on her talk show *The Oprah Conversation* to answer viewers' questions about race/ism. In the two-part interview titled "Uncomfortable Conversations with a Black Man," one guest noted that not all people who get racialized as white have power and wondered aloud if grouping all so-called white people into a single category was an effective way of addressing antiblack race/ism and "inequities that are in this country and are in this world."[14] Winfrey responded, "There are white people who are not as powerful as the system of white people—the caste system that's been put in place. But they still, no matter where they are on the rung or ladder of success, they still have their whiteness."[15] Aside from confusing the metaphor of "whiteness" as essence, as indicative of the being of people who get racialized as white, she did what many well-to-do people have done before her; she claimed that "whiteness" outweighs or trumps economic class.

Despite the billionaire Winfrey's assertion, "whiteness" does not provide meaningful succor to poor and working-class so-called white people in the face of unequal access to educational and employment opportunities, quality food and healthcare, safe and healthy environments, and so on. The advantages associated with getting racialized as white needn't be maintained in favor of slightly increasing the advantages associated with getting racialized in some other way. In other words, if our conception of justice remains trapped in "white" supremacist frameworks, we will simply be advocating for *injustice* to be doled out evenly rather than for the elimination of those injustices entirely. Money certainly doesn't guarantee a person's happiness or wellness, but the correlation between one's economic class and one's level of access to preventative medicine, health and wellness, quality education, high-income jobs, and the like is undeniable to fair-minded people. Yet, race/ism operates in ways that require both economically privileged and disadvantaged people to act as though they have more in common with people in their racialized social class (read: with people who get racialized in the same way) than with anyone else. Put another way, the poor so-called black factory worker is presumed to form a natural group with the rich so-called black investment banker and not with the poor so-called white factory worker. The question becomes, how can we address the social effects of race/ism and the problem of economic inequality without treating both in the same way? So long as the view expressed by Winfrey continues to hold sway, problems caused by poverty and problems that create poverty will remain effectively untouched and masked.

Due to the American practice of racialization and racializing of others, many Americans have inherited these faulty ways of seeing themselves and the world around them. If anything, with the proliferation of technology, globalism, and social media, this focus on social class over economic class has been amplified. Schuyler thought a lot about what it would take to stop race/ism. He writes,

> It is a development which can only end tragically unless some way can now be found to re-condition colored and white people everywhere so that they will think of themselves as the same. What chance is there of doing this? It would require a revolutionary program of re-education calling not only for wholesale destruction of the accumulated mass of racialistic propaganda in books, magazines, newspapers, motion pictures and all of the present laws and regulations which recognize the racial fiction and are based upon it, but for a complete reorganization of our social system.[16]

Although Schuyler had complicated thoughts about race/ism, he too operated within its framework. Consider, for example, the language he uses: "colored," "white," "Negro," etc. It's clear that he was still working his way through the problems that plague us. Yet, his identification of the need for the wholesale abolishment of antiblack race/ism remains true today. Ultimately, the need for reeducation persists for many reasons, including the fact that voices like Schuyler's have been ignored if not lambasted for far too long. In addition, we need to revolutionize our primary education system to stop the transmission of race/ism and racial/st ideology in the first place. To be sure, we wouldn't need "reeducation" at all if we stopped teaching our children to believe in "race" and practice racialization as requisite parts of ending or resisting race/ism. We can and should teach history, including that involving race/ism, without upholding the same problems we want to stop.

Schuyler's ideas confounded most readers then and confound many now. Like many other people who get racialized as black and who attempted to work toward a better future for everyone across both economic and social class differences, he caught the attention of the Federal Bureau of Investigation (FBI). The file on him, opened on the order of FBI director J. Edgar Hoover during World War II, read, "Subject is the most widely read Negro newspaper man in the country and his articles influence the thinking of many Negro leaders. Subject has been one of the most outspoken critics on Army and Navy [segregation] policies relating to Negroes. It is the opinion of this informant that subject is the most dangerous Negro in the country today."[17] It concluded, "whether he is in the pay of some foreign government or not, he is a helper of Hitler and Hirohito."[18] Put another way, he was perceived as an enemy of the state precisely because he threatened the state's imposition and perpetuation of race/ism—both when he was a socialist and more politically conservative.

Even today, antiblack racial/st ideology cannot be fully questioned. The elite allow only perspectives that maintain the status quo of antiblack race/ism via colorblindness or other traditional forms of antiracism to break through and pretend to change the norms of belief in "races," the practice of racialization, and the attendant power imbalances. This not only perpetuates race/ism and leads us to think the status quo—which includes even seemingly radical positions—is the natural state of affairs but also presents us with a warped black-and-white picture of reality. Put simply, how a person thinks about race/ism, including one's philosophical inclinations about "race," plays a role in how that person interprets the world. That holds true even when studying data, which should (in theory) lead to unbiased and objective interpretations but often doesn't when the data is racialized and read through our own filters.

In "An Empirical Analysis of Racial Differences in Police Use of Force,"[19] Roland Fryer Jr., a professor of economics at Harvard University, underscores how antiblack race/ism and racial/st ideology operate in this manner when he concludes: "[I]f one assumes police simply stop whomever they want for no particular reason, there seem to be large racial differences. If one assumes they are trying to prevent violent crimes, then evidence for bias is exceedingly small."[20] In other words, if you assume race/ism inspires outcomes that are predicated on the existence of "race," evidence supports that assumption. And if you assume that race/ism isn't the cause for every so-called racial disparity, evidence supports that assumption. Our racialization of data ends up maintaining our racial/st belief systems: we either end up seeing race/ism everywhere or seeing it nowhere. In either case, the conclusions are wrong. Race/ism isn't everywhere—at least not always in the ways people tend to think—nor is it nowhere. It also is not the same (i.e., black or white) everywhere. Additionally, we cannot solve it with the same system that propagates it.

A salient example of this is how data related to "race" and crime is studied and interpreted. We've seen the headlines and heard the statistics: "Black people commit 50 percent of murders in the United States," "Fifty percent of murder victims in the United States are black," "Black people commit murder at six times the rate of white people," and so on. When presented with such statistics, people either blame the structural nature of race/ism or point to the presumed inferiority of people who get racialized as black. Both responses uphold race/ism, because both generalize about how people who get racialized as black are more violent, and both accept that conclusion without question. It's either because they are poor due to systemic racism, and poor people take desperate measures, or because their culture inspires them to love violence, promiscuity, crime, and so on more than any other racialized group. These ideas about people who get racialized as black stem from the narratives that enslavers and politicians (sometimes one and the same) spread about enslaved people and people they wished to enslave. Enslaved people were presumed to be shifty, devilish, savage, and in need of saving and breaking because their "natural" inclinations almost certainly ensured their immorality, their violence, their criminality, their hypersexuality. These beliefs about people who get racialized as black remain and get carried on through our continued belief in human "races" and the practice of racialization, which maintains social and economic power imbalances.

Yet, these statistics, while technically correct, say nothing meaningful about individuals who get racialized as black. A closer look at the data shows that supposed "black" criminality simply isn't the crisis media outlets and politicians paint it to be. Moreover, examining crime through the lens of antiblack race/ism doesn't lead to more justice and equality; to the contrary, it perpetuates racist beliefs, behaviors, and policies. It's not often that we inquire about the numbers or read them in a way that does not exaggerate reality and automatically affirm our preexisting racial/st beliefs. For example, in 2019, the year before pandemic shutdowns, law enforcement reported a total of 6,816,975 arrests across nearly 11,000 agencies representing roughly two-thirds of the United States, according to the FBI's crime data.[21] That's roughly 3 arrests per 100 people for all crimes. The total number of murder and nonnegligent manslaughter arrests was 7,964, or roughly 3 arrests for every 100,000 people. For those two more serious crimes, the racialized breakdown of arrestees was as follows: 4,078 "black" or "African American" (51.2 percent), 3,650 "white" (45.8 percent), 125 "American Indian" or "Alaska Native" (1.6 percent), 83 "Asian" (1 percent), and 28 "Native Hawaiian" or "Other Pacific Islander" (0.4 percent). When looking at the murder victims that same year, we see a similar breakdown. Of the 13,927 known victims, 7,484 of them (53.7 percent) were racialized as "black" and 5,787 of them (41.6 percent) were racialized as "white," with the remaining 656 victims (4.7 percent) falling in the "unknown race" or "another race" category.[22]

With a so-called black population of roughly 46.8 million in the United States in 2019,[23] this means that roughly 13 out of every 100,000 people in the country who were racialized as black were arrested (which says nothing about their guilt) for murder or nonnegligent manslaughter that year, and roughly 24 out of every 100,000 so-called black individuals were victims of homicide that same year. By comparison, with a so-called "white" population of 259 million in the United States in 2019, roughly 2 out of every 100,000 people who were racialized as white were arrested for murder or nonnegligent manslaughter that year, and roughly 3 out of every 100,000 so-called white individuals were victims of homicide. These relative percentages hold up for most types of violent crime. Less than 3 percent of all people who get racialized as black in the United States get arrested for committing *any* violent crime. At some point, quantitative and qualitative reality must matter. The narratives about people who get racialized as black being inherently more violent, whether blamed on race/ism or "culture," is wrong and reflective of our anti-black ideological positionalities. And that there's a difference in the data that I just related between groups who get racialized differently is not indicative of causation or anything, perhaps, other than human diversity.

Yet, based on these statistics, people who get racialized as black do represent a disproportionate percentage of people committing murder and getting murdered. But if our goal is to reduce crime and victimization rates, we are unable to identify much less grapple with the underlying causes of these disparities if we focus only on racial/st variables: race/ism or culture via cultural race/ism. If we try to explain this disparity through the lens of "race/ism," we are left with simplistic racialized and race/ist explanations—for example, that the differences in murder rates are caused either by race/ism—a partial explanation in most scenarios—or by inferior genetics or culture. If our explanations are predetermined and if we can't have an honest discussion about the underlying causes, then we can never find solutions. Moreover, if we have an unclear view of what reality is and isn't, we also make and collapse problems out of that which shouldn't be collapsed or made. We should readily recognize the reality that the United States, as a whole, has a high level of violent crime relative to many other countries, but the lumping of large swaths of people together based on our largely accepted systems of oppression into "violent" and "nonviolent" "races" is a fiction that itself leads to horrific violence, whether we're talking about the Wilmington massacre of

1898,[24] the lynching of Emmett Till, or the murder of Ahmaud Arbery.

Antiblack racial/st ideologies confuse our thinking, generate fear, and uphold the causes and effects of antiblack race/ism. A so-called white woman at a workshop I once attended looked me in the eyes and told me that I must fear for my life even when at home because a cop could shoot me at any time and that she, as a so-called white person, didn't have to have such a fear. A so-called black man once thanked me profusely for my presentation about racelessness because he had been trying for a long time to tell others that the people he really must fear are those who look like him, the "real" threats. Our entire system would rather have us believe in the race/ist tropes of people who get racialized as black than encourage us to question everything—because our questioning of everything would lead to more and more people seeing everything that much more clearly, which would present an imminent danger to the status quo and hierarchical systems. We cannot solve a problem we misname or misidentify unless we do so accidentally. We need to be intentional and strategic in any measures taken. How a person thinks about a problem will inevitably influence how they go about solving or upholding a problem. For many reasons, racial/st ideology actually clouds our minds when it comes to receiving information, interpreting information, and problem solving. I would be overjoyed to see the total murder rate as close to zero as possible. Our capacity to do that will not improve without doing away with racial/st ways of seeing and being.

As Fryer's aforementioned study shows, this applies to narratives about law enforcement as well. Given the nature and amount of media coverage devoted to police shootings of people who get racialized as black, I cannot really blame the woman who told me that I should, in effect, wear a bulletproof vest at home for fear the police might storm my house and shoot me. I can imagine a world in which I might live in fear for my life from state-sponsored violence. After all, the United States consistently sponsors violence. But is it truly reasonable to assume that I should fear being shot by police at every turn and let that fear consume me? Is that good for the health of my heart? What about my mind? It might be reasonable if I based my perception of reality on media headlines and social media posts, but not if I aligned my fears with the data. According to *Statista*, 1,020 people were shot and killed by police officers in the United States in 2020, the same year that Derek Chauvin killed George Floyd. The racialized breakdown was as follows: 459 "white" (45 percent), 243 "black" (23 percent), 171 "Hispanic" (17 percent), 27 "other" (3 percent), and 120 "unknown" (12 percent). In case you think the effects of the ensuing protests and the pandemic shutdowns greatly affected these numbers and percentages, the stats from 2019 were roughly the same: of the 999 shot and killed by police that year, 424 were "white" (42 percent), 251 were "black" (25 percent), 168 were "Hispanic" (18 percent), 42 were "other" (4 percent), and 114 were "unknown" (11 percent).

People who get racialized as black constitute roughly 14 percent of the U.S. population and people who get racialized as white constitute roughly 76 percent, meaning those who get racialized as black are overrepresented in these police shooting figures. If we then lead our analysis of this disparity from the conclusion that people who get racialized as black are shot and killed *because* of race/ism, we will inevitably arrive at a circular conclusion—that they are shot and killed by law enforcement because of antiblack race/ism. As noted above, however, when we examine everything through the lens of race/ism and then analyze data with presupposed conclusions, that causes us to ignore other possible variables and doesn't allow us to find optimal solutions. It also causes us to have a flawed perception of reality. Infrequently do we talk about the probability of getting shot to death by an officer in any given year in language that doesn't uphold our preexisting beliefs: roughly 1 in 565,000 for a so-called white individual, roughly 1 in 190,000 for a so-called black individual, and so on. Do these numbers suggest, as the woman at the workshop exclaimed, that I must fear the police in a way that she does not? But even this type of "race"-based comparison is flawed, because age and gender aside, the most common denominator among those shot and killed by police is economic class, a point that gets misinterpreted as simply antiblack, mostly by those who imagine that the majority of people who get racialized as black are impoverished. And the fact that the number of people shot to death by law enforcement has been steadily increasing since at least 2015 is telling us something, something we're likely missing in favor of maintaining the status quo, which allows less obvious victimization to persist.[25] Capitalism, the economic class system of the United States, mistreats its poor and working-class folks at every level, which makes it all the more critical to free up economic class discourse and initiatives from social class discourse and initiatives without ignoring or glossing over either. It is more a question of how to be clear-eyed about how to achieve justice and remove what hinders it. Justice should never be considered in terms of *equal* victimization, which is what the logic of "racial justice" frequently reinforces or inadvertently strives to achieve.

In truth, I have little to fear from police—no more than any other average person in the United States. Indeed, each of us have a greater chance of winning a Pick-6 Lottery from a field of twenty-five numbers (1 in 177,100) than being shot and killed by police—at least when we use racial/st language and ideology to consider the odds. However, our perception of the risk is warped due to what we see on the news or on social media. Indeed, if we conducted a poll to see what percentage of people believed that 10,000 or more people who are racialized as black are killed by law enforcement each year, I bet that a staggering percentage of people would express this belief.[26] Why does such misdirection matter? Aside from allowing other life-or-death problems to persist, one of the effects of race/ism is for people who get racialized as black to live in a consistent state of fear, unwellness, and unbelonging and for people who get racialized as white to primarily see those who get racialized as black as perpetually unbelonging victims, nonhumans, or subhumans. To be sure, the number of people racialized as black who are killed by police each year is a statistic that must and can be lowered, just as the total number of homicides each year (approximately 21,000) and the percentage of people living in poverty (11.5 percent) must and can be lowered. But what guarantees that we don't have a more generative impact on any of these happenings and outcomes is the blanket washing over of every statistical difference as evidence of "race" while maintaining race/ist beliefs about so-called black people and the propagation of solutions that only ever keep, create, and obscure the reality of race/ism.

After all, if I think that law enforcement is hunting people who "look like me" in the streets—or even in my own home—everything I see will confirm my belief and will inflame my being with fear, stress, paranoia, anger, and hurt. If I think that people who get racialized as black are murdering people who get racialized as black (or anyone else) with abandon, everything I see will confirm my belief and will inflame my being with fear, stress, paranoia, anger, and hurt. I am not excusing police excesses or violent criminals here, but both ways of seeing the world are faulty and make it difficult to address race/ism and the militarization of particular communities in a productive way. Who benefits from me thinking and feeling in such a way about myself and other people? Do I benefit from thinking in such ways if neither way represents reality and if neither creates actual justice?

Here, it's useful to refer again to Fryer's research. In his work on police use of force, he found that there was no evidence of bias in law enforcement's use of lethal force in the handful of cities that he studied. I must note that his conclusions only apply to the places he studied in Florida, Texas, and California and that other economists have highlighted the limitations of Fryer's methodology. His conclusions do not reflect the reality of every place and time and may reflect potential selection bias in his study. Notably, he did find evidence that so-called black people are more likely to experience unnecessary nonlethal use of force at the hands of law enforcement,[27] yet his findings regarding lethal force flew in the face of what he expected to find when he began his study. That fact matters considering my illustration of how antiblack race/ism forces us into our camps of predetermined conclusions—race/ism is always the cause or race/ism is never the cause—with very little twilight space. Fryer acknowledges the real-world impact of race/ism when he writes,

> The importance of our results for racial inequality in America is un-clear. It is plausible that racial differences in lower-level uses of force are simply a distraction and movements such as Black Lives Matter should seek solutions within their own communities rather than changing the behaviors of police and other external forces. Much more troubling, due to their frequency and potential impact on minority *belief forma-tion*, is the possibility that racial differences in police use of non-le-thal force has spillovers on myriad dimensions of racial inequality. If, for instance, blacks use their lived experience with police as *evidence that the world is discriminatory*, then it is easy to understand why black youth invest less in human capital or black adults are more likely to believe discrimination is an important determinant of economic out-comes. Black Dignity Matters.[28]

Put simply, our beliefs and biases dictate how we see ourselves and others, how we behave, and what we support. And we mustn't pretend that the structures of our society are disconnected from how and what people think and believe. We tend to accept the status quo when the sta-tus quo corresponds with what we already think and believe. We make and maintain how things are for better or worse. We write race/ism and its effects onto and into ourselves and each other in ways that allow an-tiblack race/ism to thrive. How we are taught to see ourselves and others in relation with the broader society is part of the persistent impact of race/ism. Barbara and Karen Fields contend that racecraft turns some-one else's actions—race/ism—into someone else's being.[29] That is just one of the pernicious effects of race/ism. Its effects get written into our beings in thoroughly harmful ways. Whatever characteristics and values are as-signed to a particularly racialized group become part of that group's pre-sumed being. Everything then gets filtered through that way of seeing.

This insight is underscored by philosopher Kwame Anthony Appiah. We fall into conceptual and emotional errors when we suppose

> that at the core of each identity there is some deep similarity that binds people of that identity together. Not true.... There's no dispensing with identities, but we need to understand them better if we can hope to reconfigure them, and free ourselves from mistakes about them that are often a couple of hundred years old. Much of what is dangerous about them has to do with the way identities—religion, nation, race, class, and culture—divide us and set us against one another.... Yet these errors are also central to the way identities unite us today. We need to reform them because, at their best, they make it possible for groups, large and small, to do things together. They are the lies that bind.[30]

In the case of antiblack race/ism, it is not only a lie that binds people in paradoxical ways but also one that dehumanizes, which (to some extent) explains why people who are most adversely racialized tend to coalesce around their so-called racial identities. How does one create a barrier between oneself and an unjust and often cruel world?

The focus here should be on how large institutions and people with economic, political, and cultural power (re)enforce so-called racial identities onto folks in the first place. And people also need a way to understand experiences and perspectives that they do not share with others. The togetherness wayfinder acts as a bridge between how anyone thinks about "race" and how we can create a future without it. It isn't that race/ism is never the cause for something. Most of the time, we can translate "race" into evidence of the causes and effects of racism itself. However, there are times when "race" doesn't just translate as race/ism. It also translates into culture, ethnicity, social or economic class, or some combination of the above. Proper and full translation will only help those of us invested in generating positive changes. Ultimately, efforts toward economic and American cultural repair require precision since the effects of race/ism are virtually everywhere. These effects needn't continue to be, though. Championing and promoting racial/st ideology *with* the expressed purpose of emphasizing our shared humanity is incoherent and futile; the very conception of "race" and practice of racialization place some outside of that which is human and generate a black-and-white skewed perception of reality. Obviously, denying or hiding anti-black race/ism is also a serious nonstarter and an effective way of maintaining race/ism and inflicting material harms. An embracement and recognition of our natural state—racelessness—is the best way for us to see the world clearly. To fully unify and heal from the violence and harm caused by race/ism, we will also need to fill in the gaps in our memories and histories and break through race/ism's cycle of madness to effectively affirm our shared humanity (i.e., beingness) not just in theory but also in practice.

7

Rememory
Reconciling Our Shared Humanity

*The slave was a piece of property, a thing. Learned clerks argued long
and heatedly over whether or not he was a human being and possessed
a soul. The term Negro or "nigger" implies that he
is still a thing, a member of a robot-like mass of inherently
inferior beings essentially the same regardless of intelligence,
education, skill, profession or locality, and in any case of lower status
than any white person.*

The racial fiction has been industriously spread over the world.

—George Schuyler, *Rac[e]ing* (1944)

Antiblack racial/st ideology requires us to remain within a cycle of remembering history and personal experiences and imagining potential
solutions in black-and-white ways that bely the reality that is, more often
than not, gray or twilight. But it's possible to keep alive that which has
disappeared or been lost due to our racial/st filter through "rememory,"
a term coined by Toni Morrison in her 1987 novel *Beloved*. If our memories represent the moments that we readily recall, our rememories represent those events, experiences, and histories that have been forgotten

or repressed. Based on the character Sethe's use of the word in the novel, rememory is best understood as remembering forgotten memories and inhabiting the liminal space between past and present, transitoriness and permanence, and individual and collective experience. It involves revisiting and piecing together memories and histories held by different members of society (including those of ancestors). As Sethe explains to her daughter Denver,

> If a house burns down, it's gone, but the place—the picture of it—stays, and not just in my rememory, but out there, in the world. What I remember is a picture floating around there outside my head. I mean, even if I don't think about it, even if I die, the picture of what I did, or knew, or saw is still out there.[1]

"Rememory" is similar to Wilson Harris's theorization of the phantom limb that was created by the Middle Passage and which creates a limbo gateway of endless possibilities between the Old and New Worlds. One must (re)member the violent and troubling past to (re)attach the phantom limb and open the gateway. In effect, his theorization of limbo resonates with this project's theorization of twilight and involves a physical and metaphysical dismembering and then (re)membering through (re)memory. Unlike *memory*, "rememory" transforms an individual's understanding of their present and the (re)imagining of their future.[2]

Rememory transforms an individual's understanding of their present by filling in the gaps of their black-and-white memories or histories, a process that allows them the chance to reimagine their future or future-making potential, especially with those who don't share the same memories or histories. Rememory helps us cut through the madness caused by race/ism to get to the twilight space where unification, healing, and reconciliation happen. In practice, as something that can be shared, rememory can function as a way for everyone to do the individual *and* communal work *(Ubuntu)* necessary for true unification, healing, and reconciliation. When done well, rememory extends to one's community.

It doesn't currently function in that way because the racial/st language and ideology that attends our language is designed in ways that necessarily keep us unhealed and unreconciled, but by revisiting our memories of history and learning about how our common humanity has been undermined by race/ism, we can better imagine a raceless present and create a race(ism)less future together.

Much of what has happened in our education system, through technology, in our media, in our places of work, in our religious institutions, and in our government—in all of our most significant cultural and economic systems—from the 1600s until now has been and remains the inverse of this. Rather than encouraging us to discover and celebrate our common humanity, current programs and narratives focus on the opposite by ignoring, silencing, or raising the saliency of "race" and allowing the persistence of racialization. What remains misunderstood is that in raising the saliency of "race," one often seeks to interrogate and problematize the category itself. However, any strategy that works from within racializing frameworks have uphill battles when it comes to enabling more people to not only acknowledge but also seek to stop race/ism. Although most discourse on antiblackness is perceived as a black-and-white issue, the lives and stories of those who do not get racialized as black or white often illustrate the importance of understanding the madness caused by race/ism, playing in the twilight or the in-between spaces, and fostering rememory if we want to heal, unify, and redefine our present and future.

We see this interplay in the memoir *The Woman Warrior*,[3] in which American author Maxine Hong Kingston interweaves memoir with Chinese folktales. As a strategy for subverting and interrogating paradoxical notions of inferiority and order, she represents madness—typically in the context of foolish or dangerous behavior, disorder, mental illness, and extreme anger as a form of unmanageability and resistance—as a process of empowerment and quest for liberation. With that madness, Kingston remembers and likens her life's experiences with that of many other "women warriors," including Chinese folklore figures. Her exploration of madness offers readers a deeper understanding of not only Kingston but also of others whose authentic identities transcend divisions, classifications, and ostracization. Kingston's stitching together of various histories—various experiences and ways of seeing oneself, one's formation of identity, etc.—remains authentic to how Kingston sees herself and pushes the boundaries that would have us teach our youth that they are forever and always different or the same as one another.

She collapses the tenuous boundaries that exist between racializations and ethnicizations that are presumed to reflect homogeneity and the sort of special and immediate bond among those of the same ethnicity or racialized group. Importantly, Kingston's intragroup representation of madness suggests that the critical path to productive discourse and national, cultural, and political concord includes the recognition of both our particular and universal humanness, which is present across cultures, nations, and politics. Recalling Anna Deavere Smith's call to excavate "twilight moments,"[4] the universal moments found among all of us, and Morrison's rememory, Kingston also illustrates how racialization and ethnicization among humans require the division and separation of humans based on presumed irreconcilable differences that belie the interconnectedness and mixedness of all humans, including the presence of reconcilable differences that do exist but that don't have to include the dehumanization of people. Ultimately, madness functions by its illumination of (1) the particular (i.e., difference and individuality), (2) the universal (i.e., both the effect of anger and madness on the broader community and the individual), and (3) the tension between the particular and universal. By extension, madness and twilight underpin and are part of the togetherness wayfinder, which helps everyone willing to unify, heal, and reconcile ideas and beliefs that, until a certain point, seemed impossible.

Kingston, whose parents immigrated to the United States from China, includes talk-story in her memoir and reimagines her family's history

combining myth, orality, history, and literary techniques that extend beyond traditional conventions of memoir and disrupt binaries like true/
false, real/imagined, experience/knowledge, natural/supernatural, and
the like. In *The Woman Warrior*, the term ghost(s) symbolizes both the
supernatural and those people considered foreign, "non-Chinese," or
perceptibly different from a larger Chinese society. Synonyms of ghost,
according to Kingston's usage of the word, also include the following:
barbarian, savage, and animal. Both the synonyms of and the word ghost
call attention to the difference between the girls and women Kingston
illustrates as angry or mad and their larger societies. Her depiction of
the No Name Woman, the "village crazy lady,"[5] the No Name Girl,[6] the
woman next door, Crazy Mary, Pee-A-Nah, Moon Orchid, and herself
highlights the cathartic experience anger and madness offers society as
well as society's own madness, which inverts the othering discourse of
girls and women being different and outside of the boundaries of the
community as a strategy of resistance.

The women named above are ghosts of a sort; sometimes their names
remain unspoken and their stories untold in their entirety; sometimes
they remain silent and do not have dialogue in the book. Some seem
supernatural, and each is deemed mad, angry, or both. Ultimately, each
woman utilizes her own forms of madness and anger and in doing so
illuminates the particular, the universal, and the tension between the
two. Thus, each woman manages the unmanageable, shows herself to
be unmanageable, and exposes both the benefits and dangers associated
with madness and anger. Moreover, Kingston's representation of each
woman illustrates how racialization and ethnicization among humans
lead to, require, and reflect the division and separation of humans based
on desired power imbalances that belie the interconnectedness of all
humans.

In *The Woman Warrior*, Kingston's narrator struggles to separate the
particular from the universal and the insane from the sane. She asks,
"Chinese-Americans, when you try to understand what things in you

are Chinese, how do you separate what is peculiar to childhood, to poverty, insanities, one family, your mother who marked your growing with stories, from what is Chinese? What is Chinese tradition and what is the movies?"[7] Her line of inquiry comes in the middle of No Name Woman's story. No Name Woman, Kingston's unnamed aunt, a ghost, kills her newborn and commits suicide after giving birth while her husband has "been gone for years" and could not, therefore, be the baby's father.[8] Kingston imagines different versions of her aunt's story. The version she prefers has No Name Woman crossing "boundaries not delineated in space," combing "individuality into her bob," and being in love or sexually liberated.[9] In the other version, No Name Woman is coerced or raped by a village man and forced to keep her silence. Either way, the "village had also been counting" the numbers of months and the possible date of conception, concluding that No Name Woman is an adulterer.[10]

The village expects her to "keep the traditional [Chinese] ways" even though her "four brothers went with her father, husband, and uncles 'out on the road' and for some years became western men."[11] Her presumed eccentricity and individuality render the circumstances surrounding the pregnancy unimportant because regardless her pregnancy extends her beyond the boundaries of Chinese tradition. In response to her difference and assumed defiance or unmanageability, the village erupts in anger. In an interview with Angels Carabí, Kingston calls "No Name Woman" a story of an individual whose decision affects and changes the entire community.[12] According to Kingston, No Name Woman "becomes a cathartic experience for the villagers."[13] In anger, "people are able to hit and stab and fling blood around,"[14] making No Name Woman a sacrificial victim in what can also be described as an act of madness, foolish or dangerous behavior. They wear "white masks," ruin No Name Woman's family's house, kill animals, and smear the "blood of our animals" on the walls.[15] Her perceived difference allows the village to act out in anger and create their own disorder. More than being a sacrificial victim, though, No Name Woman is also a warrior in Kingston's rendering.

In the chapter "A Song for a Barbarian Reed Pipe," nonconformity, disorder, and Kingston's own attempt to embrace her "American-Chinese" identity create anger and a sort of madness in her.[16] Throughout this part of the memoir, Kingston tries to reconcile her own feelings of difference from the Chinese people she knows, like her mother and aunt, and Americans. She attends a Chinese school in the evenings and, along with other Chinese American female students, invents "an American-feminine speaking personality" as her way of finding a "voice, however faltering."[17] She notices that every female student invents a speaking personality "except for that one girl who could not speak up even in Chinese school."[18] Young Kingston orders this girl, whom she refers to as "No Name Girl," to talk, to explain herself, to be more manageable. By Kingston's own account, she torments the girl, who makes sounds that "come out of her mouth, sobs, chokes, noises that were almost words."[19] Kingston tries to give her words: "'Why don't you scream, Help?' I suggested. 'Say, Help. Go ahead.' She cried on. 'O.K. O.K. Don't talk. Just scream, and I'll let you go.'"[20] No Name Girl's difference and nonconformity, her choice to be silent, disturb Kingston, who "thought talking and not talking made the difference between sanity and insanity."[21] In other words, she interprets the girl's difference and silence to be indicative of madness and responds in anger similar to how the village reacts to No Name Woman's silence and difference.

Like another character in the book, No Name Woman, No Name Girl becomes yet another sacrificial victim and another woman warrior. Ultimately, the particularity and individuality of No Name Girl and her continued silence inspire Kingston's anger because she recognizes, on some level, the similarities between the girl, herself, her mother, and the village her mother tells her about. She wants to suppress those similarities because she imagines herself to be different from them and sane. Consider the parallels between how race/ism tricks some people into feeling superior and others into feeling inferior. Consider how, at its core, intragroup and intergroup oppressive action stems from one's own feelings of inadequacy or righteous difference even as one does not live in a vacuum and clearly learns those feelings from the larger context.

In the same chapter, Kingston defines insanity as an inability to explain oneself. She writes, "Insane people were the ones who couldn't explain themselves."[22] She tells stories of many girls and women that cannot explain themselves and whose disruption of order causes intragroup othering or segregation and the subsequent anger and madness the unmanageability of those perceived as different causes. The so-called mad women, ghosts, in Kingston's memoir are unmanageable because they express themselves in ways that society considers unacceptable either through how they dress, wear their hair, speak, or are silent, or how they express their sexuality, wed or unwed. In "Shaman," "the village crazy lady" wears a "headdress with small mirrors . . . [and] crazy lady clothes of reds and greens."[23] She is in constant motion; her "body sway[s] pleasantly." She sings as she gets water from the river and flings "droplets into grass and air." She "undulate[s] toward a clearing" and dances in the light captivating the attention of the villagers.[24] Poet and writer Marlene NourbeSe Philip says that "management [of the unmanageable] works to control that which is considered different and representative of Otherness."[25] Thus, a "villager whisper[s] away the spell, 'She's signaling the planes.'"[26] While Brave Orchid, Kingston's mother, tells the villagers that the woman is "'a harmless crazy lady,'" the villagers proceed to stone the woman, pounding "her temples with the rocks in their fists until she was dead."[27]

The woman is unable to explain her difference to protect herself. Instead, she shakes "her head coquettishly" and replies affirmatively, saying, "Yes . . . I have great powers" when asked if she is a spy.[28] Her language does not translate well, and people, like Brave Orchid, who try to speak her language often fail to recognize the universal through the easily perceived differences. Instead, such differences get marked with insanity or madness. Kingston illustrates iterations of girls and women, simultaneously ghosts and warriors, that remain unmanageable within their own communities and, for different reasons, do not explain themselves. A mad woman, in the novel, is not harmless and must be managed either by death (suicide or murder), anger, and/or institutionalization.

If an individual does not explain herself, she dies, invokes rage, or is institutionalized. There are four women in the book who get sent to an "asylum," a "crazyhouse."[29] First, there is the "woman next door" who makes the children "afraid, though she sa[ys] nothing, [does] nothing."[30] Her action and inaction, her voice and silence, make the kids nervous but, really, it is the "silver heat ris[ing] from her body" that causes alarm and signifies her difference, her unmanageability, and madness, which had gotten her "locked up before."[31] She gets "locked up [again] in the asylum"[32] for one to two years before being brought back home by her husband. Upon her release, she "die[s] happy, sitting on the steps after cooking dinner."[33] Second, there is "Crazy Mary," a twenty-year-old whose parents left her in China when she was a toddler and brought her to the United States when they had "made enough money."[34] Her parents hoped she could "'learn English and translate'" for them since her siblings, born in the United States, "were normal and could translate."[35]

Kingston associates Crazy Mary's madness with her transition from living in China for twenty years and then transitioning to life in the United States. Her internal madness, like with the woman next door, emanates from her body: she has a black mole that "pulls you forward with its power," points at things that are not there, hangs her head "like a bull's," wears uncomely clothes, often has rice in her hair, and smells "camphoraceous" stinking up the whole house.[36] Her difference affects the household since "houses with crazy girls have locked rooms and drawn curtains."[37] Thus, Crazy Mary gets placed in an asylum and is never released. Kingston is glad that she "was born nine months after"[38] her mother immigrated. The implication of Crazy Mary's story reflects a particular type of inability to explain oneself in a different cultural, national, and ethnic space and a desire of the broader community, even within a new space, to manage the unmanageable.

In the memoir, society's frequent inability to speak from another point of view helps inspire the identification of madness in people that are different and an outpouring of anger by those insistent about the following of traditions. Often what remains unrecognized are the similarities between traditional and cultural beliefs and that which evokes fear of particular "mad" individuals. The community reads each of Kingston's mad women and girls as different and, therefore, mad. Third, there is Pee-A-Nah who, like the village crazy lady, the woman next door, and Crazy Mary, looks different: she "rid[es] to the slough with a broom between her legs," has one cheek powered red and the other white, and black hair that stands "up and out to the sides in dry masses."[39] She also wears a "pointed hat and layers of capes, shawls, [and] sweaters buttoned at the throat like capes."[40] She is an "angry witch, not a happy one,"[41] who runs very fast and seems to fly. Pee-A-Nah, whose name is given to her by one of Kingston's brothers and "does not have a meaning,"[42] does not mask her difference and individuality.

Her agency centers on her ability to highlight the disorder and unraveling of presumed hierarchy that the community seeks to manage. That her community-given name means nothing or, at least, does not translate echoes her inability and unwillingness to explain herself and her unmanageability because what cannot be named cannot be easily controlled or translated. Eventually, she disappears and is probably "locked up in the crazyhouse too."[43] In this case, as with the other instances, the particular is easy to identify, and the universal is signified. The children think that Pee-A-Nah is a witch who is "capable of witch deeds, unspeakable boilings and tearings apart and transformations if she"[44] catches them. The stories they tell each other about Pee-A-Nah and the other so-called mad women echoes the talk-story Kingston infuses into the memoir, like that of Fa Mu Lan, who is legendary, not shamed, feared, silenced, or institutionalized, for her difference and breaking of tradition. In fact, Kingston identifies with Fa Mu Lan, saying,

What we have in common are the words at our backs. The idioms for revenge are "report a crime" and "report to five families." The reporting is the vengeance—not the beheading, not the gutting, but the words. And I have so many words—"chink" words and "gook" words too— that they do not fit on my skin.[45]

She interprets the story of Fa Mu Lan—in the chapter titled "White Tigers"—as one of the female body, language, and explanation and, therefore, relates to Fa Mu Lan beyond the easily perceived differences between herself and Fa Mu Lan. Her ability to speak another language by writing "White Tigers" also allows her to see from another perspective and to recognize the universal through the particular. In that chapter, she moves beyond Fa Mu Lan's unmanageability, primarily in what Kingston describes as a patriarchal society, beyond the rhetoric of madness and recognizes herself in Fa Mu Lan. Importantly, she redirects the anger typically directed at women who are different or mad toward the larger oppressive systems of race/ism and patriarchy. Her ability to speak another language in the way that Smith suggests is conducive to extra- and intragroup healing and discourse, though, is fleeting and strategic.

In "The Western Place," Kingston's narrative continues to weave the connections between anger, madness, difference, language, and universality or humanness through Moon Orchid's story. As lecturer and author Helena Grice argues, Moon Orchid slides into insanity and serves as a foil for Brave Orchid. She argues that Moon Orchid lives up to her name and the "lunacy" her name implies.[46] However, further analysis of Moon Orchid's madness exposes a more complex characterization of her and illuminates the paradox between what constitutes madness and difference and what constitutes normative behavior. After arriving in the United States and reuniting with Brave Orchid, her sister, after 30 years of separation, 64-year-old Moon Orchid attempts to speak from another perspective, an American one of her nieces and nephews, immediately upon arriving in California. She recognizes that the kids "must have many interesting savage things to say, raised as they'd been in the wilderness."[47] Although she thinks about them in terms associated with ghosts, foreigners, "non-Chinese," she wants to learn about them rather than outright reject their perceptible differences and, therefore, them. She follows the children around the house narrating their every move: "She liked to figure them out. She described them aloud, 'Now they're studying again. . . . He is picking up his pencil and tapping it on the desk.'"[48] Her translation of the kids' actions is even translated: "The child married to a husband who did not speak Chinese translated for him, 'Now she's saying that I'm taking a machine off the shelf.'"[49] The narrative oscillates between highlighting differences and occasional attempts to discover the universal through such differences.

However, after weeks of following "her nieces and nephews about" and saying aloud their actions and of her words getting translated into English, the children tell each other, "She's driving me nuts."[50] At that time, the family interprets her actions as eccentric and capable of driving one to madness but harmless, more or less. In other words, unlike the other scenarios of mad or angry girls/women described earlier, Moon Orchid's difference or eccentricity is not yet read as harmful. While she explains herself and her fascination with what is to her a new language— both literally and figuratively—upon her arrival, Kingston, her mother, and Kingston's siblings often respond to Moon Orchid with impatience and, yes, anger. Further, Brave Orchid actively tucks away the trinkets and gifts her sister brings with her from China, which also suggests a sort of unwillingness to empathize with Moon Orchid's perspective, transition, and language that culminates in a transformation of her difference and "madness."

Moon Orchid speaks but Brave Orchid dictates the outcome at crucial moments. At first glance, Brave Orchid appears to be living up to her own name signifying her bravery, which she undeniably embodies. In this chapter, her courage comes at the cost of Moon Orchid's own perspective, ability to explain herself, and difference, which then also extends to her sanity and manageability. Brave Orchid asserts that it is time for Moon Orchid to go to Los Angeles to confront her husband and his American wife. Moon Orchid says, "But I'm happy here with you and all your children."[51] She imagines her own future that does not include her husband and centers on Brave Orchid and her family's lives. "We're leaving on Friday,"[52] Brave Orchid replies. Indeed, the family leaves for Los Angeles on Friday. Moon Orchid expresses her fear and desires not to go during the trip only occasionally getting "into the mood" that Brave Orchid creates and imposes onto her.[53] During the confrontation with her husband, Moon Orchid is stunned into silence, like No Name Girl remains when Kingston confronts her: "[S]he seem[s] stiff and frozen," and she "open[s] and shut[s] her mouth without any words coming out."[54] The confrontation even causes the silencing of her crying.[55] Moon Orchid observes that her husband looks "like one of the ghosts passing the car windows, and she must look like a ghost from China. They had indeed entered the land of ghosts, and they had become ghosts."[56] He is a "non-Chinese" or Americanized ghost. She is a ghost from his past in China, his Chinese past, and a Chinese—foreign—woman in the United States. She recognizes their similarities through their particular differences.

The significance of her recognition involves the language Kingston uses in that observation and moment of Moon Orchid's silence and silencing. Later, Brave Orchid observes, "Perhaps Mood Orchid had already left this mad old body, and it was a ghost badmouthing her children. Brave Orchid finally called her niece who put Moon Orchid in a California state mental asylum."[57] Directly after the confrontation, Moon Orchid ceases communication with Brave Orchid, effectively ghosting her. Kingston writes, "Several months went by with no letter from Moon Orchid. When she had lived in China and Hong Kong, she had written every other week."[58] In addition to reducing her communication, she begins to fear that "Mexican ghosts" are following and conspiring to murder her.[59] Her increased paranoia seems like a distinct symptom of her madness. However, her fear of her Other—Mexicans—echoes the children's frequent exasperation of Chinese people in the same chapter and elsewhere, the villager's fear of the village crazy lady that erupts into anger, Kingston's fear of being similar to No Name Girl that explodes into anger, Brave Orchid's fear and distrust of ghosts or her Others, and so on. She comes to fear difference, as opposed to learning and speaking difference as she initially does with her nieces and nephews when she first arrives in the United States.

Her words and experience no longer translate well. Similarly, the "invisibilities" Brave Orchid talks to are reinterpreted as reflective of madness when Moon Orchid imagines that people are after her.[60] Moon Orchid's body, like that of No Name Woman, Crazy Mary, and Pee-A-Nah, begins to emanate madness: "Her [Brave Orchid's] sister's skin hung loose, like a hollowed frog's, as if she had shrunken inside it. Her clothes bagged, not fitting sharply anymore," writes Kingston. "I'm in disguise," Moon Orchid says.[61] Kingston's aunt looks, speaks, and behaves differently after the confrontation and silencing. Another part of what the family interprets as evidence of madness and, ultimately, her difference from them and an earlier version of herself includes a precise moment of recognizing and translating another language:

> "I [Moon Orchid] heard them talking about me. I snuck up on them and heard them."
> "But you don't understand Mexican words." [Brave Orchid]
> "They were speaking English."
> "You don't understand English words."
> "This time, miraculously, I understood. I decoded their [the Mexicans'] speech. I penetrated the words and understood what was happening inside."[62]

These might, in fact, be the words of a woman experiencing mental illness. However, in "A Song for a Barbarian Reed Pipe," Kingston complicates the clarity of Moon Orchid's mental health by sharing a talk-story about Ts'ai Yen, who sings "about China and her family there. Her words seemed to be Chinese, but the barbarians [ghosts] understood their sadness and anger. Sometimes they thought they could catch barbarian phrases about forever wandering."[63] Here, Moon Orchid's story connects her simultaneously to another woman warrior (Ts'ai Yen) in the text and barbarians, ghosts, foreigners. Her consistent attempts to translate and speak another language render her metaphorically mad by society's standards. Subsequently, she is institutionalized. Ironically, her language translates well only in the institution her daughter places her in and with other institutionalized women: "'[W]e understand one another here. We speak the same language, the very same. They understand me, and I understand them.'"[64] Reminiscent of how Kingston connects herself to Fa Mu Lan, Moon Orchid's story interconnects with that of Ts'ai Yen and the characterizations of the other girls and women analyzed in this chapter. Her story reflects the multifaceted function of madness in the memoir: it highlights both the particular and universal and the tension between the two.

Throughout the memoir, anger and madness often operate in tandem and oscillate between girls and women both explicitly and implicitly identified as mad. Whether due to their silence, language, physical expression—sexual and otherwise—or the anger their difference inspires, their perceived differences expose the humanness and universality between each other and Kingston, the narrator. Kingston writes, "I thought every house had to have its crazy woman or crazy girl, every village its idiot. Who would be It at our house? Probably me."[65] She then describes herself in terms like those previously reserved for Crazy Mary, Pee-A-Nah, and Moon Orchid: "I was messy, my hair tangled and dusty. My dirty hands broke things. Also I had had the mysterious illness. And there were adventurous people inside my head to whom I talked," she says.[66] When she asks her sister if she talks to "people that aren't real inside your mind," her sister asks, "Do I what?"[67] Her aunt imagines people and scenarios and gets institutionalized. NourbeSe Philip writes, "Historically, dealing with the unmanageable has run the gamut from the actual destruction of peoples when necessary—genocidal practices in the Americas, for instance—to management: putting the unmanageable into preordained places within society so that they can be more easily controlled,"[68] like institutions for the mentally ill. Kingston fears that her imagination reflects a type of madness like that of her aunt or the other institutionalized women.

Further, anger and violence manifest themselves in her interactions with No Name Girl and Brave Orchid and also occupy her nightmares where she says that "blood drip[s] from my fangs, blood of the people I was supposed to love."[69] Ultimately, her own characterization allows for the illumination and interrogation of anger and madness because she inhabits a world that is at once particular and global, of madness and sanity. In fact, her mother applies the term madness to her, saying, "Madness. I don't feel like hearing your craziness,"[70] in the midst of Kingston's version of talk-story. In the end, Kingston learns to speak from her own and other people's perspectives, including her mother's, but her mother takes a while to speak from the perspective of Others or those she considers mad (ghosts). Kingston's depiction of madness and the function anger and madness play in the memoir complicate typical understandings of madness and resist manageability.

In a 2006 interview with Nicoleta Zagni, Kingston speaks extensively about her identification as an American and as a global writer and says something that resonates with Smith's assertion that if more people spoke from another point of view, "we could accelerate the flow of ideas,"[71] and is worth closing with. She says, "I have talked before about being influenced by William Carlos Williams, who was always working on 'who is the poet of the Americas'. . . . I feel that way as I write. It is my voice, but it's also the voice of humanity."[72] Kingston's voice, like the voices of the girls and women named here, translates well, especially when one recognizes the universal through the particularity in her memoir.

Many cultures have ideas and language to describe the insider-outsider dichotomy illustrated by Kingston. The term *Americanah*, for example, is one used by Nigerians to refer to Nigerians who have come back to Nigeria after living in America.[73] In the United States, racial/ st language and ideology remain the preeminent ways that we remain divided and conquered. Race/ism impacts everything in just about all domains, whether in politics, culture, art, literature, music, technology, religion, media, education, and so on. We need to finally start to speak from each other's perspectives. We need to readily recognize and play in the twilight space to break through the cycles of madness while still honoring why madness occurs and what it is. We need to remember history and personal experiences in ways that translate well and reflect a much more expansive reality, especially as it pertains to humanity. We must embrace all of ourselves together and move forward together, vowing never to repeat the same pernicious cycles.

We're at a threshold. We can continue to practice antiracism or promote colorblindness—same coin, different sides—the same ways that we've always done, which will cause us to stay in the matrix and enable race/ism. Or we can forge a new path forward for all of us, one that centers unification, healing, and reconciliation. To create a future without race/ism, we need a way of seeing that will allow us to uncover more of what is concealed and hidden by "race," while acknowledging that no one lens alone will ever be completely able to capture our full humanity.

8

Invisible Ink
Recognizing the Reality of the Human

*Thought of self and thought of other here become obsolete
in their duality. Every Other is a citizen and no longer a
barbarian. What is here is open, as much as this there.*

—Édouard Glissant, *Poetics of Relation*, 1990

Madness results from our human desire to flatten reality with the hopes
of better understanding it, thereby simplifying it, and from managing
perceived differences and similarities in ways that actually benefit only a
very small statistical minority of people. To extricate ourselves from the
matrix of antiblack race/ism, we need to read between the lines, to make
out the "invisible ink" so that we might see ourselves and other people
in all the fullness and complexity of humanity. This will allow us to see
ourselves and others in ways that are generative and true. Some racializing frameworks aspire to achieve similar ends but fall woefully short by
design. When we are precluded from acknowledging what we share and
how everyone's own unique story has universal elements, we all lose. We
miss opportunities for sincere and healing communication and meaningful and lasting relationships. We also ensure that our children inherit
the same limiting ways of seeing themselves and knowing others, too.

To read the invisible ink, we first need to understand the concept of *opacity*, a central feature of my conceptualization of invisible ink—a critical component of the togetherness wayfinder. In his 1990 work *Poetics of Relation*, Martinican writer, philosopher, and literary critic Édouard Glissant defines opacity as a state of otherness that is unquantifiable, a diversity that exceeds categories of identifiable difference (i.e., "race," nationality, ethnicity, etc.).[1] Opacity exposes the limits of schema that attempt to define or categorize in black-and-white paradigms and acknowledges that not everything about ourselves can ever be understood or organized according to neat labels. In other words, it problematizes frameworks that reduce, essentialize, and dehumanize, which is what race/ism is designed to do, and it prevents us from understanding—even if not agreeing with—other perspectives. By acknowledging the often opaque nature of humanity, we can create a way for everyone to find and dwell in the twilight, the in-between space that black-and-white racial/st ideology prevents and masks.

Glissant's theory of opacity, along with Toni Morrison's concept of rememory,[2] Maxine Hong Kingston's depiction of madness,[3] and Anna Deavere Smith's illustration of twilight,[4] synthesize with many of the ideas and much of the imagery presented by Barbadian writer George Lamming in his 1953 partly autobiographical novel *In the Castle of My Skin* (*Castle*)[5]—specifically, as they relate to his resistance to essentialization via antiblack racial/st ideology and his presentation of the multiplicitous nature of humanity via *marronage*, the flight or liberation from enslavement and colonization, including psychological colonization, and *creolization*, the multidirectional process through which creole languages and cultures emerged through mixtures of African, European, Asian, and indigenous cultures.[6]

Lamming's writing in its foundation underscores rememory and all other tools of the togetherness wayfinder by calling attention to the similarities and differences among people across time and space. Even though Lamming, like Glissant and Kingston, occasionally falls into the racial/

st trap, we can recognize the trap and appreciate how he often avoids or escapes it and turns it on its head. Together, the synthesis of rememory, madness, twilight, marronage, and opacity lend to and reflect the process of engaging the togetherness wayfinder and the fruitfulness of doing so while also indicating the type of radical imagination one needs to imagine and create a future without race/ism.

In *Castle*, Lamming uses landscapes and the act of landscaping as a metaphor for marronage to depict the processes and outcomes of creolization. Many American and Caribbean writers use -scapes (i.e., city, sea, and land) as symbols for reflecting different aspects of the history of the Americas and the various creolized identities that stemmed from violent contact, which is not to be mistaken for saying that such writers compare humans to nonhuman entities. A landscape includes all of the visible features of an area of land, including bodies of water, human elements (such as buildings, structures, and cemeteries), flora, fauna, and transitory elements like lighting and weather. Landscapes thus include cityscapes, seascapes, skyscapes, and littoral spaces. As a verb, landscape means to change (modify) the appearance of an area of land. Through his trope of the landscape in *Castle*, Lamming presents his view of maroon consciousness as one manifestation of the creolization, the opacity—the inability to be reduced or essentialized—of the Americas. Largely reflected in the landscape, landscaping, and children—indicating a time before one gets indoctrinated into racial/st ideology, for example—of the novel, it is ultimately G, Trumper, Boy Blue, and Bob's subversive (creolized) thoughts and behavior that he suggests must survive and affect meaningful change. Like Kingston, Lamming's text suggests that twilight worldviews lead the way toward social, cultural, linguistic, and historical liberation, unification, healing, and reconciliation for both the individual and the individual's larger society.

Marronage has a deep cultural and historical significance within Barbados and in the Caribbean more broadly speaking. Several Caribbean writers extend the definition of marronage beyond its literal meaning of flight to include what is called maroon consciousness. Edward Brathwaite associates "features such as resilience, survival, resourcefulness, and innovation . . . with the Caribbean African maroon."[7] Such features seem indicative of the characteristics embodied by Maroons. Consider how Caribbean writers employ marronage in literature that extends beyond physical escape as resistance and includes the characteristics described above that are often (un)conscious aspects of one's psyche. For Michelle Cliff, "the primal mother as Nanny of the Maroons is the incarnation of historical awareness and resistant militancy."[8] According to Jarrett Brown, Claude McKay's "male characters negotiate . . . diasporan spaces with the complex consciousness and proclivities of maroons."[9] In *Caribbean Discourse*, Glissant talks about "the need for camouflage" in the Caribbean and asserts that the Maroon is the Caribbean's "tutelary hero."[10] Marronage as a trope in literature often requires what Glissant calls "reversion."[11] Reversion, according to Glissant, entails a backward glance toward a single origin: in this case, Africa. Rememory requires the same backward glance often toward multiple points of origin toward the goal of avoiding the pitfalls of the singularity of origin stories.

The character(s) must be able to first recognize the cause of marronage (the Middle Passage and slavery) to develop and carry hope for the larger community. One must be able to see the invisible ink. Marronage, as it pertains to racial/st ideology, isn't caused by any person's desire to be someone else, to not be themselves. Instead, marronage results from the impossibility and undesirability of fitting into racial/st boxes and conforming to what other people expect. It is a rejection of an unreality that would have us believe that we aren't more alike than we are different and that our differences are "racial" or racialized rather than anything else, a product of antiblack race/ism or "white" supremacy. After recognition and acknowledgment of history occurs, diversion can happen. Unlike reversion, diversion relies on "trickster [Maroon] strateg[ies]."[12] If the Maroon figure, a trickster of sorts, does not "return to the point of entanglement"[13] the trope of marronage fails.[14] In other words, the character(s) must confront the past and the present to plan for a different future.

Both Brathwaite and Glissant view modern-day Maroons as emblematic of resistance leading to liberation. Within the context of the togetherness wayfinder, marronage and maroon consciousness are paradigms "from which [societal] transformation may proceed."[15] Both include "submerged/maroon ancestral [Caribbean] heritage,"[16] signify resistance, and combine "the present, the past, and the future, simultaneously."[17] Whereas too many people would readily dismiss the togetherness wayfinder or ideas of "racelessness" that have arisen over the centuries because they misunderstand them, when best understood, the ideas of racelessness that I study align with and transcend traditional racial/st strategies of resistance. Maroon consciousness interconnects with American defiance of racial/st ideology. Based on this interpretation of his work, Lamming's definition of marronage also includes and extends beyond the literal definition. Beginning with the title of *In the Castle of My Skin*, his use of manmade constructions as a metaphor for marronage begins to unfold.

Lamming's landscape requires a simultaneous backward and forward glance. The title *In the Castle of My Skin*—a revision of Derek Walcott's line, "You, in the castle of your skin, I the swineherd"[18]—shifts the gaze of the reader from the colonizer to Caribbean people of African descent of Barbados, the Caribbean, and the Americas more broadly speaking. "Castle" is a manmade construction as is the racial/st erasing of a person's humanness via skin color, a proxy for "race," but the landscape Lamming centers by editing Walcott's line is that of the Caribbean. The sort of fortressing implied in "the castle of my [brown] skin" reflects the protective, subversive nature of marooning from the translation of phenotype into "race," which is then used to justify race/ism. It is within the castle of the Maroons' skin that the Maroons recognized their inherent humanity, despite the ideology and systems of oppression imposed by the enslavers, and they found their strength to escape. Not only did they escape, though, but they often hid close by, finding solace and safety in the dark and taking food and livestock from the fruits of their toil. Lamming's landscape, including how his words fall on each page and his topographical descriptions, becomes central as a way of speaking about marronage and creolization, which are represented throughout the entire novel. Lamming's representation of landscape and landscaping reflects marronage and maroon consciousness as part of creolization beginning with the flood in chapter one, the landscape in chapter six, and then the darkness and G's flight at the end of the novel.

Published in England, Lamming's partly autobiographical novel is a bildungsroman of a Barbadian boy named G. Set in Barbados in the 1930s, the novel begins with rain and flooding on G's ninth birthday and ends in darkness when G is seventeen years old and preparing to leave Barbados to teach English to Venezuelans in Trinidad. Lamming subverts and creolizes traditional generic conventions of the bildungs-roman by using first person (G's voice), third person, and choric voices. He also progresses through time in a nonlinear fashion (like Kingston). The landscape of the novel includes a variety of dialects, varying between formal and informal registers, and it illustrates how G's identity simul-taneously influences and is influenced by the creolization of Caribbean nations. G's narrative represents his political coming-of-age. The third person and choric narratives show the development and fabric of the vil-lage's political awareness. Just as the voices change, the landscape chang-es throughout the novel and is prominently featured. The fulcrum chap-ter of the novel, chapter six, depicts G, Trumper, Boy Blue, and Bob—all boys—transcending physical and metaphorical racial/st borders while visiting the littoral space of the island. Thus, Lamming's landscape serves as a space for the boys to transgress boundaries, a space that reflects the landscape's own crossing and creating of boundaries, and a space where boundaries are unbroken by many adults in the novel. By employing the trope of the landscape and landscaping, Lamming makes his view of marronage and maroon consciousness as an essential part of the creolization of the Caribbean space (geographically, culturally, ethnically, socially, and so on) clearer.

Water exposes Lamming's view of creolization in *Castle*. "Rain, rain, rain," Lamming begins the novel, describing the flood of G's village. G's mother and other villagers interpret the rain and subsequent flooding as a blessing: "[T]hey flattered me with the consolation that my birthday had brought showers of blessing," G explains.[19] However, G believes that the rain and flood are a curse or, perhaps, an omen; he says that the flood evokes "the image of those legendary waters which had once arisen to set a curse on the course of man."[20] Christianity is a source of colonialism in the novel; G resists Christian ideology from the very beginning when he rejects what his mother calls "the will of the Lord" by giving agency to the weather,[21] not "the eternal will of the water's source [God]."[22] In *Contradictory Omens: Cultural Diversity and Integration in the Caribbean*, in a brief subsection titled "Marronage," Brathwaite speaks of the "Africanization of Christianity."[23] Under the veil of hegemonic racial/st and classist ideology, resistance goes underground and becomes what Brathwaite calls the "submerged mother."[24] Here, Africa is submerged under and through Christianity. In *Castle*, water represents and is the physical embodiment of the type of marronage that Brathwaite describes and that is exemplified in G's thoughts. Water is without boundaries; it is fluid. It submerges and becomes submerged. Without being fully aware of his subversive thoughts, G troubles Christian beliefs and, subsequently, the beliefs of the colonialists. "As if in serious imitation of the waters,"[25] his identity is resistant and submerged. Similarly, Lamming's marronage is evident; the novel evokes images of the floods from the Bible even as the narrator questions the Bible. Water's landscaping of G's village leaves the village's scape—identity—forever altered.

The recurring facelift caused by the flood symbolizes the Middle Passage, which was the catalyst for Caribbean cultural identity since African, European, and indigenous cultures collided and inhabited the same space thereafter. G says, "[T]he season of flood could change everything."[26] Flooding is not a new occurrence in the village. Flooding serves as a reminder of history. G describes the villagers as "complacen[t]" amid describing the action of the water.[27] As G questions what people tell him about God, water rides "through the lanes and alleys," coaxing the roots of white lilies "from the earth" and "agree[ing]" to converge in "the deep black river."[28] Water uproots white lilies and converges with a black river. Africans were uprooted from Africa and placed on plantations in Barbados. They then got racialized as black, which signified their social, economic, and political status as nonhumans or subhumans.

As a result, Caribbean writers like Glissant describe a rhizomatic view of one's roots, as opposed to staying fixed on a single source. The uprooting that the water does in this chapter evokes images of the initial uprooting from Africa and Lamming's attempt to expose the multiple roots of Caribbean cultural and ethnic identity, of creolization. The water not only breaches the boundaries of nature, but it also transgresses manmade structures. Water rises "through the creases of the door" and falls through the "crevices of the roof."[29] It physically escapes what people presume are its boundaries and wreaks havoc on the inhabited land well into the night. Water is a metaphor (or trope) for Maroon consciousness in the novel. Water is without boundaries, as are Maroons. Houses are "hoisted on water."[30] Water "disintegrates" roads and advances houses "across their boundaries in an embrace of board and shingle and cactus fence."[31] Lamming's water changes the face (identity) of the village not unlike the changes caused by the Middle Passage.

Simultaneously, water also masks and exposes the village. Water camouflages: "The floods could level the stature and even conceal the identity of the village,"[32] G explains. Water submerges the village representing Brathwaite's submerged mother Africa in the image of the village. Water becomes the submerged mother visible in the landscape's "uniform wreckage" but is also imperceptible because the flood water converges with a "deep black river" and only leaves signs of its passing through the changes it has made to the landscape.[33] G pays attention to the changes. He goes to the corner "the weather had forgotten,"[34] and he tries to remember: "And what did I remember? My father who had only fathered the idea of me had left me the sole liability of my mother who really fathered me. And beyond that my memory was blank."[35] The memory of the Middle Passage and Africa are the foundation of Lamming's view of Caribbean cultural and ethnic identity and the impetus for creolization and, subsequently, marronage. Similarly, America's entire history—all of it—is the foundation for America's racial/st view of cultural and ethnic identity and the impetus for the actual creolization that continues to happen.

The United States needs to recognize and embrace marronage against racial/st ideology. G tries to remember the history of the village, predating his birth, that is suppressed by the church and the colonial education system within the novel. As he tries to remember, the voices of the village rise together in song: "[T]he voices seemed to be gathered up by a single effort and the whole village shook with song on its foundation of water,"[36] G explains. The flood waters suddenly become the village's foundation, voices rising in song as they likely did on plantations during enslavement. Through Lamming's representation of water in the first chapter, he illustrates various levels of marronage and creolization reflected throughout the novel. Ultimately, creolization and marronage are necessary for generative future-making in *Castle*.

The landscape simultaneously reflects colonialism and marronage, which then reflects creolization, an effect of colonialism and enslavement. In the fulcrum chapter, chapter six, Lamming's skyscape imagery explains why water (rain) from the first chapter would want to escape the boundaries of the sky, as a Maroon would want to escape the plantation, as embracers of racelessness, via the togetherness wayfinder, not as previously misconceptualized, would want to escape and uproot racial/st ideology. G notes, "The sky was like a great big bully choosing the life and death of these tottering shapes."[37] The "tottering shapes" are clouds, but in the clouds, G sees "shapes of islands and men and beasts."[38] Here, the sky represents the slave master or colonialist attempting to dictate the lives of the clouds representing Caribbean countries and people. While G and Bob traverse the topography on their way to the sea and the littoral space of Barbados, the scape is buzzing with the same colonialism and subsequent marronage G and Bob enact. The "parrots' scream rising like a wailing massacre to the sky" disturbs the peacefulness of Belleville[39]— meaning beautiful city—which is "where the white people" live.[40] The village, composed of people who get racialized as white, represents an attempt at homogeneity, but present in the topography (including the physical presence of the boys) is marronage and the mixing, or creolization (i.e., reality), wreaking havoc "through the light [or whiteness]."[41]

Lamming reverses traditional images of light, representing peace and purity, by creating a landscape that disturbs light and embraces darkness. The blackbirds join the noise of the parakeets making a "strained high-pitched wail as mournful as the colour of their feathers."[42] The noise of these birds symbolizes resistance; however, the docility of the doves serves a greater purpose by saving them from the snares of the villagers: "Neither the sparrows nor the blackbirds making their noise from the trees flew down to join them, and suddenly it occurred to me [G] that in the village the sparrows and blackbirds which were the commonest victims of our snares had seldom been joined by the doves,"[43] G writes. The doves carry "in their eyes all the colours of the rainbow,"[44] which reflect the same sort of fluidity the water creates and uncovers. Unlike the other birds overtly disturbing the peace, the doves move together and are peaceful but resistant because they do not get caught. The marronage of the doves is effective, but the resistance of the other loud birds still contributes to the overall subversive and creolized landscape. In addition, the topography in chapter six highlights G's maroon consciousness. Creolization—disorder and madness—exist even if we don't recognize or embrace it. Perhaps, creolization exists more when we try to resist it. Cultural and ethnic formation are multidirectional and always changing. Yet, racial/st frameworks insist that culture and ethnicity, for example, stay static and fixed to specific points in time centuries ago. That fixedness under the guise of fluidity and expansiveness is part of the design of racial/st ideology. We really think that we are out of the matrix. We aren't. But we can be.

G's maroon consciousness includes Glissant's reversion and diversion. Like how water functions in conjunction with G's maroon consciousness in chapter one, the birds' maroon nature coincides with G and Bo's actions in chapter six, which is also written into the landscape. The parakeets scream while the boys scale "the hedges and the high grass."[45] The scape is dripping in dew and the "grass rose high before us."[46] Nature's boundaries, likely landscaped to serve as boundaries by the white village these fences of sorts surround, do not keep the boys from traveling over and through them. As described earlier, Maroons took advantage of topography and hide in the landscape. They often looked down onto the plantation and could see but remained unseen. G describes the dew covering the grass as "making a sea of dots on the surface of the blades [that] looked like a thousand eyes."[47] The "thousand eyes" evokes images of escaped slaves hiding in the grass looking out to elude capture. It also mirrors the image of the village watching the landlord from the bottom of the hill unseen. Consistent with other moments in the novel, the scape of the village is supposed to reflect a racial/st hierarchy with the English landlord at the top of the hill looking down onto the village.

Marronage is subterranean and submarine, though. Creolization cannot always be perceived or readily identified depending on the gazer especially when seeing through a racial/st lens. Just as eyes from the grass peer at G's crossing of boundaries, the villagers "catching sight [of the landlord's house on the hill] through the trees of the shifting figures crept behind their fences, or stole through the wood away from the wall to see" and are "unseen."[48] The boys' crossing of "the village boundary" is an iteration of Lamming's marronage as part of the Caribbean's creolization.[49] Water in Castle changes the landscape; the boys also change the scape: "Behind us in our path the grass lay slaughtered by footprints with the water shivering over the edge of the blades."[50] In the same paragraph where he looks back, G also considers what is in front of him in the topography. This backward and forward glance is vital to Lamming's presentation of creolization and, more specifically, marronage or maroon consciousness. In the United States, we do a lot of looking back without enough forethought and imagination about how the present and future should look or will look if we continue to hold onto racial/st ideology. More importantly, we don't step outside of our beliefs into the twilight space to, for once, inspire new knowledge that pushes the boundaries of our unrealities closer to reality.

Lamming does illustrate marronage as flight from the village. Trumper and G's maroon consciousness results in Trumper going to the United States and G going to Trinidad. The novel ends in darkness and with a literal and metaphorical loss of land before G's departure, underlining Lamming's trope of the landscape and marronage: "The earth where I walked was a marvel of blackness and I knew in a sense more deep than simple departure I had said farewell, farewell to the land,"[51] G concludes. Throughout the novel, G and the other children cross boundaries, adults create boundaries, and the scapes reflect and break the same boundaries. G's flight illustrates a psychic connection between G and the Maroons, which, by extension, reflects what author Michelle Cliff calls "a matter of recognition . . . memory . . . emotion" that one is "not outside this history" of marronage.[52] Young G and Trumper recognize the country's history and how history influences the present, and both young men hope to positively impact the future of the country. Although G calls the flood at the beginning of his political coming-of-age a "watery waste" of his "ninth important day" to celebrate, G describes the effects of the rain-induced flood by turning his attention toward the landscape.[53] It is the flood and darkness that are recalled by Pa and G at the end: "'Twus a night like this . . . nine years ago when those waters roll without end all over this place,'"[54] Pa says. G's maroon consciousness coincides with the maroon nature of the water and, subsequently, the village itself. Rhetorically, Lamming diverts the reader back to the beginning of the novel or the initial point of entanglement: Rain, flood, and darkness.

Lamming's diversion to the beginning of the novel happens in the dark. At the beginning, G's "birthday mak[es] its *black* departure from the land" during the night,[55] which reflects the undergrounded, submerged resistance of his entire ethos. Similarly, *Castle* ends in darkness. The novel shows how G and other villagers navigate through a landscape of literal and metaphorical fences. The frequent breaking of boundaries is reflected within the landscape and by the boys, as are the dynamics created by colonialism, like with the birds and the clouds. For Lamming, marronage represents a desire for social, cultural, and political autonomy and is, therefore, part of creolization. The most vital aspect of Lamming's presentation of identity is this ability to camouflage, subvert, and resist by (re)membering history and planning for a future that doesn't repeat it. It is unclear if G or Trumper will return to the village to effect change; Lamming signals hope for G's return or contribution by breaking him free from the land. In other words, at the end of the novel, G reaches adulthood without boundaries just like the water and the darkness. Boundaries that the adults create for themselves in the novel, which give them a false sense of being tied to the land that is exposed by Mr. Slime and Pa, do not apply to the now man's identity. Therefore, it is his creolized maroon consciousness, which extends beyond all binaries, that survives and carries hope.

Creolization—disorder and madness—exists even if we don't recognize or embrace it. Perhaps, creolization exists more when we try to resist it. Cultural and ethnic formation are multidirectional and always changing. Yet, most racial/st frameworks insist that culture and ethnicity stay static and fixed to specific points in time centuries ago—rarely do we recognize more clearly how humans form culture and ethnicity. If we acknowledged that all of humanity comes from Africa—*that all that is human is "African" or what some would call "Black"*—then what would happen to antiblack race/ism or other types of race/isms?

The togetherness wayfinder helps people explore racialization, eth-nicization, and ideas about human identity from a global perspective to inspire increased understandings of what happens locally and nationally in any given socially constructed nation. We can explore the universal experiences and perspectives of humans to better understand specific experiences and perspectives and solutions for future-making. Invisible ink starts to become visible when the door or window opens to how others have testified to and worked to resolve similar and different but all-human issues. The themes that consistently arise include rememo-ry, twilight, madness, walking negatives, consolation, maternal energy, diaspora, nation, and home. If one is missing from a person's sphere of knowledge, they often unintentionally (usually) uphold race/ism and ra-cial/st ideology—both the effects and causes. If we can teach ourselves and our young people, though, a different way forward that includes backward glances without upholding what happened then, our present and future would be infinitely improved for everyone. We could unify, heal, and reconcile and stop race/ism in its tracks, finally.

Even if we think that we are out of the matrix, we aren't. But we can be. Through raceless antiracism or the togetherness wayfinder, we can explore the *universal* experiences and perspectives of humans to bet-ter understand *specific* experiences and perspectives and solutions for future-making. If we can teach ourselves and our young people a dif-ferent way forward that includes backward glances without upholding what happened then and how, our present and future will be infinitely improved for everyone. To create such a limitless future, we must decol-onize our imaginations from racial/st ideology so that we can see our-selves and each other more clearly.

9

Nation and Diaspora

Decolonizing Our Minds

[D]espite the terrorization which the Negro in America endured and endures sporadically until today, despite the cruel and totally inescapable ambivalence of his status in his country, the battle for his identity has long ago been won. He is not a visitor to the West, but a citizen there, an American; as American as the Americans who despise him, the Americans who fear him, the Americans who love him—the Americans who became less than themselves, or rose to be greater than themselves by virtue of the fact that the challenge he represented was inescapable.

—James Baldwin, *Notes of a Native Son*, 1955

The constructed gulf between people who get racialized differently in the United States has existed since before the creation of the country and in many ways has deepened, ironically, since emancipation. The primary cause for that gap is our continued belief in "races," our practice of racializing ourselves and others, and the continued upholding of associated power imbalances. Our continuation of the belief in human "races" and practice of racialization ensures that we frequently misdirect our focus, attention, and resources to the detriment of all of us and that we maintain power imbalances. It also ensures that we stay in us-versus-them mode, time and again. We racialize politics, culture, economics, ethnicity, nation, diaspora, and all of humanity. We often ignore or criticize disconfirming information in favor of what upholds our worldview because to challenge our worldview would require a certain level of discomfort to which most people aren't going to willingly submit.

When my students tell me that I'm a product of assimilation because I'm "black" in the United States, when all I've known is the United States and everything about me is American—for better, worse, and indifferent—I ask them how one assimilates into something that's authentic to them. I also ask how they then define *American*. How and when does one "become American?" Why do so many people still center (often subconsciously) "whiteness?" How many generations must a family be in the United States before its members "become American"? How many more decades or centuries before my children, grandchildren, great-grandchildren, great-great-grandchildren can rightfully view themselves and be viewed as American, not as a hyphenated American, a second-class citizen, or an American who "assimilated"? How have I "betrayed my race," as some students readily accept as fact, by being who and how I am *and* by simultaneously advocating for the abolishment of antiblack race/ism? In the 1950s, James Baldwin stated what was obvious then and what should be obvious today: Americans who get racialized as black are Americans, not visitors or afterthoughts or wannabes, just as Americans who get racialized in other ways are all Americans, too, for better, worse, or indifferent.

How is it not seen as an effect of antiblack race/ism to racialize me as outside of my nation, as outside of my (American) culture, as outside of my heritage? How is it not upholding antiblack race/ism to presume my culture, language, ideas, likes, and dislikes because of how people racialize me and forever see me as outside of my nation? "Race" doesn't produce culture. Culture produces race/ism. *Humans* through culture create race/ism. Your belief in human "races"—whether packaged as colorblind ideology or more explicit "race" ideology—imposes expectations on me and my children that I unequivocally refuse to accept as right or all that is possible.

Racial/st ideology impedes us from seeing ourselves and each other clearly. It stops us from ending antiblack race/ism. If we clear our minds of such antiblack race/ism and its attendant ideology, we see the reality of cultural, ethnic, and national formation more clearly. We see ourselves. We see each other. We imagine "Americanness" in a more liberating way and in a way that is closer to the reality that has always been on the ground. We acknowledge the brilliance of writers like Toni Morrison, George Schuyler, and James Baldwin who saw the shortcomings of fighting race/ism from within antiblack racial/st ideology and demanded real change of our institutions and systems. We can make race/ism something we study as history and not as something that is part of our future.

The United States is a creolized nation. *American*, therefore, is an ethnicity. It is also a culture and a nation (all constructed phenomenon). Yet, this does not infer or necessitate homogeneity. The ruling class of any country shouldn't be permitted to continue to dictate who is in and who is out, especially not while hiding its hand. Whereas racecraft turns another person's actions into another person's being, a person's self-proclaimed and presumed identity, racelessness not only rejects the notion or demand that race/ism defines our identities or being but also gives us the knowledge and insight needed to explore and see the fullness and complexity of what it is to be human in the first place. We all participate in culture in different and similar ways. This idea is reflected in Walt Whitman's "Song of Myself," a poem that simultaneously encompasses everything, nothing, and a distinguishable self. Even before enslaved people were emancipated from chattel enslavement in the United States, writers and thinkers like Whitman presented their audiences with an alternative way of seeing and being—that we are individual selves who are part of a universal self. So long as we accept black-and-white ways of seeing, we will remain trapped in a cycle of antiblack race/ism forever.

In "Song of Myself," Whitman implies that differences are written into the cosmos and, therefore, are part of human and nature's existence and that these differences connect all species. Erasing hierarchies and undermining hegemony, he specifically questions the following dyads: black/white, humans/nature, poor/rich, and Christian/non-Christian. In other words, he does not just join "all the things (body and soul, life and death, north and south, slave and slave master) his culture did its best to keep apart."[1] Through his poem, he also advances a combination of knowledge and insights that can guide our individual actions, interpersonal relationships, and our relationship with all living beings and the earth. All that Whitman imagines in the universe is united because of, not despite, difference. And the continued existence of all life forms, according to Whitman, requires an embracement of each of ourselves as beings that depend on each other to live, to survive.

In Whitman's own words, "Song of Myself" is omnivorous and, perhaps, egotistical.[2] So far, many critics agree: scholar Santiago Juan-Navarro asserts that "critics have often conceived (of) 'Song of Myself' as a narcissistic, solipsistic, and even onanistic work of art."[3] Egotism aside, critical attention has also been given to Whitman's presentation of "democracy, the Bible, mysticism, and music, along with eroticism . . . , homosexuality,"[4] and nature in "Song of Myself" and in his other poems. Whitman's use of "omnivorous" poetic conventions also suggests that Whitman attempts to create an alternate discursive space and a global politics in "Song of Myself" where he can erase hierarchies and undermine hegemony. Alternative twilight spaces and omnivorous (creolized) texts become necessary for unity, healing, and reconciliation within oppressive systems. Viewing "Song of Myself" simply through the lens of creolization is practical but would leave out important ways in which Whitman deviates and expands upon common readings of creole texts. Thus, I refer to what he's doing as *omnivorous poetics*—that is, his poem attempts to make space not only for human dichotomies of concern but also for all dichotomies in existence. Whitman's omnivorous poetics, like creolization, stems from the historical context of his time in that they reflect a transnational and transcultural identity that resulted from the Middle Passage, colonization, colonialism, and chattel enslavement. From this, a "transethnic" but really just ethnic identity was also created. This one time, I write "transethnic" to render clearer my point and meet more readers where they are when they think about ethnicity or that which is ethnic in singular and narrow terms that defy reality. Really, though, I mean that a new ethnic identity was born and is ever-forming.

First published in 1855 as part of Whitman's poetry collection *Leaves of Grass*, "Song of Myself" predates the American Civil War, with Whitman editing the poem until 1881. Collectively, the poems in *Leaves of Grass* present a very hybrid image of the universe and young American nation. During a time of intense tensions, he offered a fresh image of an all-inclusive democracy, language, literature, and cultural identity. Whitman ascribes human characteristics to grass in the poem, a metaphor that inspired the collection's title. This sort of blurring of black-and-white identities is like that found in creole texts. Referring to blades of grass as *leaves* further blurs the identity of the grass with that of leaves from trees. Had he chosen to title the collection *Blades of Grass*, there would have been a connotation of violence with the word "blades," which goes against what he is trying to accomplish: unity. As it is, his title instead also alludes to the pages of paper on which the poems themselves appear, drawing the reader's attention to the way each page (and by extension, each poem) is a unique individual "leaf" and at the same time an indispensable part of a greater whole. This appreciation of simultaneous unity and diversity, the specific and universal, a salient feature of omnivorous poetics, can be understood as a move to undermine presupposed and imagined hegemony.

While some Caribbean writers illustrate creolization to undermine hegemony, Whitman illustrates omnivorous poetics to do the same but differently. Omnivorous texts go beyond the human experience on which creolized texts typically focus. Although some creole texts indicate humanity's closeness to nature, omnivorous texts illustrate a cosmic relationship between everything in the universe. For writers like Whitman, differences are written into the cosmos and, therefore, are part of our existence. Yet, for them, these differences connect all species because there is a shared origin. Omnivorous writers aim to illustrate and bring attention to the diversity among species and unify the various elements of people by suggesting that everyone shares common elements even while testifying to violent contacts. A simplistic translation then is that people are all different but united because they are all the same. Like in creole texts, omnivorous texts, despite the essentialist quality that the former often lacks, illustrate and embrace contradiction.

Whitman was not the only writer during his lifetime who worked to collapse hegemonic views of identity. Writers like Frederick Douglass and Harriet Jacobs presented themselves as so-called black individuals with so-called white parentage while Harriet Beecher Stowe wrote characters who got racialized as mulatto/a. Like Whitman, they also recognized the rhetorical power of blurring racial/st views of humans and, ultimately, culture before the Civil War. In 1845, Douglass writes, "My father was a white man."[5] In 1852, Stowe blurs the antiblack racial/st divide by presenting several enslaved characters who she racializes as "mulatto/a," such as Eliza, who "was also so white as not to be known as of colored lineage, without a critical survey, and her child was white also."[6] In 1861, Jacobs blurs racial/st lines, writing that her uncle "inherited the complexion my grandmother had derived from Anglo-Saxon ancestors."[7]

In these instances, Douglass, Jacobs, and Stowe exemplify aspects of creolization that is true to American history and experience. Their collapsing of racial/st identities shows the "mixing" of blood—as they would've believed in the biological reality of "race"—and the perniciousness of the practice of racialization, an especially radical view for their time. In other words, these authors interrogate the belief that people who get racialized as white or black are or should be separate and distinct except within the context of America's antiblack race/ism. They also illustrate how both racialized groups are corrupted under the institution of chattel enslavement.

Whitman later participates in the same anti-enslavement discourse as Douglass, Jacobs, and Stowe, but his approach is slightly different. In "Song of Myself," Whitman furthers the blurring of "white" supremacist notions of identity by asserting that he is the same as everyone else, beginning with his opening lines: "I celebrate myself, and sing myself, / And what I assume you shall assume, / For every atom belonging to me as good belongs to you."[8] Here, Whitman's view of atomist immortality creates connections between Whitman and the reader. Likewise, "Song of Myself" is, in fact, a song of *the readers*. Instead of focusing on "mixed blood," as Douglass, Jacobs, and Stowe do, Whitman says that the basic and "good" components of the universe that exist in the speaker of the poem also exist in everyone else.

In undermining antiblack race/ism and racial/st ideology with this poem, he argues for the indivisibility of the United States. He continues this sentiment, saying, "My tongue, every atom of my blood, form'd from this soil, this air, / Born here of parents born here from parents the same, and their parents the same."[9] As his contemporaries highlight lineage from within the framework of race/ism, he illustrates *human* lineage. He also connects people with the earth and cosmos, which serves his omnivorous, all-inclusive purpose. In an Emersonian line about self-reliance, he encourages the reader to recognize the omnivorous nature of his poem and of the world: "you shall listen to all sides and filter them from your self."[10] In other words, he aims to show the reader an alternative twilight space in which to reimagine the differences the poem depicts, urging the reader to be cautious of listening to all perspectives and forming one's own conclusions.

Whitman also collapses hierarchies of assigned identity by outright critiquing society's tendency to create, inherit, or impose them in the first place: "Always a knit of identity, always distinction, always a breed of life."[11] He explains how hierarchies are human-made, because by nature people come from the same source, which, again, expresses unity, not division *and* not sameness: "Clear and sweet is my soul, and clear and sweet is all that is not my soul."[12] Whitman acknowledges the unique self-worth of each person. While Whitman illustrates how people are equally valuable, he does still fulfill Romantic values of individuality by including every difference, like occupation, race, religion, nation, gender, and sexuality, within the poem. He lays the foundation for his all-inclusive poem by connecting himself to the reader to everyone else and pointing out that differences necessarily exist but that hierarchies (i.e., power imbalances) are made and reinforced. In addition, he asserts that "Song of Myself" identifies the "origin of all poems,"[13] meaning each person is the origin of all poems because each person embodies the universe and vice versa. In asking the reader to recognize the interconnectedness of humanity and the universe, he presents a pretty radical way of seeing the world, especially for his time.

From Buddhist to deist and from prostitute to physician, "Song of Myself" references many religions and professions. Part of the omnivorous poetic conventions that Whitman employs include the cataloguing of such diversity. His poem has to consume "everything" he can think of to properly portray the universe (i.e., a stomach) and feed the reader. "One world is aware and by far the largest to me, and that is myself,"[14] he says. Here, he is not being egotistical. Rather, he is dismantling, again, hierarchies and differences otherwise used to justify social injustice and snootiness. He continues, stating, "Whoever degrades another degrades me."[15] If the reader recognizes that their identity has been collapsed with that of Whitman and that the poem itself has been collapsed with the reader since the poem's origin is the reader, the universe then has been collapsed within the poem both literally—catalogues of inclusion—and figuratively; Whitman indiscriminately highlights and bridges differences between people, species, and nature, suggesting oneness, common atoms, and one origin or at least multiple common origins.

Omnivorous poetics moves beyond the collapse of the physical and even the metaphysical aspects of assigned and inherited human identities and uses naturalistic language as another means of undoing hierarchies. Whitman's nature includes the sciences—"Hurrah for positive science!"[16]—and objects found on land, in the sea, and in outer space. His use of metaphors expands the reader's fundamental beliefs about nature and themselves. For example, the grass in the poem welcomes the dead as equals and grows indiscriminately. Scholar John Marsh posits that grass "appealed to Whitman for its democratic qualities . . . [grass] did not distinguish between high and low."[17] Indeed, Whitman's personification of the grass as "the produced babe of the vegetation" and as a "mothers' lap" signifies his vision of unity and democracy; after all, the grass grows "among black folks as among white" and seems to have a voice of its own, as one would expect in a true democracy.[18]

Here, nature acts as a model for humanity. "Song of Myself" acts as the mediator between nature and people, making the titling of *Leaves of Grass* an even more suitable representation for Whitman's omnivorous poetics. When the writer says, "I bequeath myself to the dirt to grow from the grass I love, / If you want me again look for me under your boot-soles," he is describing the possibility of being buried in the ground and "feeding" the soil from which grass grows.[19] Given his belief in atomic immortality, however, he is likely describing, again, how nature and people are all connected. The poem, thus, moves beyond razing human identities into leveling "identities" of nature and using nature as a model of unity through differences.

As with his expansion of identity, Whitman's naturalistic language is expansive; he changes the meaning of nature to include scents and sights created by nature and people. The poem's several dichotomies interact with each other in a way that lays the foundation for Whitman's attempt to blur dichotomies and hegemonic ideologies. If one views his use of nature as, in part, a model for how humans should interact with each other, his presentation of dichotomies is an extension of this purpose; see, for example, how "The play of shine and shade on the trees" and "The sniff of green leaves and dry leaves" suggest Whitman's (and the reader's, by extension) consumption of what could be considered the good and bad.[20] The shine (light) and shade (dark) play together; the writer inhales scents of vibrant and dead or dying leaves. Also, "the shore and dark-color'd sea-rocks" are both received by the writer, indicating a metaphor for undoing the antiblack racial/st ideology of white (the shore is light colored) and black, just as the grass freely receives all humans.[21] Whitman is also bringing attention to the unifying metaphors found in *Leaves of Grass*, both the title and the collection, by describing leaves and nature in this way. The scents of "atmosphere" mimic the conventions of omnivorous poetics, while also displaying them, in that readers of the poem consume everything included and cannot choose, theoretically, which lines they want to eat, just as one cannot choose which part of a scent they want to smell. Furthermore, the sounds of nature, those both coming from nature and human-made, are a sort of music and language in "Song of Myself."

For Whitman, the paradoxical nature of the universe, which for him includes the unseen and untouchable, is not lost and is present or celebrated even through sound. He includes such tensions to recognize them and then swiftly unites the differences that create the tension by presenting them as equals. He explicitly blurs the differences perceived between people and people, and people and nature:

Now I will do nothing but listen,
To accrue what I hear into this song, to let sounds contribute toward it.
I hear bravuras of birds, bustle of growing wheat, gossip of flames,
      clack of sticks cooking my meals,
I hear the sound I love, the sound of the human voice
I hear all sound running together, combined, fused or following[22]

Whitman presents people as participating in nature's cacophony, not just by listening but also by throwing snow, playing instruments, singing, and speaking. "Song of Myself" transforms into an actual song when the omnivorous poetic convention of naturalistic language is unveiled.

Whitman's passion for democracy and liberty is widely accepted by critics, because the human-made hierarchies imposed onto people by people are not applicable in nature or among animals. The writer points out that the ducks and drakes "do not call the tortoise unworthy because she is not something else, / And the jay in the woods never studies the gamut, yet trills pretty well to me."[23] In these lines, it is implied that the birds notice differences but do not create oppressive hierarchies. While he extends the metaphor of nature to animals as representative of democracy, he yearns for people to embody and imitate; his omnivorous poetics require more of all of us.

In suggesting that animals are not as different from people as one might think, he also suggests that people are not so different from animals and are dependent upon animals. The writer is again simultaneously coming and going. The text is circular in nature; no leaf is left overturned. Whitman likens human to animal and animal to human just as he conflates nature with human and vice versa.

Another part of omnivorous poetics is the use of cosmic language. He calls himself "Walt Whitman, a kosmos"[24] and describes his existence in outer space before the appearance of human beings on earth: "Afar down I see the huge first Nothing, I know I was even there, / I waited unseen and always, and slept through the lethargic mist, / And took my time, and took no hurt from the fetid carbon."[25] Since the reader's subjectivity has been conflated with that of the writer, it is the reader who exists before the presence of humans on earth in "Song of Myself." The universe aids in the preservation of humans and the creation of the earth as the reader knows it: even "stars kept aside in their own rings . . . sent influences to look after what was to hold me."[26] While the writer (and reader) essentially are the universe, the universe helps create and maintain the writer: "All forces have been steadily employ'd to complete and delight me, / Now on this spot I stand with my robust soul."[27] Thus, the cosmos is enveloped within the poem, as the poem envelops the cosmos.

The final aspects of omnivorous poetics are, like those of creolization, madness, twilight, and opacity, contradiction and tension. Ecocritic Thomas Gannon argues that Whitman conflates people who get racialized as indigenous with birds to be inclusive and that, by doing so, Whitman unintentionally others those people and creates an effect of exclusion.[28] However, if "Song of Myself" collapses all boundaries and blurs all semblance of identity between people, nature, animals, and the cosmos, perhaps Whitman is othering everybody and every body. He also illustrates people who get racialized as black using race/ist imagery. The writer remembers "perfectly well his [the runaway slave's] revolving eyes and his awkwardness," describes a "negro" as a "picturesque giant," and tells how a "half-breed straps his light boots to compete in the race."[29] He describes "[w]hite and beautiful"[30] faces, wording that contrasts with the awkward and giant descriptors of people who get racialized as black and the bird-like descriptors of American indigenous tribes. Readings which argue that Whitman either constructed a poem with wholly positive rhetoric or a poem that undermines itself with the othering of people who don't get racialized as white are easily reconciled if we understand how contradiction and tension are vital to creolization and, by extension, omnivorous poetics. Moreover, as a framework, the togetherness wayfinder encourages us to see various aspects and employment of race/ism clearly. Whitman writes against and simultaneously falls into the very trap or race/ism, something he himself acknowledges: "Do I contradict myself? / Very well then I contradict myself. / (I am large, I contain multitudes.)"[31] This type of contradiction and acknowledgment of power imbalances even as one seeks to metaphorically collapse said hierarchies is typical of antiracist creole texts and, unsurprisingly, is an essential aspect of omnivorous texts.[32]

"Song of Myself" illustrates the inherent tension between white/black and cultured/uncultured and suggests that recognition and reconciliation between these human-made imaginings is both possible and necessary for the betterment of humanity. While theories of creolization became prominent in interpreting literature well after his lifetime, "substantial colonial legislation ... was intended precisely to halt processes of cultural hybridization that were generating a cross-ethnic imagined community at the popular level" in the Caribbean during the 1800s.[33] Similarly, there have been many failed attempts at preventing integration and intermixing at every level across American history. But the reality is that Americans and what it is to be American have been ever changing and fluid across time, and countless other nations and corresponding ethnicities and cultures have and continue to contribute to that which is America. "American" needn't continue to be presumed to signify "whiteness" anymore, as America has never actually been "white," nor will it ever be.

The unifying power of creolization (when recognized and embraced) was recognized as a direct threat to colonial power in the Caribbean during the time Whitman was writing. Like Caribbean writers, Whitman and other American authors of the time recognized the power of blurring antiblack racial/st, cultural, and social and economic class divisions. Through its leveling and blurring of identities, "Song of Myself" transcends nation and "race." Reading Whitman's poem and other texts through the lens of omnivorous poetics and creolization can help us discover ourselves more fully and enrich our relationships with each other as Americans and global citizens more broadly. It can help us (re)member, (re)imagine, and create a more fruitful and unified future, one that helps people live up to the ideals we profess to value in our respective contexts.

From our DNA and ancestry to our heritage and culture, humans are mixed. Our stories are mixed and interconnected. We must decolonize our imaginations to see ourselves and each other more clearly and to create a path toward a limitless future without antiblack race/ism or other race/isms.

Once we recognize that race/ism is evitable—that it is within our power to dismantle it—the end of race/ism will be inevitable.

10

Home
Dismantling the Architecture of Race/ism

It is a development which can only end tragically unless some way can now be found to re-condition colored and white people everywhere so that they will think of themselves as the same. What chance is there of doing this? It would require a revolutionary program of re-education calling not only for wholesale destruction of the accumulated mass of racialistic propaganda in books, magazines, newspapers, motion pictures and all of the present laws and regulations which recognize the racial fiction and are based upon it, but for a complete reorganization of our social system.

—George Schuyler, *Rac[e]ing*, 1944

All of us have inherited particular ways of racializing ourselves and each other and upholding antiblack race/ism. We've been born into a house that masquerades as a home for us all but that isn't truly a home for everyone at all. Here, home isn't paradise or utopia. Instead, it's simply a metaphor for a place where we all belong as fellow humans, free from the shackles and dehumanization of race/ism. Home is what we can create when we refuse to play by the rules of "white" supremacy. We've endured a few hundred years of antiblack race/ism thus far. Given our track record, we will undoubtedly find other ways to discriminate against each other and dehumanize ourselves in the future, but must we really wait another five hundred years, or even a thousand years or more, before the maintenance and practice of this one demonstrably tragic invention reach their ignominious end.

I'm not promoting the togetherness wayfinder and racelessness because "I'm black" nor do I "want to be white." I'm promoting it because I'm a human. And I'm a human who cares deeply about ending antiblack race/ism and achieving "black" liberation in particular. All people will be freed when so-called black people are freed from the causes and effects of race/ism. If we end the causes of antiblack race/ism, all other forms of oppression will be rendered clearer, and we would seek to destroy those forms of oppression, too. The racial/st framework might be the design on which a house of race/ism has been built, but the foundation and its architecture is rotten and it will never be a home for everyone. It's time to build a new structure with a sturdy and unshakeable foundation that can be a home for all—one based on the togetherness wayfinder, the practice of raceless antiracism. This doesn't involve lambasting anyone's beliefs or experiences or ignoring the complexity of human history. It just requires us to question our own beliefs, practices, and policies and the beliefs, practices, and policies of our societies. Then it requires us to take radical action against the root causes of our oppression.

We will never be able to stop race/ism without first effectively recognizing, acknowledging, and properly defining racism or race/ism, undoing our belief in "races," and ending our practice of racialization. But once we've taken these steps, what exactly will that home look like? As with all the other key elements of the togetherness wayfinder, the world of literature offers some insights. In the future-making of "Blindsided,"[1] American writer Edward P. Jones catapults readers into a vast universe where everything is possible, expansive, and inhabitable. In so doing, he transforms America's racial/st house into an imagining of a home, a space liberated from race/ism.

Art imitates forms, so the saying goes.

In the short stories that compose *All Aunt Hagar's Children*, Edward P. Jones' exploration and presentation of racial/st ideology and its nuanced performance of social and economic power challenge what many readers know. By applying the togetherness wayfinder to "Blindsided," one of the short stories in Jones' collection, I mark a clear delineation between "race," race/ism, social and economic class, and culture within the story that illustrates the necessary undoing of "race" to undo race/ism. I argue that the prominence of geography and geotagging in Jones' work—that is, his references to specific places, streets, and landmarks[2]—coincides with the metaphorical turned literal blindness that Roxanne, the Washingtonian protagonist in "Blindsided," experiences, which transforms the story from one grounded in actual geographical locations to one based on a geography of future-making and otherworldliness.

In "The Known World in World Literature: Bakhtin, Glissant, and Edward P. Jones," literature professor Carolyn Vellenga Berman describes the backdrop of Jones' 2003 historical novel, *The Known World*—set in 1855, ten years before the emancipation of enslaved people in the United States—as "an enclosed world on the verge of implosion in which an entrenched dependence on slave labor still felt unalterable."[3] In the future world-making in "Blindsided," meanwhile, Jones maps something preceding and hauntingly like today's society that catapults readers into the vastness of the universe where everything is possible, expansive, inhabitable, and seeing. He transforms America's racial/st houses, turning the houses into an imagining of a home, a raceless or a deraced space that the writer liberates from race/ism. He gives readers a fresh imagining of liberation. Given the current political and cultural climate in the United States and, increasingly, the world, there is no better time than now to imagine alternative futures outside of the bounds of race/ism and to build vehicles to get us there.

In "Blindsided," Roxanne's—the protagonist's—characterization depicts a person bound within racial/st ways of seeing themself and others. That results in her metaphorical blindness turned literal blindness. Consequently, she can no longer use her literal sight to exact her disdain for people she deems "beneath her." Her sense of self deflates as the story progresses until she is sexually assaulted. The assault causes her to turn her third eye inward, resulting in a metaphorical and metaphysical transcending of race/ism, a product of imposing one's way of seeing onto one's being that results in eracesure. Through his fiction, Jones shows us that we can and probably should work ourselves outside of the architecture of race/ism to be more clear-eyed about what race/ism is and is not and to progress toward a more generative future for everyone. The core tenets and tools of the togetherness wayfinder illuminate the complexity of racial/st architecture and world-making within "Blindsided."

In "Edward P. Jones—The Neighborhood Preservationist," Kenton Rambsy accepts fellow author and scholar Nicole Rustin-Pashal's argument that Jones' fiction presents readers an unapologetically "black world with its norms rooted in black culture."[4] But the primary ways one's so-called "race" is identified in "Blindsided" indicate the tenuous endeavor of identifying "blackness" and "whiteness" *outside* of race/ism and social and economic happenings and beliefs that replicate race/ism and allow it to persist. Jones writes, "After the white woman Roxanne Stapleton worked for in Silver Spring gave her a ride across the northern border into Washington," Roxanne caught the bus while the racialized white woman went "far away in another world until Monday," when Roxanne would have to return to work.[5] The presence of "whiteness" starts the story in a way that harkens one's attention to the effects of race/ism at play. Namely, race/ism works within the fiction of the story to demarcate social and economic classes from each other. Also, culture and ethnicity get conflated with what is named as "race" or "racial," resulting in further eracesures, as humanity cannot be effectively reduced to a handful or less of ethnic and culture groups. The woman's so-called whiteness is not asserted to indicate some sort of biological essence. Just as Roxanne's so-called blackness might reflect Roxanne's phenotype and social or economic status but not her essence.[6] In fact, it is Roxanne's subscription to these racial/st categories as indicative of one's essence, as mirrored through the characterization of the unnamed so-called white woman, that leads to her physical blindness. Jones foreshadows, saying, "The white woman had her ideas about what black people did with their lives, especially on weekends, and just about everything they did in her mind could lead to blindness."[7] Importantly, Roxanne learns her way of seeing and being in the world through the context in which she lives: the United States government, media, education system, technology industry, and religious institutions, to name a few, all teach Roxanne to see herself through the dehumanizing apparatus of antiblack *race*/ism.

Race/ism is a social construction, not "race." Over the course of the story, through a series of breakdowns in communication, certain characters transform by losing their sight, mind, or values and, ultimately, their identities, due to their constant and consistent eracesure either by themselves or other people. Race/ism impacts the characters so that madness ensues and eracesure becomes threateningly permanent, not "race." Yet, the language many people use when speaking about race/ism is that of "race." Often, "race" is viewed as the cause of race/ism, a nefarious misdirection of focus away from the root causes of race/ism: the belief in "race" and practice of racialization. Roxanne metaphorically stands in the dark. She is signing to the blind and is blind, increasingly astute about future world-making necessitates: the undoing of the belief in "race" and practice of racialization. "I ain't just like every colored person from every corner of the world," Roxanne thinks when she recalls how "[p]eople said she got loud when she drank."[8] Her internalization of racial/st ideology leads to her belief in "race" and her desire to see herself outside of the strictures race/ism creates and necessitates for all of us. She tries to do that by seeing herself as superior to other people who get racialized as black and the stereotypes associated with said people. However, her inability to liberate herself from race/ism causes her to operate from within the strictures in ways that uphold race/ism. Just as she has to see herself as better than Agnes, her aide of sorts, she sees assimilation as the primary path forward, and she misjudges everyone who does not conform to her expectations of them, which is largely dependent on a racialized (and therefore racial/st) view of social and economic class and culture. For example, the woman who examines Roxanne's eyes on the bus when she is first blinded is described as having

> a southern accent so thick it insulted Roxanne's ears. She was much older than Roxanne was when she came to Washington with her own accent, so the woman would probably never speak any other way, as Roxanne had succeeded in doing.[9]

Rather than focus on the woman's shared humanity, her kindness, and what she says, Roxanne does what most humans do: she translates characteristics about the woman and (mis)categorizes her into a hierarchy. According to Roxanne, the woman should have worked to lose her way of speaking just as one should not be too loud for fear of not being higher on whatever hierarchy.

Our belief in human "races" and practice of racialization are not meaningless because racism and valuable aspects of humanity hide behind what we call "race." Race/ism (i.e., racism) is a socially constructed system of economic and social oppression that requires the belief in human "races" and the practice of racialization to reinforce various power imbalances. In "White Supremacy under Fire: The Unrewarded Perspective in Edward P. Jones's *The Known World*," African American and Diaspora Studies professor David Ikard examines how, in *The Known World*, Jones portrays how some people who get racialized as white "and, to a lesser extent, African American slave owners," are "slightly mad victims of their own brainwashing."[10] That correlates with understanding how people who do not get racialized as white can, in fact, be "white" supremacists. In "Blindsided," the primary perpetrator of antiblack racial/st ideology is Roxanne. And that seems to be largely of her own doing since Roxanne can choose to be a kinder and more clear-eyed person at any point. In fact, in the end, she does get closer toward seeing far more clearly than she has before, even if her sight is not literal. The story shows how race/ism is a crazy-making regime that inspires jaundiced categorizations of American life in a foolish attempt to order things by "race," something Roxanne does without realizing how her life is disordered to the detriment of herself and others.

Every instance of "race" or that which is interpreted as "racial" can and must be translated into more apt and liberatory language: class (social, economic, or both), ethnicity, culture, or race/ism itself. The togetherness wayfinder helps people free themselves from the deleterious effects of race/ism because it makes race/ism and other social ills far more clear and solvable thanks, in large part, to such clarity. Importantly, the togetherness wayfinder gives people the tools necessary to achieve a future without race/ism, a prerequisite for the unification, healing, and reconciliation so many scholars and everyday Americans say they want. And that is all something Jones seems to want for all of us too, as Roxanne's inhabitation and embracement of racial/st language and ways of being and seeing contribute to her self-eracesure and blinding. The imagery of "heavy snow" that comes "into their [people in DC] lives" in a way that "cover[s] and silence[s] the world" mirrors the metaphorical whitening or "brainwashing" that Roxanne simultaneously experiences and upholds through her consistent racialization of herself and other people and her corresponding racist beliefs about people based on how they get racialized.[11] The winter also foreshadows the death and birth or rebirth of the future, which ends the story or begins it.

It is Roxanne's newfound ability to see herself—her blindness—that truly opens the door to alternative ways of defining and redefining herself and others. She thinks, *"I am blind and that is all there is to it."*[12] Our ability and willingness to *see* ourselves outside of race/ism and racial/st ideology compel more of us to see ourselves as raceless, as part of one species: Human. That humanizing lens has material impacts. While the tentacles of race/ism currently preclude the fullness and potential of forms of humanism and freedom from race/ism as being limited only to those who get racialized as white, the effects of unintentionally upholding antiblack race/ism require people to see "race" everywhere. By extension, race/ism appears to be everywhere sometimes. The vociferousness of our belief in "race" and practice of racialization must not be understated. When read with the core tenets of the togetherness wayfinder and alternative philosophies of "race" in mind, Jones' "Blindsided" shows what has been, is now, and could be outside of the constraints that race/ism has on our imaginations and world-making.

Paradoxically, Jones describes the snow as silencing the world, but the snowflakes themselves supply "a note in a long and wondrous song, and in the moments as the song played on, she was sitting on the giant apple that was the Earth and that was taking her through the snowy universe."[13] Somehow snow becomes what could be stars, an apple the Earth, and Mars something a dog "would appreciate."[14] Snow "is warm."[15] And Roxanne moves through the universe on the apple/Earth. *And she can see.* The at once sci-fi and magical realist ending signifies the potential of the radical act of recognizing and embracing one's racelessness and liberating oneself from the strictures of race/ism, including one's own racial/st beliefs about other people. "Memory was what you made of it," Roxanne asserts as she puts "rings around it [Uranus] and give[s] it a million moons, each a different color."[16]

In countless ways, memories about the darkest and most violent aspects and events of human history continue to influence and inform today's discourse and our ability to forge a different and better path forward for everyone. Roxanne's life story, up until this point, shows that sort of struggle: she left her daughter with her parents and never returned; she was always unable to accept and embrace people (starting with herself) for who and how they are; she persistently racialized people and conflated different forms of class and culture with "race," and so on. Her struggle represents the broader American struggle to unify, heal, and reconcile as it pertains to the history and persistence of race/ism.

Even with Roxanne's metaphorical turned literal blindness, the end of the story marks a turning point: "[S]he would put a sign that said Pluto was open all the time to all of God's children. Yes, open even to the least of them,"[17] the story concludes. Pluto, an uninhabitable wintry planet, is open, according to Roxanne, to everyone.

If we suspend disbelief, Pluto symbolizes the new world-making that can and should take place in the "New World" to eradicate the hierarchy race/ism and its corresponding racial/st ideology create. I invite others to join me in (re)reading humanity from a framework that opens the possibility of a raceless future where none of us are defined or measured and none of us define or measure any human by upholding race/ism and mistranslating and racializing other meaningful social constructions (i.e., culture—including art, literature, and politics—ethnicity, social class, economic class, and race/ism itself).

Let's actively work toward a future of racelessness, a home, where antiblack race/ism is a reality of the past. To build that home, we must fully love ourselves—and others.

11

Consolation and Maternal Energy
Practicing Radical Love

I was not really ready to love or be loved in the present. I was
still mourning—clinging to the broken heart of girlhood,
to broken connections. When that mourning ceased,
I was able to love again.

—bell hooks, *All About Love: New Visions*, 1999

We enable race/ism to persist within ourselves and in our respective
nations in part because of our current inability to love ourselves unconditionally both as individuals and collectives. Our black-and-white
thinking and behaviors and policies to match leave us as fractured selves.
Talk of love might sound utopic and maybe a bit silly unless, of course,
you recognize the importance of radical unconditional self-love and
radical love for others. *Ubuntu.* This is especially true when it comes to
child-rearing. Children don't grow up as emotional robots completely
unaffected by violence, meanness, or ignorance. They need consolation,
maternal energy, and love. And we must teach them. Otherwise, they fall
victim to the world.

    Consolation involves receiving the relief of comfort after a loss or
disappointment. *Maternal energy* denotes the feelings typically associ-

ated with or typical of a mother (or mother figure) and the ability to birth change and transformative power. *Love* represents the strong and positive feelings of warmth and platonic intimacy one has about oneself and fellow humans that underpin any of our desires to be better human beings and to forge a better future for younger generations. People might cringe or otherwise become agitated when I bring up the necessity and power of radical love. Yet, intuitively, the necessity for radical self-love and love for others makes sense and aligns with many of our values, be they religiously inspired or otherwise. There is plenty of literature that shows the correlation between a lack of self-love and increased bias, hatred, and biased or hateful actions toward others. Our hearts and minds need to be educated and, indeed, changed to even want to create a better world for all.

In working toward ending race/ism, particularly antiblack race/ism, I'm inspired by the work and wisdom of bell hooks, the American social critic, author, and educator who, among other topics, theorized love: "When I travel around the nation giving lectures about ending racism and sexism, audiences, especially young listeners, become agitated when I speak about the place of love in any movement for social justice. Indeed, all the great movements for social justice in our society have strongly emphasized a love ethic."[1] It is with this ethic in mind that I want to share part of my own journey, which began without consolation, maternal energy, or love but which ultimately led to all three, and why I see each as essential to the togetherness wayfinder or raceless antiracism and our efforts to unify, heal, and reconcile.

XXX

"Who wet the bathroom rug?"

Silence. I lowered my copy of the most recent Dean Koontz novel, perking my ears to assess the severity of the situation. I was eleven and had developed hyper-hearing abilities that would alert me, most times, to when Mommy was on a rampage that was always directed toward me.

"Not me," I offered from my position on my New Kids on the Block–covered bed. The magenta pink walls of my bedroom peeked through the spaces between my many posters of the Backstreet Boys, TLC, Boyz II Men, Britney Spears, NSYNC, Brandy, Monica, Blackstreet, and Mariah Carey. Mommy was in the bathroom, which was directly across from my bedroom. The bathroom door was cracked open; I didn't need to see her to know, to sense her fury. It took little to nothing to induce her rage. I often thought that the sight of my face was enough to send her flying off the handle.

"Not me," Lucas said. He was in his bedroom nearby.[2]

"Someone did it. The floor is completely wet! Who took a shower last?"

"Lucas is the only one that showered tonight. I haven't taken mine yet."

"No, I took a shower hours ago. Sheena took a shower after me."

I continued to hold the novel in my right hand and proceeded to pretend to read when Mommy came out of the bathroom. I was unsure if anything would happen since there were, after all, conflicting stories. I hoped I would escape her rage for something I hadn't done, but since Lucas muddied the situation, as he often did, anything was possible.

Suddenly, my door flew all the way open, like the She-Hulk herself came to either save the day or Hulk smash my face. The doorknob slammed against the wall making a dreadful sound. I scurried across my bed and positioned myself at the foot of the bed, feet placed on the floor, and my left side pressed against the wall and window. I watched the green, wooden broomstick rise higher and higher before crashing down on my head like I had seen happen to Tom in *Tom and Jerry*. I balled up and started to shield my head with my arms. Mommy beat me with that broomstick until she must've felt satisfied. She left my room still cursing me out for wetting the bathroom rug. She returned quickly with it, placing it squarely in the middle of my room.

"You're going to sleep on this tonight. Lie down." I assumed the fetal position on the wet, cold rug, facing the door. She unplugged my small TV, still cussing me out, kicked me in the stomach, and carried my TV out with her.

"Mommy wants me to make sure you're still on the rug," Lucas whispered hours later in the dead of the night as he crept out of my room.

"Mommy says you can get in bed now," Lucas whispered just before dawn. I cannot remember what time of year it was. I do remember having to wear long-sleeve shirts to hide the broomstick-shaped welts that developed on my arms overnight.

XXX

Fear and trepidation flooded every cell of my body, every hair fiber, as I crept through the hallway of our double-wide trailer toward my parents' bedroom. "Do you love me?" I was thirteen years old and standing in Mommy's bedroom doorway. Poppy was at work, and my brother must've been at a friend's house for the night, a privilege I rarely enjoyed. I don't know what prompted me to have the courage to ask Mommy.

"Why?" That wasn't the response I was hoping for, but at least she didn't cuss me out.

"You have never told me you love me. You tell Lucas all of the time."

"I've said it to you once or twice." Defeated, I walked back to my room. Mommy got out of bed and followed me. We stood near my bedroom doorway facing each other.

"Why are you asking?" She asked, slowly moving toward me, forcing me to back further into the wall, as if I were melting and becoming one with it. I couldn't back away far or fast enough.

"Because you always tell Lucas you love him, and I'm an angel compared to him. I get straight As. I cook and clean. I keep your iced tea filled." I tried to paint a picture of the value I added to her life. My naivety ruled the day. My heart felt like it was going to beat out of my chest.

I didn't want her to see me cry but the tears streamed down my face. I stared her straight in her eyes, pleading for some sign of love, some sign of warmth. I so wanted her to love me, wanted her to say it even if she didn't mean it.

"You aren't an angel. You're the Devil," she sneered, holding her hands up like horns to her head. She had backed me up against the wall, literally. She made a fist and sucker punched me. Without thinking, I grabbed her wrists before she could punch me again. I was finally taller than her and, apparently, stronger. She struggled against my grasp a bit; I thought I saw fear in her eyes. She wrenched her arms away from my grip and went back to her room.

We never spoke about it again. I never heard "I love you" from her nor did I ever feel any semblance of her love.

XXX

I spent the first thirty years or so of my life believing that I was unlovable because my adoptive mother and adoptive father didn't love me. In fact, I would go so far as to say that they hated me. I spent sixteen of those years striving to earn their love, to win them over. I stuck to the script "Mommy" gave me:

"If anyone asks, tell them you fell off your bike."

"If anyone asks, tell them you were doing laundry and the dryer door was open. You slipped and fell face first into the dryer door."

"Tell anyone and you'll be in hot water" was one of Mommy's favorite sayings. That and " . . . you'll be in deep shit."

I thought that the more "perfect" I was the more likely Mommy would return my love. Despite how vile she was, I loved her with everything in me; most children tend to love the people whose responsibility it is to raise them, even when those people, by most reasonable standards, don't deserve it. I endured the beatings, neglect, and instability until I turned sixteen and could move out without their consent. Even still, I sought closure and, yes, their love. I felt incomplete for a long, long time because I didn't have parents. Rather, I had people who were fortunate enough to adopt me but who grossly mishandled their good fortune and almost ran me into the ground—literally and metaphorically.

I always knew there was more to life than what I experienced, but there were dark times when I felt I couldn't wait longer for the more to arrive. I believed in myself and my capabilities, somehow, and found within myself an unbreakable spirit and sense of determination—that I did so in those circumstances was nothing short of a miracle. By all accounts except mine, I should've been a statistic. When I dropped out of high school at the start of my senior year because I picked homelessness over remaining in what was my personal hell, my honors teachers in economics and English feared the worst. They told me that I was highly unlikely to return and finish high school. They said that knowing I was an honors student with straight As who had taken college courses for college credit that year, a varsity athlete, a kid who had never been in trouble, a band and choir member, etc. They looked me in my eyes and told me what they feared might come true. However, my school social worker would have none of it. She stated that I would finish high school. It was just a matter of when.

The power and influence of that one person, the social worker who expressed belief in me at one of the lowest moments of my life, was what I needed. It wasn't that I thought my teachers should've lied to me. No, I applaud them for telling me the truth, the risks. I remembered those risks at every turn as I made my way to financial stability and finished what I started. But Kathy Frasier, my social worker, she is one person who helped save my life.[3] One person had that impact on me. And it only takes one person to inspire a better today and tomorrow for everyone. Are you that one person?

I have been and will always be so drawn to literature because of the consolation it offered me when I was a child and continues to offer me. It is largely because I sought comfort there and love from outside of myself that I was able to see and feel the importance of consolation and love when it comes to healing. Antiblack race/ism has done and continues to do so much harm. We need to infuse more love into our discourse, our practices, our psyches to give people the tools needed to flourish as individuals and collectives. As it stands, we live in a nation that is plagued with increased mental unwellness, social instability, and violence. Antiblack race/ism buttresses that instability. Together, we must learn how to love ourselves and each other truly as ourselves and not as avatars for our respective so-called races. We can dismantle the power structures that ultimately serve the top one percent of people.

And we also need to know how to understand and receive those who see "race" and who speak about "race" differently from ourselves via racelessness translation since there is substance that hides behind "race"—culture, social class, economic class, ethnicity, and the causes and effects of racism. Because if you really understand, you won't be offended by how someone else views themselves. Rather, you will be offended that the elite continue to profit off of our consignment to the matrix they built centuries ago. In the end, we aren't each other's enemies. We must demand of the elite a new system that rightly humanizes everyone, rightly acknowledges the reality of race/ism, rightly acknowledges the multiple ways of seeing and being, and rightly destroys race/ism. Race/ism isn't another person's problem to solve. It is all of ours to solve. We would all benefit from freeing ourselves from the causes and effects of race/ism. But freedom isn't always something that comes from the outside or only from the outside.

We must learn to see ourselves outside of the labels and categorizations that create and maintain the illusion of sameness or difference and that uphold hierarchies of power and domination and disempowerment and subjugation. In *The Lies That Bind*, Kwame Anthony Appiah writes,

> If your individual character—not just your body, but your temperament, your habits of life, your artistic work—was deeply formed by your race, then we could see the shared nature of a race in each of

its members. Each of us not only belonged to a race, we expressed its nature. The result was that each member of the group was typical: representative, that is, of his or her type.[4]

That description of how the wealthy early modern Europeans that invented antiblack race/ism thought centuries ago maps easily onto how people think today about "race." We've learned and grown as humans in virtually every other respect except as it pertains to race/ism. Love for ourselves and each other (*Ubuntu*) can help pave the way toward greater forward progress and success. Whereas racial/st ideology precludes many of us from loving freely or willingly, the togetherness wayfinder or raceless antiracism removes those unnecessary barriers.

Throughout my early adulthood, I have loved people fiercely and unconditionally. Most people reciprocated my love. I made family and friends of many people who are still dear to me and still family throughout my adult years. I always suffered from low self-esteem and low self-love, which manifested in specific ways. I had internalized my unlovability courtesy of my adoptive parents. None of that hurt and heartache broke me. But it wasn't until my thirties when I finally stopped seeking the love of "Mommy and Poppy." It took my partner telling me that they didn't deserve me and that I should never put my neck on the chopping block for them again. She told me to stop going back to the trailer in search of the completeness they should've gifted me but didn't and, undoubtedly, won't.

I was still brokenhearted. The little girl in me mourned, not what she had lost but what she was never given and what was never nurtured within her. I had to give myself that which I should've readily received from my parents. I had to learn to love myself, to love all of me always and especially what I identified as my imperfections. It has been a long and winding road. Although my circumstances don't reflect everyone's experiences, I know that many, many people suffer through various types of traumas and an imperfect childhood and adulthood that impact how they see themselves, how they see others, and how they treat themselves and others. How we see ourselves is deeply connected with how we see and treat other people.

We live in a world where instead of doing work within ourselves, as individuals, we are taught to do the work outwardly, allowing our own antiblack racism to persist. It's often about rightly calling attention to what someone else does or says or believes or doesn't do, say, or believe—or rightly criticizing the systems around us. All too infrequently do we turn that critical eye inward to see how we might be furthering the projects of "white" supremacy, which center on maintaining particular social and economic hierarchies. When we do, that's what ultimately causes everything we fear and don't know or don't like about ourselves to be projected onto other people. Infrequently are we encouraged to consider how liberation radically comes from within, too. Our children inherit these incomplete ways of seeing ourselves and thinking about future-making a world without antiblack race/ism from us, even when we think we aren't passing our problems on to them. Like happened to us, we manipulate them into seeing themselves and each other from antagonistic perspectives, and it becomes natural for them to close their minds and hearts to the truth about racial/st ideology, thereby continuing the cycle. The truth is almost always on the outside of black and white—in the twilight—and is never as neat and crisp and ordered as we would prefer; it is hidden in the invisible ink.

Whether you believe that "race" exists and should be ignored because it "shouldn't matter," that "race" exists and should be embraced and celebrated, or that "race" matters because racism exists and matters, if you open your mind and heart to the possibility of being wrong about race/ism, you gain infinitely more than you might think. You gain insight about yourself and people you're taught to presume are distinct and different from you in ways they aren't. You finally start to see actual differences more clearly. You start to see similarities that matter more clearly. You stop holding onto your self-proclaimed moral high ground because you realize more of what you didn't know and would've never known had you stuck firmly to "your side" of racial/st thinking. You learn to love and to be grounded within yourself more so that you help your inner child stop mourning what they didn't but should've received. As a result, you learn to love other people more and have grounded understandings of who and how each person is, a happening that comes only with knowing a person or being able to speak fluently from positions that aren't yours. That starts with understanding yourself. You come to question every-thing, including yourself, which leads to so much more growth and free-dom. You stop racializing and "(e)racing" humans. In the face of race/ism and its attending ideology, we really have to give that consolation, maternal energy, and love to ourselves and each other.

Our future is limitless.

Conclusion: Togetherness Wayfinding

*[R]ace has functioned as a marker differentiating the human humans
from the seeming humans who are really, in one way
or another, inhuman—if not literally then at least in a
weaker sense nonetheless undermining any presumption
of their unqualified equality.*

—Charles Mills, "Race and the Human," *Human*, 2022

*Race is a political category that has been disguised
as a biological one.*

—Dorothy Roberts, *Fatal Invention*, 2011

We can end race/ism.

A system made up and maintained by humans cannot be changed without starting with individuals. The journey to race(ism)lessness, as understood within the context of the togetherness wayfinder, starts with each of us. We must come together to end our belief in "races," our practice of racialization, and our maintenance of systems of oppression that keep our attention turned inward rather than outward to the elites in the top one percent who need us to stay in the matrix that they constructed and maintain. The incoherence of antiblack racial/st understandings of the world should be enough to inspire fresh approaches for stopping the causes and effects of antiblack race/ism. Yet, people across all specializations, industries, and walks of life can miss the reality of race/ism and continue to conform to their belief in human "races" and practice of racialization.

We must all know and understand our shared history, what it is to be human, and what it is to be deemed subhuman or not at all human. If we don't, we cannot be clear-eyed about what race/ism is, what it isn't, where it is, where it isn't, how it is, and what we should do about it. Even when we think we've found our way outside of the matrix, we are often still in a different part of the matrix, still blind and signing furiously in the dark to each other. We will not end race/ism unless we recognize how undoing antiblack race/ism means that we must individually *and* collectively undo our belief in human "races" and practice of racialization to disrupt the imbalances of power and dehumanization that persist. Significant effort must be made to demand that our governments, media, corporations, religious institutions, and education systems, etc., participate in solutions rather than continue to capitalize off of our division and strife. Any and all "race" language—"white," "black," "Asian," etc.—to describe anything outside of the causes and effects of race/ism must be written into oblivion, never to return as a weapon of maintaining the causes and effects of race/ism again. We must revise the language we use to describe and teach about race/ism. In the near term, this means making effective human-centered changes to say things like "a person who gets racialized as . . ." in discussions of race/ism to avoid unintentionally upholding its causes and effects. With the successful defeat of race/ism, this language will change to "a person who once got racialized as . . ."

"But these are your/our/my people," you might say. Just as my diasporic connection changes depending on what period I pick to examine and declare, so too does yours. Your diaspora changes depending on when you pinpoint your place of "origin." If we all go back far enough, we will all find ourselves and our people in Africa, the continent with the largest diaspora to date. Remember that human history didn't begin with the Middle Passage. It began in what we now call Africa with the first humans. Some of us just have more recent connections to the continent. Yet, we are all connected to Africa, nonetheless. If that fact offends you, that's antiblack racial/st ideology telling you that there's something wrong with being connected with Africa or "blackness." Antiblack racial/st ideology precludes many people from seeing the shortcomings of limiting ourselves and our ways of seeing to colorblind ideology or commonly accepted versions of antiracist ideology. Antiblack race/ism shouldn't be how society continues to determine "one's place of origin." We shouldn't racialize culture or ethnicity, because the reality of cultural and ethnic formations is such that they belie neat, fixed, and homogenous ways of categorization.

We continue the madness of race/ism by denying the twilight. Twilight happens when we engage, measure, understand, and synthesize all ideas about a given topic, not just ideas that uphold our beliefs. When we explore the twilight more, we start to see more readily the invisible ink. We also see how we are all walking negatives to different extents, defying the laws of race/ism that were never and can never result in humanization and limitlessness. We see more clearly the architecture of racial/st ideology across time and place. We start to imagine and enact solutions that allow everyone to truly thrive—to create a home distinctly outside of the house of race/ism that other humans built for themselves and not for everyone.

We should teach American history and human history in all of its richness and nuance. This includes, of course, teaching about race/ism. We must do so from outside the confines of race/ism to examine antiblack race/ism and other types of racisms. This book is a prime example of how we can do that. We should especially encourage our youth to see themselves as raceless even as we detail how we have been erasing ourselves and each other for centuries. To that point, historically "black" universities and colleges and "Black" Studies and African American Studies programs remain as vital as ever in a nation that says, at least, it wants to live up to its ideals. There is no valid argument that I can conjure for dismantling such institutions or programs. That I came to create the to-getherness wayfinder through such institutions, programs, and studies demonstrates the generative nature and necessity of said institutions and programs. And we need effective unity, healing, and reconciliation pro-grams. Racelessness via the togetherness wayfinder is for everyone who wants to liberate themselves from the nefariousness of race/ism. That liberation should include all of us and stop being a privilege afforded primarily to people who get racialized as white.

Learn the togetherness wayfinder. Share it. Apply it across your thinking, industries, disciplines, fields, schools, curricula, diversity, eq-uity, belonging, and inclusion initiatives, and so on. You won't regret it.

If you want to join me and others in practicing the togetherness wayfinder or raceless antiracism and building a future without race/ism, here's what you must do.

Step 1: Focus on Yourself

- Complete the 45-day guide in the appendix of this book.
- Learn the ins and outs of the knowledge, rules, and tools of the to-getherness wayfinder.
- Become an abolitionist. Explore more about the philosophies of "race," especially imaginary abolitionism and synthetic abolition-ism. Use this book's recommended readings and glossary to your advantage.
- Practice and internalize the racelessness translator. In other words, practice translating what appears as "race" or "racial" into econom-ic class, social class, ethnicity, culture (including politics), and race/ism.
- Free yourself from the matrix of race/ism. Analyze and become clear-eyed about the history of human-rights efforts in your community and country and how the matrix has slowed and limited progress.
- Think about how people in your industry, discipline, etc., can apply

the togetherness wayfinder and benefit from it. Record your ideas for solutions. Future-making for any society requires the work of individuals.

- Check out the Diversity Atlas—an accessible form of racelessness translation in practice. Visit https://diversityatlas.io for more information.

- Visit www.togethernesswayfinder.org for more educational content and to learn in community with other people who engage with the togetherness wayfinder.

Step 2: Focus on Creating Change Outside of Yourself

- Share this book and its ideas within your respective spheres of influence (i.e., with family, friends, local politicians, work colleagues, social media networks, etc.). Have conversations. Post on social media. Do presentations and participate in podcasts. Create content inspired by the wayfinder for all platforms and mediums.

- Call your local K–12 educators and their respective schools into action. If you're a K–12 teacher or administrator, open the door to the togetherness wayfinder for your students. If we stop teaching our kids that they are part of a "race" and start teaching about history and current realities from a position of external racialization and assigned identities, we don't have to then do the hard work of helping kids who've grown into adults to unlearn what they've been taught to do and how they've been taught to think (i.e., how to maintain antiblack race/ism). As with anything, complex ideas and histories can be revised into grade-specific curricula. We should teach all students about philosophy of "race" to further ground them in history and the various and sometimes conflicting understandings of race/ism.

- Call your local, regional, and national politicians into action. Let them know about this book and its ideas. While politicians on both sides of the American political spectrum gain and maintain their positions of power by maintaining the status quo (i.e., race/ism), some radical and sincere politicians will be inspired to learn and change course. If you are a politician, take action.

- Demand that our governments stop requiring us to keep ourselves in a racial/st box. The U.S. Census Bureau, schools, universities, hospitals, etc., ask people to select a "race." If the goal is to end antiblack race/ism, we must strategize together toward a shared outcome of eliminating the root causes *and* effects of said race/ism. We won't be able to achieve a future without the causes and effects of race/ism overnight, but we can take immediate steps in that direction. As a start, for any form that requests the identification of "race," we must demand that there be a box that allows us to check "no race" or that such questions be reframed to focus on racialization rather than on "race" (e.g., "How are you most often racialized?" instead of "What is your race?")." A box labeled "Prefer not to say" is not a substitute for such an option because it still implies a "racial" reality or essence.[1]

- Demand that the media stop racializing every person and every story in ways that uphold race/ism. The media needs to change its language and align its narratives to reality to begin to weaken the matrix of race/ism. Like the government, the media—all media, not just "mainstream" media—benefits from maintaining the status quo for the elite. There are some independent media outlets and journalists that do not get nearly enough attention or support. Vote with your wallet and your clicks. If you are in the media, take action.

- Invite your employer's leadership team to engage with the togetherness wayfinder at www.togethernesswayfinder.org. And check out the Diversity Atlas—an accessible form of racelessness translation in practice. Visit https://diversityatlas.io for more information.

Whatever your profession and interests, consider how the belief in "races," practice of racialization, and attending power imbalances (i.e., race/ism) end up infiltrating our imaginations and broader societies through culture. Specifically, think about the ways in which newspapers, plays, books, journals, magazines, art, television, films, music, schools, political parties, corporations, governments, religions, technology, social media platforms, etc., express and perpetuate race/ism. We inherit racial/st ideology and continue it through all facets of culture. Thus, it is through all facets of culture that we must eradicate race/ism. And we can track antiblack race/ism in ways different from how we do so now, in ways that don't simultaneously help to maintain its causes and effects. Importantly, and as I've said from the outset, we cannot simply skip to the good part.

My love for humanity inspires my efforts, as do my own personal experiences with race/ism. The togetherness wayfinder allows people to recognize and embrace their racelessness and that of others without pretending that race/ism doesn't exist, isn't a problem, or is a permanent aspect of human society. It helps people become more clear-eyed and astute about what race/ism is and isn't. It allows us to keep the ethnocultural parts of us that provide value while discarding that which keeps us divided and within the throes of race/ism. For all lives to truly matter today and tomorrow, the belief in human "races" and practice of racialization that began centuries ago must cease once and for all. By confronting and acknowledging the reality of race/ism and refusing to participate in its systems and structures, we, the people, have the power to ensure that happens.

Remember: we seek not a post-racial future but a post-race/ist one. You now have the language, knowledge, and tools to act toward that end. Do not profess that you disbelieve or that you lack imagination. Refuse to uphold the machinery of race/ism. Race/ism (i.e., racism) is a socially constructed system of economic and social oppression that requires the belief in human "races" and the practice of racialization to reinforce various power imbalances.

Step into the future, one without antiblack race/ism. Help me make that future today.

Appendix: Togetherness Wayfinder 45-Day Guide

This workbook guides you through further exploration of the togetherness wayfinder, encouraging deep reflection, critical thinking, and actionable steps toward understanding and embodying the togetherness wayfinder in your life and communities.

Day 1: Understanding Race/ism

Quote from the book: "The continued belief in human 'races' and the practice of assigning 'racial' identities to humans, rendering some of us somewhat human if at all human and others fully human, causes all of us, including those who sincerely want to end racism—both its causes and effects—to remain within the machinery of racism." (p. 2)

Prompt: Reflect on your initial thoughts and feelings about the quote. Consider how the concept of "race" as an outdated yet persistent idea and practice affects societal interactions and personal identity.

Exercise: Write a short paragraph about a moment in your life when you became aware of "race" as a concept. How did it influence your view of yourself and others?

Day 2: The Invention of the Illusion of "Race"

Quote from the book: "In short, early modern Europeans of higher economic and social status invented the illusion of 'race' to maintain and reflect the economic and social systems that were on the ground during chattel enslavement, which in turn fed the belief and practice of 'race' and racialization in a now centuries-long feedback loop. It was with their belief in human 'races' and practice of assigning 'races' to humans that the social and economic hierarchies that already existed were at once reflected and maintained in those newly invented so-called racial hierarchies—'white' at the top and 'black' and all others at the bottom." (p. 6)

Prompt: Reflect on how societal structures and systems reinforce the belief in human "races" and practice of racialization. How do these structures influence the way people interact and view each other?

Exercise: Identify one social or institutional practice in your community or society that perpetuates race/ism. Consider how it could be reformed or removed.

Day 3: The Human-Made Nature of Race/ism

Quote from the book: "Race/ism (i.e., racism) is a socially constructed system of economic and social oppression that requires the belief in human 'races' and the practice of racialization to reinforce various power imbalances." (p. 10)

Prompt: Discuss the implications of understanding racism, not "race," as a human-made construct. How does this perspective impact your ability to engage with and challenge racist ideas and practices?

Exercise: Journal about a time when you encountered a racist practice or ideology. Analyze it from the perspective that racism is a constructed and maintained system. What could be done to dismantle it?

Day 4: Biological Fallacies of "Race"

Quote from the book: Revisit Chapter 4: "'Race' Is Not Biological: Embracing the Human Species"

Prompt: Explore the scientific rejection of "race" as a biological fact. How does this understanding affect the social and cultural significance of "race?"

Exercise: Create a mind map that connects the false biological notions of "race" to various societal consequences. Include education, healthcare, and employment as areas influenced by these misconceptions.

Day 5: Imagining a Race(ism)less Future

Quote from the description on the book's back cover: "To end racism, we must end the very idea of 'race' itself, our practice of racialization, and the attending power imbalances that are part and parcel of race/ism."

Prompt: Imagine a society without race/ism. How would this change the way people relate to each other and the structures of power within the society?

Exercise: Write a short story or scenario depicting a day in a truly race(ism)less society. Focus on interpersonal relationships, social policies, media, and community dynamics.

Day 6: The Togetherness Wayfinder

Quote from the book: "In a context of achieved racelessness, so-called white people wouldn't exist even in our imaginations and would be shown to have been believed to exist in history books as part of the racial/st era, with real material impacts of that belief system and practice of racialization. But people who get racialized as white now would still exist, just as people who once got racialized as white. They just wouldn't get racialized as white anymore. . . . Similarly, people wouldn't get racialized as black, indigenous, or people of color either, which means that people who get racialized as subhuman, if human at all now, would finally reap the benefits of being recognized as fully human in practice and in theory." (p. 106)

Prompt: Reflect on your initial thoughts and feelings about the togetherness wayfinder. Consider how the idea challenges or aligns with your current understanding of "race" and "racial" identity. What emotions or questions does the concept of living without "racial" categorizations evoke in you?

Exercise: List three actions you can take in your daily life to promote the principles of the togetherness wayfinder. Reflect on how these actions could influence your personal and professional relationships.

Day 7: Unpacking "Race" as Imaginary

Prompt: Consider the argument that while "race" itself is not real, the effects of racism are. How does this distinction between "race" as imaginary and race/ism as real shape your understanding of social justice efforts?

Exercise: Debate this concept with a friend or colleague. Write down the key points of agreement or disagreement and reflect on how these discussions could be used to educate yourself and others.

Day 8: The Role of Education in Ending Race/ism

Quote from the book: "Part of why we continue to stay within the cycle of race/ism comes down to how some people are programmed to believe that 'race' is not a factor or should not be, and others are programmed to believe that 'race' is always a factor and should not be a negative impact but could be embraced as a positive aspect of society." (p. 11)

Prompt: Explore how education systems can either perpetuate or challenge racial/st ideologies. What role does education play in maintaining or dismantling race/ism?

Exercise: Propose three changes or additions to the current educational curriculum that could help promote a deeper understanding of race/ism as a construct and encourage racelessness, the end of race/ism.

Day 9: The Power of Raceless Unity

Prompt: Discuss how the practice of the togetherness wayfinder could unify diverse communities. What barriers exist that might prevent this unification, and how can they be overcome?

Exercise: Organize a community event or workshop aimed at discussing and promoting unity. Plan the agenda and outline the discussion topics.

Day 10: Exploring Personal Identities without "Race"

Prompt: Reflect on how personal identities might evolve in a raceless society. How would people express and define themselves without so-called racial categories while simultaneously reflecting on external impacts and hierarchies?

Exercise: Create a personal identity map that includes your interests, values, skills, and cultural influences without referencing "race." Share this with a group to discuss how identity is multifaceted and expansive.

Day 11: Self-Love and Healing in a Raceless World

Quote from the book: "People might cringe or otherwise become agitated when I bring up the necessity and power of radical love. Yet, intuitively, the necessity for radical self-love and love for others makes sense and aligns with many of our values, be they religiously inspired or otherwise. There is plenty of literature that shows the correlation between a lack of self-love and increased bias and even hatred toward others. Our hearts and minds need to be educated and, indeed, changed to even want to create a better world for all." (p. 185)

Prompt: Consider the relationship between self-love and the rejection of race/ism. How does embracing the togetherness wayfinder impact self-esteem and interpersonal relationships?

Exercise: Write a letter to yourself from the perspective of someone living in a society without any race/ism. What would you want to tell your current self about self-love and acceptance?

Day 12: The Myth of Biological Human "Races"

Prompt: Reflect on how the belief in biological "races" for the human species has influenced societal structures and personal interactions. Why is it important to debunk this myth?

Exercise: Research and compile a list of scientific studies that refute the biological basis of "race." Prepare a presentation or blog post summarizing these findings.

Day 13: Race/ism as a System of Power

Quote from the book: "As the philosopher Charles Mills writes, '[R]ace has functioned as a marker differentiating the humans from the seeming humans who are really in one way or another inhuman—if not literally then at least in a weaker sense nonetheless undermining any presumption of their unqualified equality.'" (p. xviii)

Prompt: Analyze the role of "race" in establishing and maintaining power structures. How does race/ism benefit certain groups at the expense of others?

Exercise: Draw a diagram that maps out the flow of power in society and how racial categorizations can influence this flow. Discuss how different levels of power are maintained through racial/st ideologies.

Day 14: Challenging Race/ism

Exercise: Create a campaign aimed at challenging common race/ist stereotypes in your community or workplace. Include posters, social media posts, and discussion guides.

Day 15: Imagining New Forms of Community

Prompt: Discuss what it means to "decolonize our minds" from racial/st ideology. How can communities benefit from such a transformation?

Exercise: Host a community dialogue or roundtable discussion where participants are invited to envision new forms of community that transcend race/ism. Document the ideas and publish them in a community newsletter or blog.

Day 16: The Inevitability of the End of Race/ism

Prompt: Explore the statement that the end of race/ism is inevitable. What factors contribute to this inevitability? Do you agree with this assessment? Why?

Exercise: Write an op-ed for a local newspaper or online platform arguing for or against the inevitability of racelessness in practice, using examples from current events and historical trends to support your position.

Day 17: Intersectionality and Racelessness

Prompt: Reflect on how intersectionality—a framework that explores how various forms of social stratification, such as "race," gender, and class, interact—might be understood in a raceless society. How can intersectional thinking help in the transition toward racelessness? How might this connect with the racelessness translator?

Exercise: Create a diagram that shows your personal identity layers, including but not limited to "race," gender, economic status, social class, etc. Discuss how these layers intersect and how racelessness might alter and enhance the diagram.

Day 18: The Role of Media in Shaping Racial Perceptions

Prompt: Analyze the role of media in reinforcing or challenging so-called racial perceptions. How can media be leveraged to promote a society without race/ism?

Exercise: Design a media project (e.g., video, podcast, article series) that challenges traditional so-called racial narratives and promotes a deeper understanding of race/ism and racelessness.

Day 19: Reimagining Equality and Justice

Prompt: Consider what equality and justice would look like in a raceless society. How would laws, policies, and social norms change?

Exercise: Write a proposal for a new law or policy that embodies the principles of the togetherness wayfinder, detailing how it would promote equality and justice.

Day 20: The Psychology of Race/ism and Identity

Prompt: Discuss the psychological impact of so-called racial categorizations on individual identity and community dynamics. How does moving toward racelessness affect our psychological well-being?

Exercise: Participate in or facilitate a workshop focused on identity and racelessness, using psychological tools and exercises to explore how identities might be constructed in a raceless world.

Day 21: Global Perspectives on Race/ism

Prompt: Explore how the concept of racelessness might apply in different cultural or national contexts. What are the challenges and opportunities of promoting the togetherness wayfinder globally?

Exercise: Research and present a case study of a country or culture that approaches "race" differently from the United States. Discuss what aspects of their approach could be adopted or avoided in the push toward a future without race/ism.

Day 22: Challenging Historical Narratives

Prompt: Consider how historical narratives have shaped our understanding of race/ism. How would a revised history curriculum that emphasizes ending race/ism look?

Exercise: Choose a significant historical event seldomly or commonly taught in schools. Rewrite a section of a textbook to reflect a raceless antiracist perspective, focusing on human actions and societal impacts.

Day 23: The Economics of Race/ism

Prompt: Explore the economic implications of a raceless society. How might economic policies change if we engaged the togetherness wayfinder?

Exercise: Create an economic plan for a small community that aims to reduce economic disparities. Include proposals for education, employment, and housing.

Day 24: Personal Narratives and Racelessness

Prompt: Reflect on the power of personal narratives in shaping our perceptions of race/ism. How can sharing personal stories contribute to the togetherness wayfinder movement?

Exercise: Write your own personal narrative that focuses on your experiences with race/ism, and how you envision overcoming this construction. Consider sharing this with a local community group or online.

Day 25: Art and Culture in a World without Race/ism

Prompt: Discuss how art and culture would evolve in a society without the causes and effects of race/ism. What new forms of cultural expression might emerge? How might we discuss culture?

Exercise: Create an art piece—be it a drawing, painting, poem, or song—that represents what the togetherness wayfinder means to you. Organize a virtual or local art exhibit with works focused on envisioning a society without race/ism.

Day 26: The Role of Technology in Promoting the End of Race/ism

Prompt: Analyze the role of technology in either perpetuating or dismantling race/ism. How can technology be used positively in the move-ment toward a future without race/ism?

Exercise: Design a concept for an app or software that helps users explore and understand the concept of racelessness and the togetherness wayfin-der. Outline the features, target audience, and intended impact.

Day 27: Legal Frameworks and the End of Race/ism

Quote from the book: "Culture doesn't stem from one's 'race.' Try as they might, anthropologists, other social scientists, and scholars continue to fail to answer this call-to-action."

Prompt: How do you define your cultural identity, and what influences it beyond race/ism? Discuss the role of experiences, language, traditions, and beliefs in shaping who you are.

Day 28: Health and the End of Race/ism

Prompt: Explore how healthcare systems are influenced by race/ism. What would a raceless approach to healthcare look like? What impact might that have on health disparities that stem from race/ism?

Exercise: Develop a proposal for a public health campaign that addresses a common health issue. Include strategies for outreach, education, and treatment that are inclusive and effective for everyone.

Day 29: Education Reform for Ending Race/ism

Prompt: Discuss the needed reforms in the education system to support a raceless society. How can education help dismantle entrenched race/ism?

Exercise: Design a workshop or lesson plan for middle or high school students that teaches about the togetherness wayfinder. Include interactive activities that help students understand the social construction of race/ism and the benefits of a raceless approach toward creating a future without race/ism.

Day 30: Media Representation and Ending Race/ism

Prompt: Plan a conversation with someone from a different background, focusing on shared experiences or interests. Reflect on how this approach influences the connection and understanding between you.

Day 31: Political Advocacy for Ending Race/ism

Prompt: Explore the role of political advocacy in promoting racelessness. What political strategies could effectively reduce race/ism?

Exercise: Plan a campaign or advocacy strategy aimed at promoting the togetherness wayfinder in local or national politics. This could involve running awareness campaigns.

Day 32: Community Engagement and Ending Race/ism

Prompt: Spend the day consciously avoiding so-called racial assumptions about people you see or interact with. Note any challenges or insights you encounter.

Day 33: Racial Identity and Personal Growth

Exercise: Write a reflective essay on your own so-called racial identity and how it has shaped your experiences. Consider what aspects of your identity would change or remain the same in a society without the causes and effects of race/ism.

Day 34: Sports and Ending Race/ism

Prompt: Analyze the role of sports in reinforcing or challenging race/ism. How can sports become a vehicle for promoting a future without race/ism?

Exercise: Develop a campaign for a local sports team or league that focuses on promoting unity and the togetherness wayfinder. Include initiatives such as community outreach, educational programs, and inclusive team policies.

Day 35: The Role of Religion in Ending Race/ism

Prompt: Consider how religious institutions and beliefs influence so-called racial identity and race/ism. How can religious communities contribute to a society without race/ism?

Exercise: Plan a series of interfaith workshops that focus on the togetherness wayfinder. Aim to explore how different religious teachings can support the concept of universal humanity and discourage race/ism.

Day 36: Racelessness in Literature and the Arts

Prompt: Explore how literature and the arts can serve as powerful tools for promoting racelessness. What changes would you like to see in how race/ism is addressed in literature and the arts?

Exercise: Curate a virtual or physical exhibition of artworks or literary pieces that challenge traditional notions of "race" or promote a future without race/ism. Include works from diverse artists and provide explanations of how each work contributes to the theme.

Day 37: Racelessness and Globalization

Prompt: Discuss the impact of globalization on so-called racial identity. How does the global movement of people, goods, and ideas affect so-called racial categorizations and perceptions?

Exercise: Develop a research paper or presentation that examines a case study of a global issue (e.g., migration, international trade, global media) through a raceless lens. Analyze how global interactions can either perpetuate or dismantle race/ism.

Day 38: Racelessness and Environmental Justice

Prompt: Examine the intersection of environmental justice and the togetherness wayfinder. How does race/ism affect environmental policies and practices?

Exercise: Plan an environmental justice campaign that emphasizes the togetherness wayfinder. Focus on how communities can unite to address environmental issues, including collaborative projects and inclusive education efforts.

Day 39: Technological Innovation and Racelessness

Exercise: Write an example for each philosophy of "race." Hereditary, synthetic, imaginary, preservation, reformation, and abolition. Examples: "We shouldn't judge people by their skin color" is an example of a hereditary view of "race." "My skin color is white" is another example of a hereditary view of "race." The language of "race" ("white") inadequately describes the literal complexion of most people who get racialized as white.

Day 40: Racelessness in Business and Entrepreneurship

Prompt: Curate a list of books, films, and music from various cultures without focusing on the background or politics of the creators. Reflect on how this diversity enriches your understanding of human creativity.

Day 41: Historical Reconciliation and Racelessness

Prompt: Reflect on the importance of historical reconciliation in the journey toward a future without antiblack race/ism. How can societies address past injustices while moving toward such a future?

Exercise: Design a community-based project that aims to reconcile historical injustices through education, art, and public discussions that advocate for a perspective that centers the togetherness wayfinder.

Day 42: Racelessness and Mental Health

Prompt: Consider the impact of the togetherness wayfinder on mental health. How might that paradigm shift affect individual and community well-being?

Exercise: Organize a workshop or seminar that addresses mental health from a togetherness wayfinder perspective. Include discussions on the psychological impacts of racial categorization and strategies for fostering a more inclusive, supportive community.

Day 43: The Future of Racelessness

Exercise: Write a speculative fiction story set in a future where the end of race/ism has been achieved. Explore the societal, cultural, and personal dimensions of this world.

Day 44: Building Raceless Communities

Prompt: Discuss strategies for building communities that embrace the togetherness wayfinder. What practical steps can individuals and communities take to foster inclusivity and unity?

Exercise: Plan a community event that promotes the togetherness wayfinder. This could include workshops, cultural displays, guest speakers, and community-building activities.

Day 45: Reflecting on the Togetherness Wayfinder

Prompt: Reflect on everything you have learned over the last 44 days. How has your understanding of race/ism changed?

Exercise: Create a personal action plan outlining how you will continue to advocate for the togetherness wayfinder in your own life and community. Include specific goals, actions, and timelines.

Glossary

Antirace/ism (i.e., antiracism). The policy, practice, and process of stopping the belief in human "races" and practice of racialization to undo the causes and effects of race/ism, including and especially the various attendant power imbalances.

Biracialism. The advancing belief in separate and distinct "races," namely, "white" and "black," and the correlated hierarchies that underpin such ideas.

Creolization. The process through which creole languages and cultures emerge. This is a term often used to refer to the Caribbean even though it is not exclusive to the Caribbean; it refers to the process through which creole languages and cultures emerge. Social scientists use the term to describe new cultural expressions brought about by contact between societies and relocated peoples. It has been associated with cultural mixtures of African, European, and indigenous (in addition to other lineages in different locations) ancestry. Today, *creolization* tends to refer to that mixture of different people and different cultures that merge to become one (i.e., New Yorican or Miami Spanish).

Eracesure (eracing, erace, eraced, etc.). An act or instance of being erased by being "raced," which happens when a person is racialized by society and themselves.

Ideology. A set of beliefs, values, and ideas that form the basis of a social, economic, or political system. It influences the way people think, act, and perceive the world around them. It often provides a framework for understanding society, prescribing how it should function, and guiding behavior and policy. An ideology can be explicit, such as through formal manifestos or doctrines, or implicit, such as through subconscious attitudes and assumptions. Examples of ideologies include capitalism, socialism, liberalism, conservatism, feminism, and environmentalism, among others.

Race. An imaginary component of the socially constructed reality of racism (i.e., race/ism).

Racecraft. The illusion of "race" produced by the practice of racism (as coined by Barbara and Karen Fields).

Race/ism (i.e., racism). A socially constructed system of economic and social oppression that requires the belief in human "races" and the practice of racialization to reinforce various power imbalances.

Raceless (racelessness, etc.). Human, as seen outside of the paradigm of race/ism and without upholding and perpetuating the causes and effects of race/ism (i.e., synthetic abolitionism or imaginary abolitionism).

Racialism. A belief that "race" determines human traits and capacity.

Racialization. The process of applying an inescapable economic and social class hierarchy to humans that creates or reinforces power imbalances.

Racial/st. The interconnection between that which is racist and "racial." For something to be racial/st, it must include a hierarchy of humans based on the belief in "races," the practice of racialization, and the subsequent upholding of various power imbalances.

Notes

Preface

1. When I speak of people of "more recent African decent," I'm referring specifically to those individuals who have ancestors that came from the continent of Africa within the last 550 years or so. I say "more recent" because all humans originated in Africa.

2. Ideology refers to a set of beliefs, values, and ideas that form the basis of a social, economic, or political system. It influences the way people think, act, and perceive the world around them. Ideologies often provide a framework for understanding society, prescribing how it should function, and guiding behavior and policy. They can be explicit, such as in manifestos or doctrines, or implicit, shaping attitudes and assumptions subconsciously. Examples of ideologies include capitalism, socialism, liberalism, conservatism, feminism, and environmentalism, among others.

3. Charles Mills, "Reflection: Race and the Human," in *Human: A History*, ed. Karolina Hübner (Oxford: Oxford University Press, 2022).

4. Antirace/ism (i.e., antiracism) is the policy, practice, and process of stopping the belief in human "races" and practice of racialization to undo the causes and effects of race/ism (i.e., racism), including and especially the various attendant power imbalances.

5. Virginia Kennedy, in private correspondence with the author.

6. Paul Gilroy, *Against Race: Imagining Political Culture Beyond the Color Line* (Harvard University Press, 2000), 6–7.

Introduction

1. Carlos Hoyt, *The Arc of a Bad Idea: Understanding and Transcending Race* (Oxford University Press, 2015).

2. Francisco Bethencourt, *Racisms: From the Crusades to the Twentieth Century* (Princeton University Press, 2015).

3. See works on Afrofuturism.

4. Anika Prather, "Discovering the Theory of Racelessness," in *Dr. Anika Prather Blog* (2023), drprather.com/2024/01/20/discovering-theory-of-racelessness/.

5. Sheena Michele Mason, *The Theory of Racelessness: A Case for Antirace(ism)* (Palgrave, 2022).

6. It is worth noting that Ibram X. Kendi did not coin the term or practice of *antiracism*. He simply helped to popularize it.

7. Jim Mandelaro, "Ibram X. Kendi: 'The Very Heartbeat of Racism Is Denial,'" in *University of Rochester News Center* (2021), www.rochester.edu/newscenter/ibram-x-kendi-the-very-heartbeat-of-racism-is-denial-470332/.

8. *Eracesure* and the related terms *erace* and *eracing* are inspired, in part, by Percival Everett's novel *Erasure* (Graywolf Press, 2001) and the movie adaptation *American Fiction* (Amazon MGM Studios and Orion Pictures, 2023).

9. See, for example, Brianna Atkinson, "UNC–Chapel Hill BOT Votes to Divert DEI Funding, Redirecting It to Campus Public Safety," *WUNC* North Carolina Public Radio, May 13, 2024, www.wunc.org/education/2024-05-13/dei-unc-chapel-hill-trustees-vote-redirect-funding-police.

10. Toni Morrison on *The Colbert Report*, Comedy Central, November 19, 2014.

11. See Carlos Hoyt, *The Arc of a Bad Idea: Understanding and Transcending Race* (Oxford University Press, 2015).

12. Toni Morrison, "Foreword," *Paradise* (Vintage, 2014).

Chapter 1

1. See my book *The Theory of Racelessness* for more on the connections between "white" supremacy and patriarchy and how recognizing their sameness can help us create a better future for all.

2. See, for example, Kristin Leong, "Whitewashing of Asian Students and a Report That Launched a Reckoning," *KUOW*, February 5, 2021, www.kuow.org/stories/whitewashing-of-asian-students-and-the-report-that-launched-a-reckoning.

3. The idea that "Asian American" is a coherent category does not align with the reality. Connie Hanzhang Jin, "6 Charts That Dismantle the Trope of Asian Americans as a Model Minority," *NPR*, May 25, 2021, www.npr.org/2021/05/25/999874296/6-charts-that-dismantle-the-trope-of-asian-americans-as-a-model-minority.

4. Studies that examine the sources of "racial" disparities often identify "gaps" across racial/st lines. Consider, for example, how the following study might still be able to address race/ism and inform public policy without upholding the causes of race/ism: Raj Chetty et al., "Race and Economic Opportunity in the United States: An Intergenerational Perspective," *Quarterly Journal of Economics* 135, no. 2 (May 2020): 711–783, doi.org/10.1093/qje/qjz042.

5. Ibram X. Kendi, *Stamped from the Beginning: The Definitive History of Racist Ideas in America* (Bold Type Books, 2016).

6. The following passage is from Mason, *The Theory of Racelessness*, 8–10.

7. Ibid., 9–10.

8. The median net worth of so-called white families was $284,310 in 2022 and $44,100 for so-called black families. Board of Governors of the Federal Reserve Board, "Survey of Consumer Finances, 1989-2022," Federal Reserve, November 22, 2023 (last updated), www.federalreserve.gov/econres/scf/dataviz/scf/chart/#series:Before_Tax_Income;demographic:racecl4;population:all;units:median.

9. See Cord Jefferson's *American Fiction* (Amazon MGM Studios, 2023), a film adaptation of Percival Everett's novel *Erasure* (Graywolf Press, 2001).

10. Andre M. Perry et al., "Black Wealth Is Increasing, but So Is the Racial Wealth Gap," Brookings, January 9, 2024, www.brookings.edu/articles/black-wealth-is-increasing-but-so-is-the-racial-wealth-gap/.

11. Matt Bruenig, "The Racial Wealth Gap Is about the Upper Classes," People's Policy Project, June 29, 2020, www.peoplespolicyproject.org/2020/06/29/the-racial-wealth-gap-is-about-the-upper-classes/.

12. Emily A. Shrider and John Creamer, *Poverty in the United States: 2022*, Current Population Reports P60-280 (U.S. Census Bureau, September 2023),

www.census.gov/content/dam/Census/library/publications/2023/demo/p60-280.pdf.

13. Gilroy, *Against Race*, 21.

14. Ibid., 22.

15. Mills, "Reflection: Race and the Human," 71.

Chapter 2

1. In the United States, there is good reason for this. People who get racialized as black and their allies historically needed to mobilize collectively to fight for human rights. It may also be a strong carryover from modes of seeing and being in Africa that prioritize the individual's role within a broader community and the community's role in the development of individuals.

2. Rugare Mugumbate and Admire Chereni, "Editorial: Now, the Theory of Ubuntu Has Its Space in Social Work," *African Journal of Social Work* (April 2020): 10.

3. M. O. Eze, *Intellectual History in Contemporary South Africa* (Palgrave, 2010), 190–191.

4. The polarization includes our racialized political system.

5. Barbara and Karen Fields, *Racecraft: The Soul of Inequality in American Life* (Verso, 2014), 16.

6. Kwame Anthony Appiah, *In My Father's House: Africa in the Philosophy of Culture* (Oxford University Press, 1993).

7. Mike Laws, "Why We capitalize 'Black' (and Not 'White')," *Columbia Journalism Review* (2020), www.cjr.org/analysis/capital-b-black-styleguide.php.

8. "ABC Suspends Whoopi Goldberg for Comments on Jews, Race and the Holocaust," PBS, February 2, 2022, www.pbs.org/newshour/arts/abc-suspends-whoopi-goldberg-for-comments-on-jews-race-and-the-holocaust.

9. Roland Dixon, *The Racial History of Man* (Charles Scribner's Sons, 1923), 501.

10. Ibid., 502-3.

11. Alain Locke, "The Problem of Race Classification," in *The Works of Alain Locke*, ed. Charles Molesworth (Oxford UP, 2021), 280.

12. Ibid., 281.

13. Ibram X. Kendi, *How to Be an Antiracist* (One World, 2019), 20.

14. See Kendi, *Stamped from the Beginning.*

15. Barbara and Karen Fields, *Racecraft*, 17.

16. Kendi, *Stamped from the Beginning*, emphasis in original.

17. Frantz Fanon, *Black Skin, White Masks* (Grove Press, 2008).

18. Harriet Jacobs, *Incidents in the Life of a Slave Girl. The Norton Anthology of American Literature*, ed. Nina Baym and Robert S. Levine (W.W. Norton and Co., 2012), 922.

19. For more information, see U.S. Census Bureau, "Measuring Race and Ethnicity Across the Decades: 1790–2010," www.census.gov/data-tools/demo/race/MREAD_1790_2010.html.

20. U.S. Census classifications map onto U.S. Office of Management and Budget (OMB) standards, which require, at a minimum, the following five categories of "race" for the purposes of collecting data for federal reporting: "White," "Black of African American," "American Indian or Alaska Native," "Asian," and "Native Hawaiian or Other Pacific Islander." It also makes an allowance for the selection of "other races" or for the selection of two or more "races" and gives two categories for ethnicity: "Hispanic or Latino" and "Not Hispanic or Latino."

21. See U.S. Census Bureau, "Measuring Race and Ethnicity Across the Decades: 1790-2010."

22. Hansi Lo Wang, "Next U.S. Census Will Have New Boxes for 'Middle Eastern or North African,' 'Latino,'" NPR, March 28, 2024, www.npr.org/2024/03/28/1237218459/census-race-categories-ethnicity-middle-east-north-africa.

23. Hansi Lo Wang, "Biden Officials May Change How the U.S. Defines Racial and Ethnic Groups by 2024," NPR, June 15, 2022, www.npr.org/2022/06/15/1105104863/racial- ethnic-categories-omb-directive-15.

24. Kat Chow and Gene Demby, "Overthinking It: Using Food as a Racial Metaphor," NPR, September 12, 2014, www.npr.org/sections/codeswitch/2014/09/12/348008432/overthinking-it-using-food-as-a-racial-metaphor.

25. See Charles W. Mills, *The Racial Contract* (Cornell University Press, 1999).

Chapter 3

1. Scott Hershberger, "Humans Are All More Closely Related Than We Commonly Think," *Scientific American*, October 5, 2020, www.scientificamerican.com/article/humans-are-all-more-closely-related-than-we-commonly-think/.

2. Ibid.

3. For example, see Theresa M. Duello et al, "Race and Genetics versus 'Race' in Genetics: A Systematic Review of the Use of African Ancestry in Genetic Studies," *Evolution, Medicine, and Public Health*: 9, no. 1 (2021): 232–245, doi: 10.1093/emph/eoab018.

4. Jonathan Jarry M. Sc., "Are You There, Race? It's Me, DNA," McGill, August 9, 2019, www.mcgill.ca/oss/article/health-general-science/are-you-there-race-its-me-dna#.

5. Johann Friedrich Blumenbach, "De Generis Humani Varietate Nativa," 1793/1795, available at www.biodiversitylibrary.org/item/81492#page/7/mode/1up.

6. Mateus Gouveia et. al., "Unappreciated Subcontinental Admixture in Europeans and European Americans and Implications for Genetic Epidemiology Studies," *Nature Communications* 14, no. 6802 (2023), www.nature.com/articles/s41467-023-42491-0.

7. Marieke Van de Loosdrecht et al., "Pleistocene North African Genomes Link Near Eastern and Sub-Saharan African Human Populations," *Science* 360, no. 6388 (March 2018): 548–552, doi: 10.1126/science.aar8380.

8. Ibid.

9. Joseph Pickrell et al., "Ancient West Eurasian Ancestry in Southern and Eastern Africa," *Proceedings of the National Academy of Sciences* 111, no. 7 (February 2014): 2632–2637, doi.org/10.1073/pnas.1313787111.

10. Nicholas Crawford et al., "Loci Associated with Skin Pigmentation Identified in African Populations," *Science* 358, no. 6365 (October 2017): 867, doi.org/10.1126/science.aan8433.

11. Selina Brace, "Population Replacement in Early Neolithic Britain," *BioRxiv*, February 2018, doi.org/10.1101/267443.

12. M. De Braekeleer et al., "The French Canadian Tay-Sachs Disease Deletion Mutation: Identification of Probable Founders," *Human Genetics* 89, no. 1

(1992): 83, doi:10.1007/BF00207048.

13. G. A. McDowell et al., "The Presence of Two Different Infantile Tay-Sachs Disease Mutations in a Cajun Population," *American Journal of Human Genetics* 51, no. 5 (1992).

14. Gabrielle Birkner, "Non-Jews Hit by 'Jewish' Diseases Fall Through the Cracks of Genetic Screening," *Forward*, August 11, 2013, forward.com/culture/181751/non-jews-hit-by-jewish-diseases-fall-through/.

15. Douglas L. T. Rohde et al., "Modelling the Recent Common Ancestry of All Living Humans," *Nature* 431, no. 7008 (2004), doi:10.1038/nature02842.

16. See *Ordering the Human: The Global Spread of Racial Science*, ed. Eram Alam, Dorothy Roberts, and Natalie Shibley (Columbia University Press, 2024).

17. B. A. Julian et al., "Effect of Replacing Race with Apolipoprotein L1 Genotype in Calculation of Kidney Donor Risk Index," *American Journal of Transplantation: Official Journal of the American Society of Transplantation and the American Society of Transplant Surgeons* 17, no. 6 (2017), doi:10.1111/ajt.14113.

Chapter 4

1. Martin Luther King Jr., "I Have a Dream" (1963), available at *Talk of the Nation*, www.npr.org/2010/01/18/122701268/i-have-a-dream-speech-in-its-entirety.

2. Frederick Douglass, "West India Emancipation" (1857), available at University of Rochester Frederick Douglass Project, rbscp.lib.rochester.edu/4398.

3. Sheena Michele Mason, "Undoing Racism Means Undoing Race: Opinion," *Newsweek*, 2021, www.newsweek.com/undoing-racism-means-undoing-race-opinion-1656598.

4. Mills, "Reflection: Race and the Human," 71.

5. Cara Murez, "Race Plays Big Role in Whether Kids Learn to Swim," *Health Day*, December 15, 2022, www.healthday.com/health-news/child-health/swimming-2658900805.html.

6. Francisco Bethencourt, *Racisms: From the Crusades to the Twentieth Century* (Princeton University Press, 2015).

7. Jessica Sullivan, Leigh Wilton, and Evan Apfelbaum, "Adults Delay

Conversations about Race Because They Underestimate Children's Processing of Race," *Journal of Experimental Psychology: General,* 2020.

Chapter 5

1. Anna Deveare Smith, *Twilight: Los Angeles, 1992* (Anchor, 1994), xxv.
2. Langston Hughes, "The Negro Artist and the Racial Mountain" (1926), available at Poetry Foundation, www.poetryfoundation.org/articles/69395/the-negro-artist-and-the-racial-mountain.
3. Actors Nia Long and Idris Elba have also expressed this wish, among others.
4. Georgina Lawton, *Raceless: In Search of Family, Identity, and the Truth About Where I Belong* (Harper Perennial, 2021). Lawton's memoir was published almost one hundred years after Hughes' essay. The type of thinking around "race" has appeared to change radically over the decades but there is much evidence to the contrary.
5. Lawton, *Raceless,* 11.
6. Ibid., 11.
7. Ibid., 23.
8. Peggy McIntosh, "White Privilege: Unpacking the Invisible Knapsack," *Independent School* 49, no. 2 (Winter 1990): 31.
9. Lawton, *Raceless,* 278.
10. Ibid., 279.
11. See Toni Morrison's "The Site of Memory," in *The Source of Self-Regard: Selected Essays, Speeches, and Meditations* (Vintage, 2020).
12. For a discussion of what this might look like in practice, see Kwame Anthony Appiah, *Cosmopolitanism: Ethics in a World of Strangers* (W. W. Norton & Company, 2007), and Gilroy, *Against Race.*

Chapter 6

1. See *Ordering the Human: The Global Spread of Racial Science,* ed. Eram Alam, Dorothy Roberts, and Natalie Shibley (Columbia University Press, 2024).
2. See Mason, *The Theory of Racelessness.*

3. David Livingstone Smith (@DavidLSmith_Iam), post on X, July 14, 2022.

4. See Touré, *Who's Afraid of Post-Blackness?: What It Means to Be Black Now* (Atria, 2012).

5. President Joe Biden later apologized for this statement. Astead W. Herndon and Katie Glueck, "Biden Apologizes for Saying Black Voters 'Ain't Black If They're Considering Trump,'" *New York Times*, May 22, 2021, www.nytimes.com/2020/05/22/us/politics/joe-biden-black-breakfast-club.html.

6. See chapter 3 in Mason, *The Theory of Racelessness.*

7. See Kerry Ann Rockquemore, *Beyond Black: Biracial Identity in America,* 2nd ed. (Rowman & Littlefield, 2007).

8. See Andrea Pena-Vasquez and Maryann H. Kwakwa, "Barack Obama and Kamala Harris Both identify as Black. The News Media Doesn't Describe Both That Way," *Washington Post*, September 16, 2020, www.washingtonpost.com/politics/2020/09/16/barack-obama-kamala-harris-both-identify-black-news-media-doesnt-describe-both-that-way/.

9. Sam Roberts and Peter Baker, "Asked to Declare His Race, Obama Checks 'Black,'" *New York Times*, April 3, 2010, www.nytimes.com/2010/04/03/us/politics/03census.html.

10. See, for example, *Rac[e]ing to the Right: Selected Essays of George Schuyler*, ed. Jeffrey B. Leak (University of Tennessee Press, 2001).

11. George Schuyler, "The Caucasian Problem," in ibid., 49.

12. Schuyler's assessment aligns with W. E. B. Du Bois' theory of double consciousness. See W. E. B. Du Bois, *The Souls of Black Folk* (Dover Publications, 2016).

13. The leader of Patriot Front explained their views in an interview with *News Share.* See the video thread by Ford Fischer (@FordFischer) on X, January 19, 2024, x.com/FordFischer/status/1748466654458048835?s=20.

14. McKenzie Jean-Philippe, "Emmanuel Acho and Oprah Talk White Privilege in The Oprah Conversation," *Oprah Daily*, 2020, www.oprahdaily.com/entertainment/tv-movies/a33473509/emmanuel-acho-the-oprah-conversation-white-privelege/.

15. Ibid.

16. Schuyler, "The Caucasian Problem," 49.

17. "George S. Schuyler," F.B. Eyes Digital Archive: FBI Files on African

American Authors and Literary Institutions Obtained through the U.S. Freedom of Information Act [FOIA], 1942–1967, omeka.wustl.edu/omeka/exhibits/show/fbeyes/schuyler.

18. Ibid.

19. Roland Fryer, "An Empirical Analysis of Racial Differences in Police Use of Force," *Harvard Scholar*, 2017, scholar.harvard.edu/files/fryer/files/empirical_analysis_tables_figures.pdf.

20. Ibid., 2.

21. "Crime in the United States: 2019," FBI.gov, ucr.fbi.gov/crime-in-the-u.s/2019/crime-in-the-u.s.-2019/tables/table-43.

22. "Expanded Homicide Data: 2019," FBI.gov, ucr.fbi.gov/crime-in-the-u.s/2019/crime-in-the-u.s.-2019/tables/expanded-homicide-data-table-6.xls.

23. "U.S. Census Bureau Releases Key Statistics on Nation's African American Population in Honor of Black History Month," U.S. Department of Commerce (2021), www.commerce.gov/news/blog/2021/02/us-census-bureau-releases-key-statistics-nations-african-american-population#:~:text=48.2%20million,the%20United%20States%20in%202019.

24. See NC Department of Natural and Cultural Resources, "1898 Wilmington Coup," www.dncr.nc.gov/1898-wilmington-coup, and Library of Congress, Chronicling America: Historic American Newspapers, *The News and Observer*, September 27, 1898, chroniclingamerica.loc.gov/lccn/sn85042104/1898-09-27/ed-1/seq-1/.

25. "Police Shootings Database," *Washington Post*, 2024, www.washingtonpost.com/graphics/investigations/police-shootings-database/.

26. Kevin McCaffree and Anonda Saide, "How Informed Are Americans about Race and Policing?" Skeptic Research Center, Research Report: CUPES-007, February 20, 2021, www.skeptic.com/research-center/reports/Research-Report-CUPES-007.pdf.

27. "On nonlethal uses of force, blacks and Hispanics are more than 50 percent more likely to experience some form of force in interactions with police. Adding controls that account for important context and civilian behavior reduces, but cannot fully explain, these disparities. On the most extreme use of force—officer-involved shootings—we find no racial differences either in the raw data or when contextual factors are taken into account." Roland Fryer, "An Empirical Analysis of Racial Differences in Police Use of Force," *Journal of*

Political Economy, 127, no. 3 (January 2019), www.journals.uchicago.edu/doi/abs/10.1086/701423?mobileUi=0&.

28.   Ibid., emphasis added, 40.

29.   Barbara and Karen Fields, *Racecraft*.

30.   Kwame Anthony Appiah, *The Lies That Bind: Rethinking Identity Creed, Country, Color, Class, Culture* (Profile, 2018).

Chapter 7

1.   Toni Morrison, *Beloved* (Vintage, 2004).

2.   Mason, *The Theory of Racelessness*.

3.   Maxine Hong Kingston, *The Woman Warrior: Memoirs of a Girlhood Among Ghosts* (Vintage, 1976).

4.   Smith, *Twilight*.

5.   Kingston, *The Woman Warrior*, 92.

6.   Ibid., 172.

7.   Ibid., 6.

8.   Ibid., 3,

9.   Ibid., 8 and 9.

10.   Ibid., 3.

11.   Ibid., 8.

12.   Ibid., 143.

13.   Angels Carabí, "Interview with Maxine Hong Kingston," in *American Women Writers* (New York: Garland Publishing, 1994), 110.

14.   Kingston, *The Woman Warrior*, 143.

15.   Ibid., 4.

16.   Ibid., 172.

17.   Ibid., 172.

18.   Ibid., 172.

19.   Ibid., 178.

20.   Ibid., 179.

21.   Ibid., 186.

22.   Ibid., 186.

23.   Ibid., 94.

24.   Ibid., 94.

25. Marlene Nourbese Philip, "Managing the Unmanageable," in *Caribbean Women Writers*, ed. Selwyn Cudjoe (Calaloux, 1990), 295.

26. Kingston, *The Woman Warrior*, 95.

27. Ibid., 96.

28. Ibid., 95.

29. Ibid., 187.

30. Ibid., 186.

31. Ibid., 186.

32. Ibid., 186.

33. Ibid., 186.

34. Ibid., 187.

35. Ibid., 187.

36. Ibid., 187.

37. Ibid., 187.

38. Ibid., 187.

39. Ibid., 188.

40. Ibid., 188.

41. Ibid., emphasis added, 189.

42. Ibid., 188.

43. Ibid., 189.

44. Ibid., 188.

45. Ibid., emphasis in the original, 53.

46. Helena Grice, *Maxine Hong Kingston* (Manchester University Press, 2006), 127–134. See Kingston, *The Woman Warrior*, 26.

47. Kingston, *The Woman Warrior*, 131.

48. Ibid., 140.

49. Ibid., 149.

50. Ibid., 141.

51. Ibid., 142.

52. Ibid., 143.

53. Ibid., 144.

54. Ibid., 152.

55. Ibid., 152.

56. Ibid., 153.

57. Ibid., 159.

58. Ibid., 154.

59. Ibid., 155.

60. Ibid., 121.

61. Ibid., 155.

62. Ibid., 156.

63. Ibid., 209.

64. Ibid., 160.

65. Ibid., 189.

66. Ibid., 189.

67. Ibid., emphasis in the original, 190.

68. Philip, "Managing the Unmanageable," 295.

69. Kingston, *The Woman Warrior*, 190.

70. Ibid., 200.

71. Smith, *Twilight*, xxv.

72. Nicoleta Alexoae Zagni and Maxine Hong Kingston, "An Interview with Maxine Hong Kingston," *Revue Française 'études Américaines*, no. 110, (December 2006): 97–106, 100 (emphasis added), www.jstor.org/stable/20875713.

73. See Chimamanda Ngozi Adichie, *Americanah* (Vintage, 2013), for example.

Chapter 8

1. Édouard Glissant, *Poetics of Relation* (University of Michigan Press, 1990).

2. Morrison, *Beloved.*

3. Kingston, *The Woman Warrior.*

4. Smith, *Twilight.*

5. George Lamming, *In the Castle of My Skin* (McGraw-Hill Book Company, Inc., 1953).

6. *Creolization* is the process through which creole languages and cultures emerge. It is a term often used to refer to the Caribbean even though it is not exclusive to the Caribbean. Social scientists use the term to describe new cultural expressions brought about by contact between societies and relocated peoples. It has been associated with cultural mixtures of African, European, and indigenous (in addition to other lineages in different locations) ancestry. To-

day, creolization tends to refer to that mixture of different people and different cultures that merge to become one (i.e., New Yorican or Miami Spanish). See Juan Flores, *The Diaspora Strikes Back: Caribeño Tales of Learning and Turning* (Routledge, 2009). I go more in-depth about the complexity of cultural, ethnic, and national formation in other chapters.

7. Edward Kamau Brathwaite, *Roots* (University of Michigan Press, 1993), 232.

8. Sandra Pouchet Paquet, *Caribbean Autobiography: Cultural Identity and Self-Representation* (University of Wisconsin Press, 2002), 12.

9. Jarrett H. Brown, *Black Masculinities as Marronage: Claude McKay's Representation of Black Male Subjectivities in Metropolitan Spaces* (College of William and Mary, 2011).

10. Édouard Glissant, *Caribbean Discourse* (University of Virginia Press, 1999), 21 (emphasis added) and 87.

11. Ibid., 16.

12. Ibid., 23.

13. Ibid., 26.

14. For example, returning to the plantation to collapse colonialism and slavery that resulted from the Middle Passage.

15. Brathwaite, *Roots*, 232.

16. Ibid., 44.

17. Cynthia James, *The Maroon Narrative: Caribbean Literature in English Across Boundaries, Ethnicities, and Centuries* (Heinemann, 2002), 16.

18. Derek Walcott, *Epitaph for the Young: XII Cantos* (Advocate Company, 1949).

19. Lamming, *In the Castle of My Skin*, 1.

20. Ibid., 2.

21. Ibid., 1.

22. Ibid., 2.

23. Edward Kamau Brathwaite, *Contradictory Omens: Cultural Diversity and Integration in the Caribbean* (Savacou, 1977), 31.

24. Ibid., 17.

25. Lamming, *In the Castle of My Skin*, 2.

26. Ibid., 3.

27. Ibid., 3.

28. Ibid., 1.
29. Ibid., 2.
30. Ibid., 2.
31. Ibid., 2.
32. Ibid., 3.
33. Ibid., 1.
34. Ibid., 3.
35. Ibid., 3.
36. Ibid., 4.
37. Ibid., 109.
38. Ibid., 109.
39. Ibid., 107.
40. Ibid., 108.
41. Ibid., 108.
42. Ibid., 109.
43. Ibid., 109.
44. Ibid., 109.
45. Ibid., 107.
46. Ibid., 107.
47. Ibid., 107.
48. Ibid., 18.
49. Ibid., 107.
50. Ibid., 107.
51. Ibid., 312.
52. Michelle Cliff, *No Telephone to Heaven* (Plume, 1987), 194.
53. Lamming, *In the Castle of My Skin*, 1.
54. Ibid., 311.
55. Ibid., emphasis added, 7.

Chapter 9

1. John Marsh, "Interlude II: Was Walt Whitman Gay?" in *In Walt We Trust: How a Queer Socialist Poet Can Save America from Itself* (New York University Press, 2015), 149.

2. Walt Whitman, "Song of Myself," available at University of Washing-

ton, depts.washington.edu/lsearlec/TEXTS/WHITMAN/SONGSELF.HTM.

3.   Santiago Juan-Navarro, "Beyond the Myth of Narcissus: The Role of the Reader in Walt Whitman's 'Song of Myself'" *Atlantis* 12, no. 1 (1990): 109.

4.   George Fortenberry, "American Literary Realism, 1870–1910," *American Literary Realism, 1870–1910*, 24, no. 1 (1991): 96.

5.   Frederick Douglass, *Narrative of the Life of Frederick Douglass, An American Slave*, in *The Norton Anthology of American Literature*, ed. Nina Baym and Robert S. Levine (W. W. Norton and Co., 2012), 1182.

6.   Harriet Beecher Stowe, *Uncle Tom's Cabin*, in *The Norton Anthology of American Literature*, ed. Nina Baym and Robert S. Levine (W. W. Norton and Co., 2012), 820.

7.   Harriet Jacobs, *Incidents in the Life of a Slave Girl*, in *The Norton Anthology of American Literature*, ed. Nina Baym and Robert S. Levine (W. W. Norton and Co., 2012), 922.

8.   Whitman, "Song of Myself," lines 1–3.

9.   Ibid., lines 6–7.

10.   Ibid., line 37.

11.   Ibid., line 47.

12.   Ibid., line 52.

13.   Ibid., line 33.

14.   Ibid., line 416.

15.   Ibid., line 503.

16.   Ibid., line 485.

17.   Marsh, "Interlude II: Was Walt Whitman Gay?" 157.

18.   Whitman, "Song of Myself," line 105 and 108.

19.   Ibid., lines 1339–40.

20.   Ibid., lines 27 and 24.

21.   Ibid., line 24.

22.   Ibid., lines 582–586.

23.   Ibid., lines 242–43.

24.   Ibid., line 497.

25.   Ibid., lines 1153–55.

26.   Ibid., lines 1160–1161.

27.   Ibid., lines 1168–1169.

28.   Thomas C. Gannon. "Complaints from the Spotted Hawk: Flights and

Feathers in Whitman's 1855 *Leaves of Grass,*" in *Leaves of Grass: The Sesqui-centennial Essays,* ed. Susan Belasco et al. (University of Nebraska Press, 2007), 141–176.

29. Whitman, "Song of Myself," lines 195, 230, and 282.

30. Ibid., line 854.

31. Ibid., lines 1324–26.

32. See, for example, Derek Walcott's introduction to *Dream on Monkey Mountain* (Farrar, Straus and Giroux, 1971).

33. Carolyn Allen, "Creole Then and Now: The Problem of Definition," *Caribbean Quarterly* 44, no. 1/2 (1998): 33–49.

Chapter 10

1. Edward P. Jones, "Blindsided," in *All Aunt Hagar's Children* (Amistad, 2007), 293–321.

2. See, for example, Paul Ardoin, "Space, Aesthetic Power, and True Fal-sity in the Known World," *Studies in the Novel* 45, no. 4 (2013): 638–54. Kim Gallon, "Recovering Black Humanity in Lost in the City: A Review of Lost in the City: An Exploration of Edward P. Jones's Short Fiction," *Fire!!!* 5, no. 2 (2020): 121–24. Kenton Rambsy, "Edward P. Jones—The Neighborhood Preservation-ist," *Fire!!!* 5, no. 2 (2020): 40–52.

3. Carolyn Vellenga Berman, "The Known World in World Literature: Bakhtin, Glissant, and Edward P. Jones," *NOVEL: A Forum on Fiction* 42, no. 2, (2009): 233.

4. Kenton Rambsy, "Edward P. Jones—The Neighborhood Preservation-ist," *Fire!!!* 5, no. 2 (2020): 40.

5. Jones. "Blindsided," 293.

6. Ibid., 293.

7. Ibid., 293.

8. Ibid., 297.

9. Ibid., 294.

10. David Ikard. "White Supremacy under Fire: The Unrewarded Perspec-tive in Edward P. Jones's *The Known World,*" *MELUS,* vol. 36, no. 3, (Oxford UP), 2011, 68.

11. Jones, "Blindsided," 320.

12. Ibid., emphasis in the original, 320.

13. Ibid., 320.

14. Ibid., 320.

15. Ibid., 320.

16. Ibid., 321.

17. Ibid., 321.

Chapter 11

1. bell hooks, *All About Love: New Visions*, (William Morrow Paperbacks, 2018), xviii–xix.

2. I changed their names to protect their identities.

3. I did not change Kathy Frasier's (or Frazier's) name. And I would love to reunite with her to tell her directly how much she has impacted me. She was a social worker at South Glens Falls High School in 2000.

4. Appiah, *The Lies That Bind*.

Conclusion

1. For more information, see Carlos Hoyt, *The Arc of a Bad Idea: Understanding and Transcending Race* (Oxford University Press, 2015).

Further Reading

Alam, Eram, Dorothy Roberts, and Natalie Shibley. *Ordering the Human: The Global Spread of Racial Science.* Columbia University Press, 2024.

Allen, Carolyn. "Creole Then and Now: The Problem of Definition." *Caribbean Quarterly* 44, no. 1/2 (1998): 33-49. Accessed May 27, 2024. www.jstor.org/stable/40654020.

Aslakson, Kenneth. *Making Race in the Courtroom.* New York: NYU Press, 2014.

Baldwin, James. *The Cross of Redemption: Uncollected Writings.* New York: Pantheon Books, 2010.

—. "The Price May Be Too High." *The New York Times,* 1969.

Bantum, Brian. *The Death of Race: Building a New Christianity in a Racial World.* Minneapolis: Fortress Press, 2016.

Baugh, Edward. "The West Indian and His Quarrel with History." *Small Axe* 16, no. 2 (2012): 60-74. Accessed May 27, 2024. muse.jhu.edu/article/483217.

Blum, Edward J., and Paul Harvey. *The Color of Christ: The Son of God and the Saga of Race in America.* Chapel Hill: University of North Carolina Press, 2012.

Blumhardt, Christoph Friedrich. *Everyone Belongs to God: Discovering the Hidden Christ.* Walden, NY: Plough Publishing House, 2015.

Brown Douglas, Kelly. *The Black Christ.* 9th ed. Maryknoll, NY: Orbis Books, 2002.

Carter, Jacoby. "Between Reconstruction and Elimination: Alain Locke's Philosophy of Race." In *The Oxford Handbook of Philosophy and Race,* edited by Naomi Zack, 195-203. Oxford: Oxford University Press, 2017.

Carter, Jacoby, and Darryl Scriven. *Insurrectionist Ethics: Radical Perspectives on Social Justice*. New York: Palgrave Macmillan, 2023.

Cone, James H. *God of the Oppressed*. 3rd ed. Maryknoll, NY: Orbis Books, 1999.

Copeland, M. Shawn. *Enfleshing Freedom: Body, Race, and Being*. Minneapolis: Fortress Press, 2010.

Daas, Angelica. "Humanae." *Angelica Dass (AD)*, 2023. Accessed May 27, 2024. angelicadass.com/photography/humanae/.

Du Bois, W.E.B.. *Dusk of Dawn: An Essay Toward an Autobiography of a Race Concept*. New Brunswick, NJ: Transaction Publishers, 2005.

Emerson, Michael O., and Christian Smith. *Divided by Faith: Evangelical Religion and the Problem of Race in America*. Oxford: Oxford University Press, 2000.

Everett, Percival. *Erasure*. New York: Hyperion, 2001.

Fanon, Frantz. *Black Skin, White Masks*. New York: Grove Press, 2008.

—. *The Wretched of the Earth*. New York: Grove Press, 2021.

Felder, Cain Hope. *Troubling the Biblical Waters: Race, Class, and Family*. Maryknoll, NY: Orbis Books, 1993.

Ferguson, Everett. *Baptism in the Early Church: History, Theology, and Liturgy in the First Five Centuries*. Grand Rapids, MI: William B. Eerdmans Publishing Company, 2009.

Fields, Karen, and Barbara Fields. *Racecraft: The Soul of Inequality in American Life*. London: Verso, 2014.

Fitch, David E. *The Church of Us vs. Them: Freedom from a Faith That Feeds on Making Enemies*. Grand Rapids, MI: Brazos Press, 2019.

Fuller, Kathleen. "Eradicating Essentialism from Cultural Competency Education." *Academic Medicine* 77, no. 3 (2002).

Gates, Henry Louis, Jr.. *Loose Canons: Notes on the Culture Wars*. Oxford: Oxford University Press, 1992.

Gerbner, Katherine. *Christian Slavery: Conversion and Race in the Protestant Atlantic World*. Philadelphia: University of Pennsylvania Press, 2018.

Gilroy, Paul. *Against Race: Imagining Political Culture Beyond the Color Line*. Cambridge, MA: Belknap Press, 2002.

Glasgow, Joshua. "A Third Way in the Race Debate." *The Journal of Political Philosophy* 14, no. 2 (2006): 163-185.

Glissant, Édouard. *Poetics of Relation*. Ann Arbor: University of Michigan Press, 1997.

Goetz, Rebecca Anne. *The Baptism of Early Virginia: How Christianity Created Race*. Baltimore: Johns Hopkins University Press, 2012.

Goranson Jacob, Haley. *Conformed to the Image of His Son: Reconsidering Paul's Theology of Glory in Romans*. Downers Grove, IL: IVP Academic, 2018.

Gossett, Thomas. *Race: The History of an Idea in America*. New York: Oxford University Press, 1997.

Graves, Joseph, Jr.. *The Emperor's New Clothes: Biological Theories of Race at the Millennium*. New Brunswick, NJ: Rutgers University Press, 2003.

Hanke, Lewis. *Aristotle and the American Indians: A Study in Race Prejudice in the Modern World*. Bloomington: Indiana University Press, 1959.

Hannah-Jones, Nikole, Caitlin Roper, Ilena Silverman, and Jake Silverstein, eds. *The 1619 Project: A New Origin Story*. New York: One World, 2021.

Harris, Leonard. "Necro-Being: An Actuarial Account of Racism." *Res Philosophica* 95, no. 2 (2018): 273-302.

---and Lee A. McBride III. *A Philosophy of Struggle: The Leonard Harris Reader*. New York: Bloomsbury Academic, 2020.

Harris, Wilson. "History, Fable and Myth in the Caribbean and Guianas." *Caribbean Quarterly* 54, no. 1/2 (2008): 5-38. Accessed May 27, 2024. www.jstor.org/stable/40655139.

—. *The Womb of Space: The Cross-Cultural Imagination*. New York: Praeger, 1983.

Haynes, Leonard L., Jr.. *The Negro Community within American Protestantism, 1619-1844*. Boston: Christopher Publishing House, 1953.

Haynes, Stephen R.. *The Last Segregated Hour: The Memphis Kneel-Ins and the Campaign for Southern Church Desegregation*. New York: Oxford University Press, 2012.

Herskovits, Melville. *The Myth of the Negro Past*. Boston: Beacon Press, 1958.

Hochman, Adam. "Has Social Constructionism about Race Outlived Its Usefulness? Perspectives from a Race Skeptic." *Biology & Philosophy* 37, no. 6 (2022): 1-20.

hooks, bell. *All About Love: New Visions*. New York: William Morrow Paperbacks, 2018.

Hopkins, Dwight N.. *Down, Up, and Over: Slave Religion and Black Theology.* Minneapolis: Fortress Press, 2000.

Jarrett, Gene. *African American Literature beyond Race.* New York: NYU Press, 2006.

—. *Deans and Truants: Race and Realism in African American Literature.* Philadelphia: University of Pennsylvania Press, 2013.

—. "Loosening the Straightjacket: Rethinking Racial Representation in African American Anthologies." In *Publishing Blackness: Textual Constructions of Race Since 1850,* edited by George Hutchinson and John K. Young, 160-174. Ann Arbor: University of Michigan Press, 2013. Accessed May 27, 2024. www.jstor.org/stable/j.ctv3znzrx.11.

—. "Toward a New Political History of African American Literature." In *Representing the Race: A New Political History of African American Literature,* 1-19. New York: NYU Press, 2011.

Jennings, Willie James. *After Whiteness: An Education in Belonging.* Grand Rapids, MI: William B. Eerdmans Publishing Company, 2020.

Jones, Robert P.. *White Too Long: The Legacy of White Supremacy in American Christianity.* New York: Simon & Schuster, 2020.

Jones, William R.. *Is God a White Racist? A Preamble to Black Theology.* Boston: Beacon Press, 1998.

Jordan, Winthrop. *The White Man's Burden: Historical Origins of Racism in the United States.* New York: Oxford University Press, 1974.

Juster, Susan, and Lisa MacFarlane, eds. *A Mighty Baptism: Race, Gender, and the Creation of American Protestantism.* Ithaca: Cornell University Press, 1996.

Kelsey, George D.. *Racism and the Christian Understanding of Man.* New York: Charles Scribner's Sons, 1965.

Kiernan, V. G.. *The Lords of Human Kind: Black Man, Yellow Man, and White Man in an Age of Empire.* New York: Columbia University Press, 1986.

Lincoln, C. Eric. *Coming Through the Fire: Surviving Race and Place in America.* Durham: Duke University Press, 1996.

Locke, Alain. *The Works of Alain Locke,* edited by Charles Molesworth. Oxford: Oxford University Press, 2021.

Loomba, Ania, and Jonathan Burton. *Race in Early Modern England: A Documentary Companion.* New York: Palgrave Macmillan, 2007.

Lopez, Ian Haney. *White By Law: The Legal Construction of Race, Revised and Updated*. New York: New York University Press, 2006.

Mallon, Ronald. "Passing, Traveling and Reality: Social Constructionism and the Metaphysics of Race." *NOUS* 38, no. 4 (2004): 644-673.

Mason, Sheena Michele. *Theory of Racelessness: A Case for Philosophies of Anti-race(ism)*. New York: Palgrave Macmillan, 2022.

—. "The Racelessness Translator." *Discourse Magazine*, 2023. Accessed May 27, 2024. www.discoursemagazine.com/ideas/2023/05/25/the-racelessness-translator/.

—. "Reexamining 'Race' and Crime." *Discourse Magazine*, 2023. Accessed May 27, 2024. www.discoursemagazine.com/ideas/2023/03/13/reexamining-race-and-crime/.

—. "ReVisioning Unalignment and Freedom: Insurrectionist Ethics in Marlon James' *The Book of Night Women*." In *Insurrectionist Ethics: Radical Perspectives on Social Justice Interventions*, edited by Jacoby Carter and Leonard Harris. New York: Palgrave Macmillan, 2023.

Mason, Sheena Michele, and Dana Williams. "Black Liberation Movements." In *The Cambridge Companion to the Twentieth-Century American Novel and Politics*, edited by Bryan Santin, Cambridge: Cambridge University Press, 2023.

Mason, Sheena Michele, and Jacoby Carter. "Harlem Renaissance: An Interpretation of Racialized Art and Ethics." In *Oxford Handbook of Ethics and Art*, edited by James Harold, Oxford: Oxford University Press, 2023.

Mitchell, Henry H. *Black Church Beginnings: The Long-Hidden Realities of the First Years*. Grand Rapids, MI: William B. Eerdmans Publishing Company, 2004.

Moahloli, Refiloe, and Zinelda McDonald. *I Am You: A [Children's] Book about Ubuntu*. Amazon Crossing Kids, 2022.

Moore, Charles E., ed. *Called to Community: The Life Jesus Wants for His People*. Walden, NY: Plough Publishing, 2016.

Morrison, Toni. *The Origin of Others*. Cambridge, MA: Harvard University Press, 2017.

—. *Playing in the Dark: Whiteness and the Literary Imagination*. New York: Vintage Books, 1992.

—. *The Source of Self-Regard: Selected Speeches, Essays, and Meditations.* New York: Alfred Knopf, 2019.

Mudimbe, V. Y. *The Invention of Africa: Gnosis, Philosophy, and the Order of Knowledge.* Bloomington: Indiana University Press, 1988.

Mukhopadhyay, Carol, Rosemary Henze, and Yolanda Moses. *How Real Is Race?: A Sourcebook on Race, Culture, and Biology.* 2nd ed. Lanham, MD: Rowman & Littlefield Publishers, 2013.

Ngomane, Mungi. *Everyday Ubuntu: Living Better Together, the African Way.* New York: Harper, 2020.

Omi, Michael, and Howard Winant. *Racial Formation in the United States: From the 1960s to the 1990s.* New York: Routledge, 1994.

Patterson, Orlando. *The Ordeal Of Integration: Progress And Resentment In America's "Racial" Crisis.* New York: Civitas Books, 1998.

—. "Ecumenical America: Global Culture and the American Cosmos." *World Policy Journal* 11, no. 2 (1994): 103–117. Accessed May 27, 2024. www.jstor.org/stable/40468616.

—. *Slavery and Social Death: A Comparative Study with a New Preface.* Cambridge, MA: Harvard University Press, 2018.

Patterson, Stephen J.. *The Forgotten Creed: Christianity's Original Struggle against Bigotry, Slavery & Sexism.* New York: Oxford University Press, 2018.

Pearce, Marsha. "Transnational/Transcultural Identities: The Black Atlantic and Pythagoras's Theorem." *Callaloo* 30, no. 2 (2007): 547-554. doi:10.1353/cal.2007.0215.

Pierce, Jeremy. *A Realist Metaphysics of Race: A Context-Sensitive, Short-Term Retentionist, Long-Term Revisionist Approach.* Lexington: Lexington Books, 2014.

Perkinson, James K.. *White Theology: Outing White Supremacy in Modernity.* New York: Palgrave Macmillan, 2004.

Phillips, Anne. "What's Wrong with Essentialism?" *Distinktion: Scandinavian Journal of Social Theory* 11 (2010): 47-60. doi:10.1080/1600910X.2010.9672755.

Pope, Liston. *The Kingdom Beyond Caste.* New York: Friendship Press, 1957.

Prothero, Stephen. *American Jesus: How the Son of God Became a National Icon.* New York: Farrar, Straus and Giroux, 2003.

Puri, Shalini. *The Caribbean Postcolonial: Social Equality, Post-Nationalism, and Cultural Hybridity.* New York: Palgrave Macmillan, 2004.

Raboteau, Albert J.. *Canaan Land: A Religious History of African Americans.* New York: Oxford University Press, 2001.

—. *Slave Religion: The "Invisible Institution" in the Antebellum South.* New York: Oxford University Press, 1978.

Rhodes, Marjorie, and Kelsey Moty. "What is Social Essentialism and How Does It Develop?" *Advances in Child Development and Behavior* 59 (2020).

Roberts, Dorothy. *Fatal Invention: How Science, Politics, and Big Business Re-create Race in the Twenty-first Century.* New York: The New Press, 2012.

Rockquemore, Kerry Ann. *Beyond Black: Biracial Identity in America.* 2nd ed. Lanham, MD: Rowman & Littlefield Publishers, 2007.

Roediger, David R. *Working Towards Whiteness: How America's Immigrants Became White.* New York: Basic Books, 2005.

—, ed. *Black on White: Black Writers on What It Means to Be White.* New York: Schocken Books, 1998.

Ryan, Thomas, ed. *Reclaiming the Body in Christian Spirituality.* New York: Paulist Press, 2004.

Singh, Gurnam. "Post-racial Pedagogy–Challenges and Possibilities." *Race Ethnicity and Education* (2016). doi: 10.1080/13613324.2016.1248830.

Smith, Anna Deavere. *Twilight: Los Angeles, 1992.* New York: Anchor Books, 1994.

Snowden Jr., Frank M.. *Before Color Prejudice: The Ancient View of Blacks.* Cambridge, MA: Harvard University Press, 1983.

Spencer, Rainier. *Spurious Issues: Race and Multiracial Identity Politics in the United States.* New York: Routledge, 2000.

Thiong'o, Ngũgĩ wa. *Decolonizing the Mind: The Politics of Language in African Literature.* Oxford: James Curry Limited, 1986.

Touré. *Who's Afraid of Post-Blackness?: What It Means to Be Black Now.* New York: Atria Books, 2012.

Trent, Tererai. *Ubuntu: On Whose Shoulders We Stand.* Karen McDermott, 2023.

West, Cornel. *Prophesy Deliverance! An Afro-American Revolutionary Christianity (Anniversary Edition).* Louisville, KY: Westminster John Knox Press, 2002.

Wilkerson, Isabel. *Caste: The Origins of Our Discontents*. New York: Random House, 2020.

Williams, Delores S.. *Sisters in the Wilderness: The Challenge of Womanist God-Talk*. New York: Orbis Books, 2005.

Zack, Naomi, ed. *American Mixed Race: The Culture of Microdiversity*. Lanham, MD: Rowman & Littlefield, 1995.

Index

shift away from current forms of, xxii; the problem of racialization in, 19, 43, 47, 62, 63, 90, 108, 120, 147; raceless, xix, 47, 70, 89, 161, 176, 185, 191, 197

Appiah, Kwame Anthony, 51, 129, 190, 224n6, 228n12, 231n30, 238n4

Arbery, Ahmaud, 93, 95, 123

Arbery, Marcus, 93, 94

architecture, 12, 14, 56, 62, 176, 178, 196

Asians, as "white adjacent," 33–34

assimilation, 34, 57, 163, 180

authenticity, 46, 114

Baldwin, James, xvii, xx, 45, 88, 162, 163, 164

Bantum, Brian, xiv

Baraka, Amiri, xx

Barbados, 152, 153, 155, 157; Barbadian, 149, 153

Belonging. See diversity, equity, inclusion, and belonging

Berman, Carolyn Vellenga, 177

Bey, Marquis, ix

Biden, Joe, 68, 115, 228n5

biology, "whiteness" as, 108

biracialism, 116, 219

"Black," capitalization of, 53, 62

black lives matter, 6, 92, 93, 94, 128

Black Lives Matter Movement, 62

Black Power Movement, 62, 92

"blackness," assignment of impoverishment to, 32, 41; attempts to remake, 62, 65–66; author's experience with, 16; banner of, 54; caricatures and archetypes attached to, 53; celebrity rejection of, 104; in contrast to "whiteness," xvii, 34, 38, 46, 59, 64, 178; Fanon on, 59; fixed nature of, 37, 66; Gilroy on, 28, 41; "inauthentic," 47;

Lawton on, 105; not a synonym for "black" people, 96; as outside humanity, 64, 95, 114; in quote from *In the Castle of My Skin*, 159; racial/st discomfort with, 196; reformation of, 17, 93; as a so-called racial term, xvii; translation of, 7, 13, 20; Tyla on, 61; in Vanuatu and Melanesia, 79; 159, 178, 196

Black Skin, White Masks (Fanon), 59

boundaries, crossing of, 136, 153, 158

Brathwaite, Edward Kamau, 151, 152, 154, 155

Brown, William Wells, xx

Buddhist, 169

Butler, Octavia, xx

Cajun, 85

Canadians, 79, 85

capitalism, 126, 220, 221n2

Carabí, Angels, 136

Carribean, 150, 151, 152, 153, 154, 155, 156, 157, 158, 166, 174, 219, 233n6

caste, xi, 118,

census, 37, 67-69, 199

changing same, 33

Chereni, Admire, 224

Chesnutt, Charles, xx

Chinese, 67, 134, 135-37, 142-45

Christianity, 154, 165

civil rights, 19, 37, 41, 98

Civil Rights Movement, 62

Cliff, Michelle, 151, 159

Clifton, Lucille, xx

Cobb, Montague, 73

colonialism, xi, 154, 156, 157, 160, 166

colonization, xi, xviii, 29, 60, 85, 149, 166

colorblindness, as distinct from humanism, 91; as distinct from racelessness, 89–90; logic of, 94;

reforming "race," 7, 14–17, 37, 42–45, 56, 61, 63, 90, 108, 129, 202, 214; requires belief in "race" and the practice of racialization, xix, 5, 8, 10, 20, 21, 22, 24, 44, 51, 62, 70, 98, 117, 122, 180, 200, 202, 218; seeing ourselves outside the paradigm of, 12; in South Africa, 61; systemic, 23, 45, 46, 50, 63, 70, 91, 121; translating "race," 10, 11, 13–16, 24, 25, 47, 55, 97, 98, 190, 197, 198, 208; universalism of, 61

Raceless: In Search of Family, Identity, and the Truth About Where I Belong (Lawton), 104, 106–8, 228n4

racelessness, antirace/ism as synonym for, 18; author's, 22; author's call to work toward, 183; author's reasons for promoting, 176; as compared to racecraft, 164; as a form of resistance, 152; as freedom from race/ism, 57; implies an imaginary-abolitionist or synthetic-abolitionist philosophy, 15; lesson from "Blindsided" about, 182; Maroons as reflective of, 156; not a post-racial vision, 1; as only effective path forward, 25; as our natural state, 130; Prather quote on, 12–13; proper way to understand, 21; should not be mistaken for colorblindness, 89; story from author's presentation about, 124; theory of, xii, xix; within the togetherness wayfinder, 24, 96, 197, 200; togetherness wayfinder 45-day guide and, 203, 205, 207–215, 218; truth of, 95; universality of, 96, 100, 103, 113; "whiteness" mistakenly conflated with, 29, 38, 103, 105–107, 109. *See also* racelessness translator

racelessness translator, 10, 11, 13–16, 24, 25, 47, 55, 97, 98, 190, 197, 198, 208

racial categories, xviii, xxi, 9, 33, 37, 67–69, 225n20

Racial History of Man, The (Dixon), 55

racial/st ideology. *See* antiblackness *and* race/ism

racism. *See* race/ism

Racism (Memmi), 72

reconstruction, 42

reconstructionism. *See* reformation philosophy of "race"

redlining, 39

reformation philosophy of "race," 14, 16, 43, 90, 217

reformers of "race," 15, 17, 56

religion, 2, 25, 52, 97, 129, 147, 169, 200, 215

rememory, 14, 25, 131, 132, 133, 134, 149–151

reparations, 22

representation, 41, 214

Roberts, Dorothy, 3, 194, 227n16

Rwanda, 52, 96

Sanchez, Sonia, xx

-scape, 150

Schuyler, George, xx, 116, 117, 119, 131, 164, 175

science, xii, 112, 170

Seethal, Tyla Laura, 61

segregation, 82, 120, 138

Semang, 79

serfdom, 39, 84

shared humanity, 5, 23, 49, 50, 130, 180. *See also* common humanity

sickle cell disease, 74, 75, 84, 85

skepticism, 8, 14

skin color, belief that "race" is, 43; biological reality of, 15, 107; colorblindness and, 89; genetic variants

About the Author

Sheena Michele Mason is an assistant professor of English at SUNY Oneonta. She holds a PhD with distinction in English from Howard University in Washington, DC, and specializes in Africana and American studies and philosophy of "race." She is published with Oxford University Press, Palgrave MacMillan, Cambridge University Press, and the University of Warsaw, among other presses. She is the series editor of The Anthem Impact in Africana Philosophy and Racial Eliminativism, a series that offers pioneering research in the Africana philosophy of "race," with a particular emphasis on the critical examination of racism and the concept of "racial" eliminativism. She is the innovator of the togetherness wayfinder and founder of Togetherness Wayfinder (www.togetherness-wayfinder.org), an educational firm. She enjoys spending quality time with her wife, their triplets, and their two dogs.